The Angelo Herndon Case and Southern Justice

LOUISIANA STATE UNIVERSITY PRESS
BATON ROUGE

THE
Angelo Herndon Case
AND *Southern Justice*

CHARLES H. MARTIN, 1945-

This book was designed by Dwight Agner, and
composed in VIP Times Roman by Moran Industries, Inc.
It was printed by Edwards Brothers, Inc.,
and bound by Universal Bookbindery, Inc.

LIBRARY OF CONGRESS CATALOGING IN PUBLICATION DATA
Martin, Charles H   1945–
    The Angelo Herndon case and southern justice.

    Based on the author's thesis, Tulane University, 1972.
    Bibliography: p.
    Includes index.
    1. Herndon, Angelo, 1913–   I. Title.
KF224.H47M3   342′.73′0850269   73–91777
ISBN 0–8071–0174–5

In memory of my mother and father

Contents

Preface   xi

ONE   One Damning Word: C-O-M-M-U-N-I-S-T   1

TWO   Atlanta, 1930 and 1932   17

THREE   In a Georgia Courtroom   36

FOUR   "A Shameful Verdict"   62

FIVE   Building a Local Defense Movement   83

SIX   Free on Bail   97

SEVEN   Red Scare, 1934   121

EIGHT   The Supreme Court Evades a Ruling   140

NINE   A Narrow Victory   168

TEN   Conclusion   191

Epilogue   211

Selected Bibliography   217

Index   227

Illustrations

Following page 96

Angelo Herndon at press conference
Benjamin J. Davis, Jr.
John Geer
Angelo Herndon, 1935
William L. Patterson
W. T. Anderson
Angelo Herndon and an attorney
Angelo Herndon
Crowd greeting Herndon at Penn Central Station
Milton Herndon, Angelo Herndon, and Ruby Bates
The Process Server!

Preface

THE STRUGGLE of black Americans for equality has been a central theme in modern American history. Fundamental to this quest has been the fight for equality before the law. Historically, the greatest barriers to full legal rights for blacks have been found in the South, where most whites accepted without question the legitimacy of white supremacy and the accompanying need for rigid social control of blacks. Any attempt to modify the repressive status quo of the South often produced fanatical resistance from recalcitrant white southerners who regarded any proposed change as an attempt to subvert the social system if not southern civilization itself. Though color-blind in theory, the South's legal system could not escape being molded by the prevailing social milieu. Consequently, "southern justice" often served as an overt tool of white supremacy, especially during periods of crisis and confrontation.

During the 1930s there were numerous social upheavals in the United States. In the midst of the decade's uncertainties, the Communist party of the United States proclaimed itself the champion of the downtrodden and the exploited. Particularly impressed with the plight of black Americans, Communists made a special effort to recruit them by launching a major campaign against racial discrimination and exploitation, especially in the South. In so doing Communists emphasized the denial of equal justice to black defendants in southern courtrooms as proof of the American system's failure. Predictably this radical activity provoked bitter antagonism from aroused southern whites.

The hysteria and controversy generated by Communist efforts in behalf of southern blacks were best symbolized in the early thirties by the notorious Scottsboro case, in which nine black youths were accused of raping two white women on a freight train in northern Alabama. After a rancorous feud with the NAACP, the Communist-dominated International Labor Defense (ILD) seized control of the case and energetically defended the "Scottsboro boys." Through the ILD's diligence, the affair gained national and even international renown as a shocking example of southern repression and Jim Crow justice.

Another significant ILD effort came in Georgia, where the organization intervened in a dispute involving Angelo Herndon, a nineteen-year-old black Communist charged with attempting to incite an insurrection. Unlike the sensationalistic Scottsboro case, the Herndon case was not automatically predestined to earn national attention. When Atlanta authorities jailed the obscure young Communist recruiter in July, 1932, shortly after he had led a large, biracial relief demonstration, his arrest inspired few headlines. Although many black Americans soon displayed interest in his persecution, their concern alone was not sufficient to arouse national awareness. Only after several years of vigorous publicity efforts and skillful legal maneuvers did the ILD succeed in bringing the affair to the attention of many white Americans, thus establishing it as a *cause célèbre*. By 1935 white liberals, labor leaders, and other citizens joined blacks and radicals in viewing the conviction as a serious threat to basic civil liberties, especially the rights of free speech and free assembly.

Herndon's conviction was not an isolated event in Atlanta during the 1930s but the best known of several prosecutions by local authorities designed to silence all challenges, real and imagined, to the conservative status quo of a Deep South city. Because of this hostility, radical activists and politically conscious blacks often made common cause. Sometimes white liberals joined them. Although internal differences within this shaky alliance—mainly the ILD's dogmatism and narrow sectarianism—eventually drove blacks and radicals apart, their temporary unity terrified conservative whites and spurred them to greater repression utilizing Georgia's old antiinsurrection law. Ultimately, action by the United States Supreme Court was needed to curb these violations of basic constitutional rights.

A study of the Angelo Herndon case and its accompanying prosecutions touches on a variety of issues. Although not designed primarily as a legalistic survey, this account does deal with the precarious status of free speech legislation during a period of unsettled social and economic conditions. In addition, since the fight for Herndon's freedom temporarily forged an alliance between blacks, radicals (Communist and non-Communist), and white liberals, an analysis of this unstable *ménage à trois* reveals much about the values and tactics of each group as well as the nature of social protest during the depression.

The relationship between Communists and blacks is another thorny problem. Traditionally, most historians have treated Communist efforts as nothing more than crude, cynical attempts to exploit blacks for propaganda purposes without actually securing anything tangible for them. Recent historians such as Dan T. Carter have suggested that the reality was more complex than previously depicted and that Communists did sometimes produce results. If a new synthesis is to emerge, it should be based not merely on rewriting older accounts but also on new research and detailed case studies. It is hoped that this examination of the Herndon case will provide fresh information which will assist this reexamination. Moreover, a study of the Herndon case documents the conservative social, political, and legal milieu of the Deep South, especially the pervasive fear of biracial economic cooperation and the Communist slogan of "self-determination for the Black Belt." Since law did not function in a vacuum, these mores shaped a peculiar legal system best characterized as "southern justice." Precisely what this phrase meant to a nineteen-year-old black Communist and to the individuals who saw him as a symbol of injustice is the subject of this book.

If traditionalists will forgive me, I would like to reverse the usual pattern and begin my acknowledgments by sincerely thanking my wife Cheryl English Martin for her considerable assistance. In addition to working on her own dissertation, she still found time to suggest ways to improve the manuscript (not all of which were heeded), to correct my faltering spelling, and to assist me in typing the manuscript. Most important, she tolerated the intrusions of the Herndon case into our lives. Professor Bennett H. Wall of Tulane University read the manuscript several times in its original form as a doctoral dissertation and continued to provide kind assistance in the later stages of rewriting. His patience and faith in my ability I hope has been warranted. Gerald Carpenter, Bill Malone, William E. Nicholas, Blake Touchstone, Duncan Jamieson, and Maxine Rose generously consented to read portions of the manuscript and saved me from several embarrassing errors with their incisive comments.

Many individuals aided me in my research. Professor Clarence A. Bacote of Atlanta University introduced me to officials at the Fulton County Courthouse and oriented me to Atlanta sources. Henry Cobb, clerk of the Georgia Superior Court, directed me to state records and advised me concerning several possible subjects for interviews. Joseph Brennan of the law firm of Sutherland, Asbill, and Brennan (formerly Sutherland, Tuttle, and Brennan) discussed the case with me and permitted me to photocopy their copy of the official transcripts, briefs, petitions, etc., thereby providing me with a personal reference copy of the entire case proceedings. Hugh Murray located several sources for me and sharpened my understanding of radical protest through several enlightening discussions. Librarians at the following institutions also provided assistance: Tulane University, Xavier University, Emory University, Atlanta University, Atlanta Public Library, Georgia State Archives, University of North Carolina, Duke University, Princeton University, Columbia University, American Civil Liberties Union, New York Public Library, and Library of Congress.

Since the printed word does not always tell the full story, I supplemented the written documents in this case with interviews of participants or contemporary observers. The following persons kindly consented to be interviewed, for which I am most grateful: Whitney North Seymour, Walter Gellhorn, Howard N. Meyer, Don West, Elbert P. Tuttle, Joseph Brennan, J. Walter LeCraw, Nannie Leah Young Washburn, H. L. Mitchell, Glenn W. Rainey, C. Vann Woodward, R. A. Day, William H. Jones, and Edgar A. Johnson, Jr. Ralph Ellison provided a few spur-of-the-moment recollections in a hasty conversation in an elevator. I also benefited from correspondence with Roger N. Baldwin, Walter Gellhorn, J. Walter LeCraw, Clifford W. Mackay, Floyd W. Crawford, Mary Vaughn Bennett, William L. Patterson, and

Clarence Mitchell. Angelo Herndon, who now lives in a midwestern city, declined to be interviewed for personal reasons. John C. Edwards and Howard N. Meyer contributed material they had collected on the Herndon case and offered suggestions on possible sources, as did Dan T. Carter and John H. Moore, whose papers on the Scottsboro and Herndon cases at the 1968 Southern Historical Association convention in New Orleans first interested me in this topic. Vicci Gowen also helped me type the manuscript. A John T. Monroe Dissertation Fellowship from the Graduate School of Tulane University provided financial assistance during much of the researching and writing of the dissertation version of this study. Of course, the ultimate responsibility for the observations contained herein lies solely with myself.

CHAPTER ONE

One Damning Word:
C-O-M-M-U-N-I-S-T

THE CHILLING specter of economic depression lay across the South in the early 1930s. Fear, doubt, and despair gripped millions. No one seemed able to predict the future. Many people talked of changes; some even contemplated revolution. "Folks are restless," said Governor Theodore G. Bilbo of Mississippi in 1931. "Communism is gaining a foothold. Right here in Mississippi some people are about ready to lead a mob. In fact, I'm getting a little pink myself." [1]

By 1932 the lingering hope that somehow prosperity was just around the corner had evaporated. As industrial production continued to decline, unemployment steadily rose. Prices of agricultural products remained depressed, and mounting bank failures struck at the very basis of the country's financial system. On and on went the sad tale. While the shrinking economy reduced the tax base and income of most municipalities, growing numbers of unemployed workers demanded additional public assistance. Results were predictable. Across the country and across Dixie, "states and local governments were neither prepared nor able to cope with human distress." The needs of the jobless simply overwhelmed their shaky financial resources. By June, 1932, numerous cities including New Orleans and Birmingham had exhausted their relief funds. The governments of the city of Atlanta, Georgia, and Fulton County (encompassing Atlanta) experienced similar difficulties. In early

1. Quoted in George B. Tindall, *The Emergence of the New South, 1913–1945* (Baton Rouge: Louisiana State University Press, 1967), 386, Vol. X of Wendell Holmes Stephenson and E. Merton Coulter (eds.), *A History of the South* (10 vols.; Baton Rouge: Louisiana State University Press, 1949–).

June Atlanta banks refused to honor county paychecks until the Fulton county commissioners corrected a projected deficit of $428,000 for the year. To meet this demand, the officials slashed relief appropriations by about one-third, or $116,300, offsetting part of the deficit. By Monday, June 6, employees were finally permitted to cash their paychecks, but the county's financial woes were far from finished.[2]

Local residents hotly debated the commissioners' wisdom. The Atlanta *Constitution* reflected one common attitude when it pleaded, "Certainly there are other ways to balance the budget than by adding to the suffering of thousands of the county's helpless people." The newspaper added that every dollar of the original appropriation would be needed, if not more, since thousands of families were dependent on organized relief for food and shelter. On the other hand, some citizens complained that county government already taxed its wage earners too heavily. Understandably perplexed, George F. Longino, finance chairman of the county commission, lamented, "The county board is met on one hand with demands from reputable organizations that it reduce its expenditures and on the other with an urgent demand for appropriations for worthy causes." It was not an enviable position.[3]

Several local groups offered more dramatic solutions to the city's problems. A white supremacist organization, the American Order of Fascisti, or Black Shirts, tried to revive its tattered fortunes by advocating the replacement of black workers with unemployed whites. The group, which supposedly had collapsed two years previously, attempted to stage a rally at the state capitol. City police promptly arrested Holt J. Gewinner, the Black Shirts' self-styled "adjutant general," and several others on minor charges. Although only one member of the society was eventually convicted (for disorderly conduct), the police action swiftly aborted the Black Shirts' attempted resurrection. Other Atlanta residents decided to take their complaints directly to the nation's capital. Inspired by the example of Bonus Army marchers who passed through Atlanta on June 2, a local contingent chose to join this "march on Washington" to demand immediate payment of a bonus to veterans. The delegation's leaders devoted considerable effort to screening local radicals

2. *Ibid.*, 369–71; Atlanta *Constitution*, June 2, 3, and 7, 1932.
3. Atlanta *Constitution*, June 6, 1932.

—affiliated with the Workers' Ex-Servicemen's League—from the marchers' ranks. One of the protest organizers warned, "Anyone who starts talking 'red' and anybody who takes a crack at the Constitution of the United States is going to get a swift kick and get it quick too." The veterans thus hoped to discredit the charges already emanating from Washington that the march was Communist dominated. On June 7 nearly two hundred former servicemen finally departed in trucks for the nation's capital. Both black and white delegations participated, but in separate units.[4]

Meanwhile, Atlanta's relief crisis worsened. The city's emergency relief center at 23 Pryor Street encountered constant funding problems. Finally, on June 16, the chairman of the Emergency Relief Committee, T. K. Glenn, announced that the agency had not only exhausted its funds but was operating at a deficit. Because of the bleak financial situation, Glenn announced that the relief center would be forced to suspend operations at the end of the week. Some 3,951 families or a total of 21,730 persons would be affected; most were without any other source of support. Characterizing this as a "critical situation," the Atlanta *Constitution* demanded immediate action: "Something must be done and done AT ONCE to meet this situation!" The *Constitution*'s Sunday edition on June 19 headlined the crisis, proclaiming, "Hunger and misery today is stalking through the capital city of Georgia." It reported that the closing of the emergency relief station had created sheer desperation among former recipients. To meet these needs the *Constitution* courageously advocated one of the most unpopular measures of the depression years—higher taxes. County commissioners had previously considered but rejected a proposed additional one-mill assessment on county taxes. Now the commissioners began to waver. The *Constitution* strongly urged county and city officials to meet the needs of these desperate families. "Every effort must be made to avoid an increase in the tax rate, but if there is no other way in which to meet the present relief emergency, there can be no doubt that the one-mill increase will be approved," it said. The leading publication of the Atlanta labor move-

---

4. *Ibid.*, June 1, 3, 5, 7, 8, and 10, 1932; Atlanta *Daily World*, June 7, 1932; John Hammond Moore, "Communists and Fascists in a Southern City: Atlanta, 1930," *South Atlantic Quarterly*, LXVII (Summer, 1968), 437–54.

ment, the *Journal of Labor*, likewise advocated a more liberal spending policy, repeatedly criticizing the commissioners for their obsession with "balancing the budget."[5]

Beset with pressures from all directions, the county commissioners struggled to find some way out of their quandary. So great was their desperation that they decided to reduce the salaries of county officials. Solicitor General John A. Boykin (the equivalent of a district attorney) and Superior Court Judge Hugh M. Dorsey saw their yearly salaries slashed from $12,000 to $9,000. Other officials and judges suffered similar fates. The commissioners saved $162,000 for the year by these austerity measures, but none of the savings could be devoted to relief appropriations, since the reductions merely offset the projected deficit. Consequently the commission considered a tax increase at its June 25 meeting. During the three-hour hearing, nearly sixty citizens presented their opinions. The speakers divided into two camps—those in favor of greater relief expenditures and those opposed to any increase in taxes. T. K. Glenn, chairman of the board of the First National Bank and a leader in emergency relief work, requested the commission to reinstate the relief money by pruning its budget. He promised to support an additional tax levy if no other source of revenue could be found. R. C. Mizell, president of the Taxpayers' League, presented a different view. Mizell conceded that an emergency existed but maintained that its extent had been exaggerated. Commissioner Walter C. Hendrix likewise asserted that community leaders had "been misled about the huge army of gaunt, suffering people in our city." Questioning the presence of widespread hunger, he suggested that anyone possessing such evidence bring it forward. Later in the evening he remarked, "I do not believe that there is any vast army of starving in our midst." At the meeting's conclusion, the commission tabled the proposed tax increase.[6]

Commissioner Hendrix's words denying the existence of hunger and urging dissatisfied citizens to produce evidence to the contrary were taken as a challenge by radical activists in the city. Although their activities were on a limited scale, several Communists and other leftists had formed a local Unemployed Council. Like its sister groups across

5. Atlanta *Constitution*, June 17, 18, 19, 20, and 25, 1932; *Journal of Labor*, July 14, 1932.
6. Atlanta *Constitution*, June 23 and 26, 1932.

the country, the council acted as a self-appointed militant spokesman for the economic needs of the destitute, severely criticizing political and economic leaders for their failures and working independently to help the unemployed obtain assistance or jobs.[7] Spurred by the relief crisis and the county commissioners' response, the Unemployed Council's leaders plotted direct action.

Several days later, while Democrats in Chicago were nominating Franklin D. Roosevelt for the presidency, a small delegation of fifty people petitioned the commissioners for food or money to relieve suffering among unemployed cotton mill workers. The following day, Thursday, June 30, dawned quietly, offering no hint of what lay in store for county officials. By mid-morning the warm sunshine had broken through the overcast sky, and the temperature was climbing into the eighties. For leaders of the Unemployed Council, it had been a long, busy night. Under cover of darkness they had spent several hours distributing thousands of leaflets calling for a rally of the jobless at the Fulton County Courthouse the next morning. Seeking to enlighten Commissioner Hendrix, the council urged that "all of us, whites and Negroes together, with our women folk and children go to his office . . . and show this faker that there is plenty of suffering in the city of Atlanta and demand that he gives [*sic*] us immediate relief." The demonstration's chief organizer, a trim, bespectacled young black man named Angelo Herndon, tossed restlessly in bed. Serious beyond his nineteen years, Herndon found little rest that night. At daybreak he hastily dressed and made his way downtown to the protest site where he waited nervously for developments. He was not disappointed.[8] By nine o'clock, one hour before the announced time, scores of haggard-looking men and women, black and white alike, ignored the possibility of rain and began to assemble near the courthouse under the partly cloudy sky.

7. For an account of the formation of the Unemployed councils nationally, see Daniel J. Leab, "'United We Eat': The Creation and Organization of the Unemployed Councils in 1930," *Labor History,* VIII (Fall, 1967), 300–15. Concerning the suppression of the Greenville, S.C., Unemployed Council, see Erwin D. Hoffman, "The Genesis of the Modern Movement for Equal Rights in South Carolina, 1930–1939," in Bernard Sternsher (ed.), *The Negro in Depression and War* (Chicago: Quadrangle, 1969), 203–206.

8. Angelo Herndon, *Let Me Live* (New York: Arno Press, 1969), 189–92; mimeographed circular in the printed transcript of *Herndon* v. *Georgia,* U.S. Supreme Court, October term, 1934, No. 665, p. 124, copy in law office of Sutherland, Asbill, and Brennan, Atlanta, Ga.

By the scheduled hour nearly one thousand people had quietly gathered. A large portion of the demonstrators flowed through the courthouse door and up the stairway to the fifth floor. There they assembled before the county commissioners' offices and asked to see Walter C. Hendrix, hoping to dramatically convince the skeptical commissioner that hunger and starvation really existed in the city.[9]

The unexpected appearance of such a large crowd caused much confusion in the commission offices. The group patiently waited in the corridors while nervous officials hastily conferred. After thirty minutes, an official emerged and summoned a small delegation of white workers. Black demonstrators were barred. Inside, Commissioner Walter Steward spoke with the white group. He promised that a special session of the county commissioners would be called immediately to deal with the emergency. He urged anyone present who had relatives on a farm to see about returning there, hinting that the county might provide transportation if needed. Steward added that any relief granted would go equally to both black and white recipients, a promise greeted with some skepticism. When the demonstrators departed, harried officials were greatly relieved, but the large gathering—purportedly the biggest biracial demonstration in the South in several decades—had captured their attention. The beleaguered commissioners approved the following day an emergency appropriation of six thousand dollars to provide immediate relief via grocery orders for families cut off by the earlier action. At the same time, the commissioners assured the public that every effort would be made to prevent the unemployed from flocking into the city to enjoy these generous relief benefits.[10]

Although the commission's action temporarily eased the relief crisis, the incident had once again reminded local law enforcement officials of the presence and influence of Communists in Atlanta. The size of the demonstration, as well as its interracial composition, frightened these officials. Fearful of additional radical activity and possible class solidarity among the poor and jobless, they apparently decided to

9. *Ibid.*; Atlanta *Daily World*, June 30, 1932; Atlanta *Constitution*, June 26, 1932; *Daily Worker*, July 2, 1932.

10. Atlanta *Daily World*, June 30, 1932; *Daily Worker*, July 2, 1932; Atlanta *Constitution*, July 1, 2, and 12, 1932. The *Constitution* gave the smallest estimate of the crowd—three hundred persons.

destroy the movement. Subsequently, Atlanta policemen began to shadow suspected leaders of the Unemployed Council. A special watch was placed on the post office, since the leaflet announcing the relief protest listed a return address of P.O. Box 339. Eventually this diligence produced results. On the night of July 11, 1932, eleven days after the courthouse demonstration, Detectives John Chester and Frank B. Watson stepped forward and arrested a young black man as he withdrew mail from Box 339. The initial charge lodged against the suspect was the vague phrase, "on suspicion." But the ledger book at police headquarters told the story. Across from his name was scribbled one damning word—"C-O-M-M-U-N-I-S-T." The strange and perplexing case of Angelo Herndon versus the state of Georgia had begun.[11]

With Herndon behind bars, the prosecution proceeded slowly. The Fulton County Grand Jury considered Herndon's indictment on July 12 but took no action. Meanwhile, Herndon remained in jail without bail. In three subsequent meetings, the grand jury failed even to discuss the case. Finally, on July 21, white attorney Oliver C. Hancock, assisted by black lawyers John H. Geer and Benjamin J. Davis, Jr., filed a habeas corpus petition seeking to free Herndon, who now had been held eleven days without bond "for investigation." Judge Virlyn E. Moore of the Fulton County Superior Court denied the petition but ordered the solicitor general's office to secure an indictment by the following day or free Herndon. Meanwhile, he set bond for the black Communist at three thousand dollars. After hearing testimony from several witnesses including Assistant Solicitor General E. A. Stephens, the grand jury returned a true bill on Friday, July 22. The indictment formally charged the prisoner with the offense of attempting to incite insurrection, a capital crime. It stated that on July 16 (a date on which he was securely housed in jail) Herndon attempted to incite insurrection and tried to induce others to join in combined resistance to the lawful authority of the state of Georgia. To support these charges the indictment declared that Herndon had called meetings and made speeches in order to establish a group of white and colored persons under the name of the Communist party of America. These actions were allegedly designed to incite riots,

11. Atlanta *Constitution*, July 2 and 12, 1932; Atlanta *Daily World*, July 12, 1932; *Daily Worker*, July 15, 1932; Herndon, *Let Me Live*, 193; John Hammond Moore, "The Angelo Herndon Case, 1932–1937," *Phylon*, XXXII (Spring, 1971), 62.

to impede the orderly processes of the courts, and to overthrow by force and violence the lawfully constituted authority of the state.[12]

The indictment further charged Herndon with soliciting unknown persons to join the Communist party and the Young Communist League for the purpose of waging war against the state. Their eventual goal was purportedly to create by violence and revolution "a new government known as United Soviets Soviet Russia [*sic*], sometimes called and known as 'The Dictatorship of the Propertyless People.'" The state further contended that Herndon had circulated certain pamphlets with the aim of inciting insurrection, riots, and uprisings against the state. These works included *The Life and Struggles of Negro Toilers* by George Padmore, *Communism and Christianism* by Bishop William Montgomery Brown, the *Daily Worker*, and the *Southern Worker*. All of these actions were said to have been planned in order to deny and overthrow the lawful authority of the state of Georgia.[13] In short, Herndon was a danger to the state and his Communist activities were viewed as inherently insurrectionary.

The path that led Angelo Herndon to the Fulton County Jail began nineteen years earlier in the little mining town of Wyoming, Ohio, near Cincinnati, where Eugene Angelo Braxton Herndon was born on May 6, 1913, apparently the fifth of seven children in the Paul Herndon family. Angelo's father was a black coal miner; his mother Harriet, a mulatto of black, white, and Indian ancestry, worked as a maid. Poverty and religion dominated Herndon's childhood. His mother was an extremely devout person whose strong faith impressed her young son. His uncle Jeremiah became a preacher, and it was at his emotional first sermon that the nine-year-old Angelo "got religion" and was "saved." Along with childhood illnesses and financial worries, religion helped mold Angelo into a serious youth. His father's meager wages kept the family chronically impoverished, and Paul Herndon's death in 1922 precipitated another economic decline for the family. At the age of thirteen, Herndon

12. Atlanta *Daily World*, July 21 and 24, 1932; Oliver C. Hancock to Abraham Isserman, July 27, 1932, in American Civil Liberties Union Archives, Princeton University Library; copy of indictment in printed brief of *Herndon* v. *Georgia*, in law office of Sutherland, Asbill, and Brennan.

13. Copy of indictment in printed brief of *Herndon* v. *Georgia*, in law office of Sutherland, Asbill, and Brennan.

and an older brother left home for nearby Kentucky, where they found work in the coal mines. After several months of hard physical labor, the two journeyed southward to Birmingham to live with relatives. But, instead of improved employment opportunities in Alabama's mines, they found only long hours of work, low wages, and demeaning working conditions.[14]

Increasingly the black teenager became distressed by widespread bigotry and economic exploitation of black workers. As he searched for a solution to these problems, he found the emotional religion of his youth, with its accommodation to the social system, inadequate and inconsistent with his new, outspoken temperament. At this stage in Herndon's life a new creed presented itself. On a sultry day in June, 1930, he stumbled upon several handbills advertising a meeting of the Birmingham Unemployed Council to discuss solutions to starvation and unemployment. Not really understanding what the meeting was all about but believing that he had nothing to lose, Herndon decided to attend. At the rally that evening, he was amazed to hear the main speaker, a white man, denounce segregation and urge black and white workers to unite to solve their common economic difficulties. This was the first time Herndon had heard a white person advocate such views, and the speaker's words had a profound effect on the youth. Only once before had he felt such an intense emotional experience—as a child when he had been "saved" by his uncle. Communism now replaced Christianity, but Herndon believed that this recent conversion was based on a superior world view. To this neophyte, Communist teachings explained many of the problems that had been troubling him. Communism's absolute certainty gave him a new purpose and a sense of mission as he plunged into the activities of the Unemployed Council. During the summer he attended a national meeting of the councils in Chicago, where he met many important Communist leaders and was further impressed by interracial cooperation among Communists. Shortly after returning to Birmingham, he was arrested along with Joseph Carr, a white activist already indicted in Georgia under that

14. The following paragraphs on Herndon's early life are based on Herndon, *Let Me Live*, 3–164, and Angelo Herndon, "You Cannot Kill the Working Class," reprinted in August Meier, Elliott Rudwick, and Francis L. Broderick (eds.), *Black Protest Thought in the Twentieth Century* (2nd ed.; Indianapolis: Bobbs-Merrill, 1971), 132–47.

state's notorious insurrection law, as they tried to organize workers at a Tennessee Coal, Iron, and Railroad Company mine. This was the first of Herndon's many encounters with law enforcement officials. Instead of discouraging him, the arrest motivated the black teenager formally to join the Communist party.

By the end of 1930, Birmingham police had recognized Herndon as a leading local "Red." Periodic arrests and frequent surveillance made sustained activity difficult. Consequently, party leaders sent him to New Orleans, where a longshoremen's strike was in progress. While in the Crescent City, Herndon first learned of the Scottsboro rape case, which was later to be compared with his own case. Returning to Birmingham, Herndon worked in the International Labor Defense (ILD) Scottsboro campaign, but heightened public hysteria and increased police harassment made it virtually impossible for him to continue. As a result, in late 1931 or early 1932, he departed for Georgia to carry on his activities for the Unemployed councils and the Communist party.

In Atlanta Herndon concentrated his efforts on black and white workers. In addition to recruiting members for the Unemployed Council and the party, he also assisted the Communist party's 1932 presidential candidates, William Z. Foster and James W. Ford, by organizing Foster-Ford clubs. Then the city and county underwent their relief crisis, and Herndon embarked on his collision course with local officials.

Unlike that of the Scottsboro boys, Herndon's arrest was not a dramatic event. Few people outside the Atlanta area took note of it. Yet within three years the Herndon case had been made into a liberal-leftist *cause célèbre* symbolizing southern injustice and oppression. The credit for this national awareness belonged primarily to the leftist International Labor Defense. Herndon's arrest incensed the ILD. The organization's national office promptly called for protests by progressive organizations. The ILD urged that Solicitor General John A. Boykin and Governor Richard B. Russell be deluged with complaints. The Communist newspaper *Daily Worker* endorsed the protest effort, asserting that the "text of the indictment reveals in glaring nakedness the frame-up character of the charges." In order to supervise legal arrangements, the ILD dispatched its fiery, outspoken national secretary, William L. Patterson, to Atlanta. There he denounced the affair as a "frame-up" and charged that almost "every bit of so-called 'Red' literature found in his room after his arrest may be found in books, magazines and pamphlets at the public library. Why not arrest the librarian?" Patterson further claimed that authorities were trying to persecute blacks in order to distract the attention of white workers from their own economic plight. The ILD official had difficulty locating a cooperative lawyer to defend Herndon but finally hired a prominent white attorney, H. A. Allen, for a sizable retainer. [15]

Then Patterson met Benjamin J. Davis, Jr., a black graduate of the Harvard Law School and the son of Benjamin J. Davis, Sr., former Republican national committeeman from Georgia. After reading of Herndon's arrest and visiting him in jail, Davis offered his legal services without charge to the young Communist. Herndon arranged for Davis to talk with Patterson, with the result that the ILD head agreed to retain the young attorney and his partner John Geer as defense counsel. When Patterson informed Allen of the ILD's desire to see the two black lawyers serve as co-counsel, Allen balked at breaking traditional southern mores. In the Deep South any white lawyer who participated as an equal with a black attorney risked social disapproval and a loss of business as well. Allen declined to return the ILD retainer, much to Patterson's disgust, as the ILD was perpetually short of funds. According to legal etiquette, however, Allen was not obligated to return the money. [16]

Shortly after Patterson's visit, an anonymous southern correspondent filed a confidential analysis of these developments with the ILD. The writer, probably ILD attorney Frank Irwin, stressed that the great importance of the case had not yet been fully recognized, blaming the Birmingham party leader Donald Burke for this. "Give Burke hell for falling down on this case," he wrote. "[He] did not consider it important enough to even inquire about it." Praising Allen's departure from the case, Irwin urged that Geer and Davis be given firm support. He also proposed that a prominent writer, such as Sherwood Anderson, be hired

---

15. *Daily Worker*, August 3, 1932; Atlanta *Daily World*, August 30, 1932.
16. William L. Patterson to the author, May 25, 1970; Benjamin J. Davis, *Communist Councilman from Harlem* (New York: International Publishers, 1969), 53–55.

to cover the trial and that Bishop William Montgomery Brown, author of one of the "insurrectionary" books cited in the Herndon indictment, be asked to appear as a defense witness. These last two suggestions, however, were ignored.[17]

After lengthy discussions with ILD officials during the fall, Davis and Geer agreed to base the defense on the unconstitutionality of the insurrection statute, the systematic exclusion of blacks from juries, and the right of citizens to assemble and peacefully petition their government for redress of grievances. But, in mapping its strategy, the defense refused to limit its efforts solely to traditional courtroom measures, desiring also to confront the political aspects of the trial. The chief targets of this political counteroffensive were the harsh economic conditions, at which Herndon's protest had been aimed, and Georgia's white supremacy system. In short, Herndon's defenders planned a twofold strategy—legal efforts at justice within the court system and political efforts outside it aimed at undermining the socioeconomic forces which had originally inspired the prosecution.[18]

The entry of the International Labor Defense into the Herndon case reinforced for many blacks and whites that group's image as the most outspoken defender of black rights and freedoms in the country. It also dramatized the ILD's militant and aggressive tactics, in contrast to the less flamboyant, gradualistic methods of the National Association for the Advancement of Colored People (NAACP). Formed in 1925 and based in New York, the ILD was a leftist group designed to defend Communists, radicals, and other "class war prisoners" through regular legal procedures and by "mass protest." Although Communist party members controlled its leadership, many non-Communists were members. Understandably, Communist leaders hoped that such members might ultimately be recruited into the party's ranks. Since ILD leaders viewed the courts as dominated by hostile capitalist forces, they felt that legal maneuvers alone could not be expected to free victims of politically oriented arrests. Hence mass protest was a necessary strategy

17. [?] to International Labor Defense, undated, in International Labor Defense Papers, Schomburg Collection, New York Public Library, hereinafter cited as ILD Papers.
18. Davis, *Communist Councilman from Harlem*, 55.

designed to attack the political basis of such prosecutions. Only by these methods, they maintained, could hostile courts be forced to grant the just legal points advanced by ILD lawyers.[19]

The Central Committee of the Communist party used the Scottsboro case as an example in explaining this strategy in 1932. It declared, "Confidence in the courts cannot bring justice. Only confidence in the might and power of the organized efforts of the American working class is the method of obtaining the freedom of these innocent boys." The ILD took a special interest in black defendants during the 1930s and gained several victories. This fact brought the organization greater popularity with blacks than other leftist organizations, since ILD efforts were aimed at immediate, visible results.[20] Groups that promised improvements only "after the revolution" found a less receptive black audience. William L. Patterson, the ILD's black stormy petrel, symbolized that group's militancy. As a young Harlem attorney, Patterson first encountered Communists while working in the campaign to save the lives of Nicola Sacco and Bartolomeo Vanzetti. Impressed by Communist dedication to social justice, he joined the Communist party in the mid-1920s. In September, 1932, Patterson was named national secretary of the ILD, reflecting the ILD's growing interest in black Americans. Volatile, outspoken, and sometimes dogmatic, Patterson left his imprint on black protest during the 1930s. He continued to participate in Communist activities in following decades and served as head of the Communist-influenced Civil Rights Congress, remaining an outspoken critic of American racism and discrimination for nearly half a century.[21]

19. Wilson Record, *The Negro and the Communist Party* (Chapel Hill: University of North Carolina Press, 1951), 34–36, 86; Theodore Draper, *American Communism and Soviet Russia* (New York: Viking, 1960), 180–83; William Z. Foster, *The Negro People in American History* (New York: International Publishers, 1954), 460–61.

20. Dan T. Carter, *Scottsboro: A Tragedy of the American South* (Baton Rouge: Louisiana State University Press, 1969), 138; *Daily Worker*, January 20, 1932. "We always sought the development of mass action as an inseparable part of 'legal' defense. Mass defense is of vital significance in a political case, and virtually all cases involving blacks are political cases." Patterson to the author, May 25, 1970.

21. Carter, *Scottsboro*, 147. See also William L. Patterson, *The Man Who Cried Genocide* (New York: International Publishers, 1971). In 1951, along with the noted actor Paul Roberson, Patterson presented a petition to the United Nations charging that the United States government at all levels practiced genocide against Afro-Americans. The 1960s and 1970s witnessed a revival of these politico-legal defense tactics. As Patterson observed in 1970, "The ILD-Civil Rights

The most prominent example of ILD involvement in behalf of southern blacks came in Alabama's notorious Scottsboro rape case. The organization also assisted in a significant but relatively unknown case involving Euel Lee (Orphan Jones) in Maryland, as well as in the Herndon affair. But the Scottsboro case emerged as the ILD's greatest triumph. The plight of the nine Scottsboro boys drew sympathy not only from most sections of the United States but also from foreign countries. To many Americans, Scottsboro symbolized "southern racism, repression, and injustice" at its worst, though to others it showed the dangers "of Communism and the accompanying dreaded 'social equality.'" The nine black defendants were accused of raping two white women on a freight train in northern Alabama in March, 1931. After a speedy trial, eight of the nine youths were convicted and sentenced to death. Before other national organizations could act, the ILD seized control of the case and, despite a bitter struggle with the NAACP, retained exclusive control of it until 1935. Utilizing the services of several noted authorities on constitutional law, the ILD appealed the case to the United States Supreme Court. In November, 1932, the high court issued a landmark decision known as *Powell* v. *Alabama*, which granted a new trial to the defendants because the failure of local officials to provide the defendants with adequate counsel had denied them due process of law. This decision enhanced the ILD's and Communist party's claims to be the true defenders of basic rights for blacks in the United States.[22]

The Euel Lee case likewise affirmed the ILD's reputation as a militant defender of blacks against injustice. Euel Lee was a black Maryland farmhand accused of murdering his employer. He barely escaped a lynch mob while being conveyed to jail. ILD attorneys Bernard Ades and David Levinson defended Lee. At the first trial in January, 1932, Ades challenged the systematic exclusion of blacks from the petit jury. Although the trial judge admitted that he could not remember a single black juror having served in the last twenty-six years,

---

Congress methodology in political cases is very much alive today and will be so long as the Courts are in the hands of racists, and those who use Courts as a class weapon. The Chicago Seven and New Haven cases are political, not legal cases, and will be decided on the basis of the relation of forces in the arena of struggle." Patterson to the author, May 25, 1970.

22. See Carter, *Scottsboro*, and Hugh Murray, "The NAACP Versus the Communist Party: The Scottsboro Rape Case, 1931–1932," *Phylon*, XXVIII (Fall, 1967), 276–87.

he said that he nonetheless saw no discrimination in the system of selecting jurors. Lee was subsequently convicted and sentenced to death. The ILD promptly appealed to the Maryland Court of Appeals, with Joseph R. Brodsky, head of the ILD legal staff, supervising the arguments. Brodsky's efforts were rewarded with an unexpected legal victory. The appeals court threw out Lee's conviction and ordered a new trial, ruling that the procedures used to select jurors, coupled with the long absence of blacks from these juries, confined "selections to white men as effectively as if such a restriction were prescribed by statute." Thus the defendant had been deprived of his constitutional rights under the Fourteenth Amendment, and the conviction was voided.[23]

Communist leaders cited this favorable ruling as proof that their tactics were superior to the "reformist" methods of the NAACP. Earl Browder claimed in the *Daily Worker* that the ILD was responsible for taking the case out of obscurity and making it a trial not merely of Euel Lee but of Jim Crow justice. "The higher court was forced by the pressure of aroused mass opinion and protest to set aside the verdict and order a new trial," Browder asserted. Patterson concurred. "Not legal pressure alone, but mass pressure, into which the legal defense is merged, has forced the capitalist courts of Maryland to grant a new trial," he said. Patterson added that orthodox courtroom measures only rarely won victories for blacks or the working class in America, but "legal defense linked up with mass pressure has won many victories." Unfortunately the ILD soon discovered that its own triumphs could prove illusory. Maryland authorities quickly reindicted Euel Lee in September, 1932. This time three token blacks were included on the new jury panel of two hundred persons. Since the prosecution had ten peremptory challenges, three of which it used to disqualify these prospective black jurors, the ILD felt cheated. Despite a vigorous defense by Ades and Levinson, the all-white jury again found Lee guilty and sentenced him to death. The appeals court upheld the verdict, legal and mass protests notwithstanding.[24]

23. *Daily Worker*, January 18 and 22, February 4, and May 21, 1932; Atlanta *Constitution*, July 7, 1932; New York *Times*, July 12, 1932, p. 16; *Lee* v. *Maryland*, 161 Atl. 284 (1932); Atlanta *Daily World*, October 4, 1932.
24. *Daily Worker*, August 3 and 4, September 26 and 30, October 1 and 24, 1932; Atlanta *Daily World*, October 4, 1932.

Despite this setback the ILD had demonstrated during 1932 its firm determination to defend the rights of southern blacks. These actions came at an appropriate time, for it seemed that blacks in Atlanta and across the nation were becoming more outspoken in their attacks on discrimination and prejudice. The time now seemed ripe for a broad assault on racism and Jim Crow justice. The Angelo Herndon case in Georgia provided an excellent opportunity for precisely such a campaign.

CHAPTER TWO
Atlanta,
1930 and 1932

ALTHOUGH later generations came to view Atlanta as "the city too busy to hate," observers during the 1930s knew a different city. In 1930 Atlanta was a bustling, optimistic city of 270,000 residents, the physical embodiment of the New South. Despite its appearance, the city remained chained to its Deep South heritage. Not progressive administration or racial harmony but narrow-minded leadership, racial friction, corruption in city government, and labor unrest characterized Atlanta during the decade. In 1937 a report by the American Civil Liberties Union (ACLU), noting the prosecutions of Angelo Herndon and other radicals in the early thirties, named the city one of the nation's ten worst centers of repression. But this negative image was not a product of the depression years alone. Unfortunately the Angelo Herndon case was just one of several twentieth-century incidents that brought disrepute to the metropolis. [1]

Shortly after the turn of the century, Atlanta had been the site of a bloody race riot. On September 22 and 23, 1906, thousands of frenzied whites roamed the streets of downtown Atlanta, chasing and beating every black person they could capture. This massive outburst left an estimated twenty-five blacks dead and well over one hundred seriously injured. Irresponsible civic leaders, an emotional political campaign,

---

1. American Civil Liberties Union, *Let Freedom Ring!: The Story of Civil Liberty, 1936–1937* (New York: American Civil Liberties Union, 1937), 12. For information on Atlanta during the depression, see Work Projects Administration Writers' Program, *Atlanta: A City of the Modern South* (New York: Smith and Durrell, 1942), and Elizabeth Stevenson, "A Personal History of Change in Atlanta," *Virginia Quarterly Review*, XL (Autumn, 1965), 580–95.

and a sensationalistic local press had contributed heavily to this racial explosion.[2] The notorious Leo Frank case of 1913–1915 did little to improve the city's tarnished reputation. Frank, the manager of a local pencil factory, was accused of murdering fourteen-year-old Mary Phagan. The trial proceeded in an atmosphere marked by yellow journalism, widespread hysteria, and anti-Semitism. On the trial's final day, thousands packed the area surrounding the courthouse. Because of the danger to their safety, the defendant and his attorneys were excused from being present in court that day. When Governor John M. Slaton later commuted Frank's sentence to life imprisonment in June, 1915, a mob repeatedly tried to storm the governor's home. Two months later, on August 16, a band of twenty-five armed men daringly seized Frank from the state penitentiary and boldly drove him across the state to Marietta where they hanged him from a tree. Not one of the lynchers was ever brought to trial.[3]

On a cool November evening several months later, William J. Simmons, an insurance salesman and former history teacher, conducted atop Stone Mountain (just east of Atlanta) a solemn ceremony that formally reestablished the Ku Klux Klan (KKK). For the next ten years, Atlanta served as headquarters for the group. Many city residents held national offices in the order, and Imperial Wizard Simmons lived in a mansion on Peachtree Road. Although the Atlanta *Georgian* occasionally challenged the Klan's views, it was joined by few other civic spokesmen. Public opinion, no doubt influenced by the fact that "the Invisible Empire contributed substantially to the city's economy," heavily favored the organization. When opposition eventually arose, it centered on personalities rather than ideology. By the 1930s the Klan was only a pale imitation of its former self, but it did rally its tattered legions for occasional public demonstrations.[4]

During the depression years radical organizers clashed repeatedly with conservative southern officials. Although the frequency of these

2. Charles Crowe, "Racial Massacre in Atlanta, September 22, 1906," *Journal of Negro History*, LIV (April, 1969), 150–73.

3. C. Vann Woodward, *Tom Watson: Agrarian Rebel* (New York: Oxford University Press, 1963), 435–48. See also Leonard Dinnerstein, *The Leo Frank Case* (New York: Columbia University Press, 1968).

4. Kenneth T. Jackson, *The Ku Klux Klan in the City, 1915–1930* (New York: Oxford University Press, 1967), 29–44.

confrontations may not have matched those of other areas, their intensity could not be surpassed anywhere. Beginning with Communist involvement in the famous Gastonia strike of 1929 and continuing during the expanded Communist activity of the following decade, conservative white southerners saw their region as being invaded by dangerous "outsiders" attempting to stir up discontent. Particularly disturbing to these southerners were Communist teachings on racial equality and Communist efforts to combat the numerous abuses of the Jim Crow system.[5] "The hitherto guerrilla warfare is announced now as a deliberate invasion by a horde of reds determined to destroy the peace, to wreck the prosperity and to subjugate the Americanism of the American Southern States," warned the *Manufacturer's Record* in September, 1930. Although most of this Communist activity focused on Birmingham, Atlanta received some attention too.[6]

The first clash between Atlanta officials and Communist activists began on March 9, 1930, when local police raided a Communist-sponsored meeting in the black business district. Officers arrested the gathering's two leaders—Joseph Carr, eighteen, of Wheeling, West Virginia, and M. H. Powers, twenty-four, of St. Paul, Minnesota. Following some initial confusion about what charges to file against the two young white radicals, officials reached into the most obscure sections of the state penal code and dusted off a statute unused since 1869. Specifically, Carr and Powers were charged with "attempting to incite insurrection" against the state of Georgia—a capital offense—and with "circulating insurrectionary literature," a crime that carried a lengthy jail sentence. Assistant Solicitor General John H. Hudson took credit for rediscovering this ancient law, which the state subsequently used to prosecute other alleged radicals including Angelo Herndon.[7]

5. The congressional committee headed by Congressman Hamilton Fish, which was investigating Communist activities, visited Atlanta and several other southern cities in November, 1930. It concluded that the Communist party, by making serious appeals to southern blacks as well as southern workers, was behind Negro and labor unrest. See United States House of Representatives, *Investigation of Communistic Propaganda: Hearings Before a Special Committee to Investigate Communistic Activities in the United States*, 71st Cong., 2nd Sess., Pt. 6, Vol. I.

6. George B. Tindall, *The Emergence of the New South, 1913–1945* (Baton Rouge: Louisiana State University Press, 1967), 378, Vol. X of Wendell Holmes Stephenson and E. Merton Coulter (eds.), *A History of the South* (10 vols.; Baton Rouge: Louisiana State University Press, 1949–).

7. Atlanta *Constitution*, March 10 and 12, 1930; Walter Wilson, "Atlanta's Communists," *Nation*, June 25, 1930, pp. 730–31; Macon *Telegraph*, March 10, 1930; New York *Times*, March

The indictment of Carr and Powers focused attention on the history of the almost forgotten insurrection statute. In the 1830s, numerous southern legislatures, frightened by the bloody Nat Turner rebellion and the emergence of a militant trend in the abolitionist movement, had tightened the regulations concerning slave revolts, hoping to avoid such an upheaval in their own states. Georgia lawmakers revised the state penal code in 1833 to read: "Exciting an insurrection or revolt of slaves, or any attempt by writing, speaking, or otherwise, to excite an insurrection or revolt of slaves, shall be punished with death." The code's next section, aimed at abolitionist publications, likewise punished by death any introduction or circulation within the state of any pamphlet or written paper for the purpose of inciting resistance, revolt, or insurrection among the slaves or free persons of color.[8]

The next stage in the insurrection law's development came immediately after the Civil War when southern states revised their statutes to acknowledge the new status of blacks. Certain new rights were granted; others were denied. Meeting in Milledgeville in November and December, 1866, the Georgia legislature rewrote many of that state's laws, including the slave revolt statutes. When specific references to slaves were dropped, the concept of "insurrection" became the heart of the statute. Lawmakers defined insurrection as combined resistance to the lawful authority of the state. The legislature then specified, "Any attempt, by persuasion or otherwise, to induce others to join in any combined resistance to the lawful authority of the State, shall constitute an attempt to incite insurrection." Punishment for insurrection or attempted insurrection was death, unless the jury recommended mercy. No specific punishment for an *attempt* to incite an insurrection was specified, since the legislature probably assumed that it would fall under the previous stipulations. The legislators also modified the accompanying section prohibiting the circulation of insurrectionary literature, substituting a five-to-twenty-year prison term for the death penalty.[9]

12, 1930, p. 3; Walter Wilson to American Civil Liberties Union, June 26, 1930, in American Civil Liberties Union Archives, Princeton University Library, hereinafter cited as ACLU Archives.

8. *Acts of the General Assembly of the State of Georgia, Passed in Milledgeville, at an Annual Session in November and December, 1833* (Macon: Polhill and Fort, 1834), 215.

9. *Acts of the General Assembly of the State of Georgia, Passed in Milledgeville, at an Annual Session in November and December, 1866* (Macon: J. W. Burke and Co., 1867), 152–53.

The first and only case known to have arisen under the insurrection law during the sixty-four years from 1866 to 1930 occurred in 1868. The defendant in that case was John T. Gibson, identified by the appeal record as a preacher and "a free person of color." Authorities charged Gibson with inciting about one hundred blacks to break into the Early County Jail on August 18, 1868, in order to rescue Charles Fryer, a black man. At the alleged urging of Gibson, an armed mob had advanced upon the jail, but, when a guard had fired a single shot at the crowd, it had promptly dispersed. No other violent acts resulted. Following his conviction on a charge of *attempting* to incite an insurrection, Gibson was sentenced to be executed.[10]

Gibson's attorneys appealed the conviction to the Supreme Court of Georgia in June, 1869. They contended that the state penal code failed specifically to provide a penalty for an *attempt* to incite insurrection, as distinguished from the offenses of insurrection and attempted insurrection. Chief Justice Joseph E. Brown, a former wartime governor appointed to the bench by a Republican governor in 1868, wrote the court's decision, which upheld the defense contention and freed Gibson. Chief Justice Brown applied a rule of strict construction to the law, agreeing that no punishment had been specified for an attempt to incite insurrection; hence the conviction was void. In so ruling he called the attention of the legislature to the omission and voiced his hope for corrective action.[11]

Slow to act on the matter, the Georgia legislature waited until December 12, 1871, before revising the statute. It inserted the appropriate language, establishing an attempt to incite insurrection as a capital offense.[12] There the matter rested for fifty-nine years, until Fulton County officials resurrected the law in 1930. The chief reason for reviving the statute was the absense of sedition or criminal syndicalism laws in Georgia. During or shortly after the First World War, many states across the nation enacted these statutes; Georgia did not. In the 1930s, these states used such laws to combat increased radical activity.

10. *Gibson* v. *Georgia*, Ga. 572–73 (1869).

11. *Ibid.*, 573–74. Brown later rejoined the Democratic party and was elected to the U.S. Senate.

12. *Acts and Resolutions of the General Assembly of the State of Georgia, at a Session in November and December, 1871* (Atlanta: W. A. Hemphill and Co., 1872), 19–20.

Georgia officials could not do so and were somewhat handicapped in their antiradical efforts until John H. Hudson reactivated the insurrection law. [13]

During April and May, 1930, various law enforcement officials expressed great concern over continuing Communist activity in Atlanta. On May 21, police raided another Communist-sponsored labor meeting, netting four additional suspects. Those arrested were Mary Dalton, twenty, of New York City, and Ann Burlack, nineteen, of Greenville, South Carolina, both organizers for the National Textile Workers' Union; Herbert Newton of New York City (who originally gave his name as Gilmer Brady), an organizer for the American Negro Labor Congress; and Henry Story, an Atlanta printer. [14] All were ultimately charged with "attempting to incite insurrection." The fact that Dalton and Burlack were young white females and Newton and Story were black males deeply disturbed Atlanta authorities, already troubled over Communist teachings concerning political and social equality. Efforts by these radicals to organize industrial workers in Atlanta likewise worried officials. "As far as I can see," declared Police Captain Grover Fain, "the Communists are attempting to create a chaotic situation in the South by constant agitation on the labor situation. We're going to spike any such attempts, and we mean business!" [15]

Public reaction to the arrest and indictment of these four additional radicals—who, along with Joseph Carr and M. H. Powers, were referred to as the "Atlanta Six"—seemed generally favorable. The major

13. Zechariah Chafee, Jr., *Free Speech in the United States* (Cambridge: Harvard University Press, 1941), 389; Macon *Telegraph*, June 5, 1930. Assistant Solicitor J. Walter LeCraw later explained that the statute had lain unused for sixty years because there had been "no occasion" to use it during that period. Author's interview with J. Walter LeCraw, Atlanta, Ga., August 25, 1970.

14. Atlanta *Constitution*, May 22, 1930; Atlanta *Journal*, May 22, 1930; Atlanta *Georgian*, May 22, 1930; Wilson, "Atlanta's Communists," 731; New York *Times*, March 12, 1930, p. 3. Julius and Lizette Klarin of Atlanta were also arrested at the same time; however, charges against them were later dropped because of the efforts of their landlady Mrs. J. E. Andrews, president of the Atlanta Women's Civic Council. Apparently the fact that they were local residents, not "outsiders," also aided their release. Ironically, records introduced at the trial of Angelo Herndon in 1933 identified Julius Klarin as a member of the Communist party.

15. Atlanta *Constitution*, May 23, 1930; Atlanta *Journal*, May 22, 1930; Atlanta *Georgian*, May 23, 1930; hearing transcript, in ACLU Archives. The state even refused for over a month to permit bail for these four radicals.

newspapers supported such attacks on communism, and there was little public criticism of the move. Yet there were a few dissenting voices. W. T. Anderson, the outspoken liberal editor of the Macon *Telegraph*, dared to denounce the arrests. Anderson declared that the prosecution of the Atlanta Six illustrated how an archaic statute, "resurrected to suit the purposes of an over-zealous prosecuting officer, may be a weapon of oppression for the prisoner and embarrassment for the state." During the following months, Anderson continued to deride Atlanta officials for their actions.[16]

Although Anderson remained the main public critic within the state, two national organizations shared his concern over the arrests. Both the International Labor Defense and the American Civil Liberties Union viewed the prosecutions as a violation of fundamental legal rights. The ILD also saw the arrests as a threat to radical and labor activities in Georgia. Initially, the ILD retained Oliver C. Hancock of Atlanta as legal counsel for the Six. Subsequently the ACLU volunteered its assistance. Since the short-funded ILD was in a far weaker financial position than the ACLU, it gladly permitted the ACLU to underwrite the cost of retaining W. A. McClellan, an outstanding criminal lawyer from Macon, as additional counsel in the case.[17]

Despite occasional correspondence with several Atlantans committed to the cause of civil liberties, the ACLU lacked a local chapter. Thus, in order to build public support for the Atlanta Six, as well as for basic constitutional rights, the national ACLU office dispatched a representative to the city. Walter Wilson, a journalist and field agent for the union, traveled to Atlanta in May, 1930, to coordinate local efforts. Friendly and outgoing, Wilson carefully cultivated the favor of labor leaders, liberals, and sympathetic citizens.[18] His behind-the-scenes activities slowly bore fruit, as many prominent Atlantans privately indicated their

16. Macon *Telegraph*, June 5 and 21, 1930. For an extended discussion of the prosecution of the Atlanta Six, see Charles H. Martin, "The Angelo Herndon Case and Georgia Justice, 1930–1937" (Ph.D. dissertation, Tulane University, 1972), 5–38.

17. Thomas W. Hardwick to Roger N. Baldwin, April 8, 11, and 14, 1930, Baldwin to Oliver C. Hancock, April 8, 1930, Hancock to ACLU, April 22, 1930, Forrest Bailey to Hancock, April 23, 1930, Bailey to Walter Wilson, June 11, 1930, and W. A. McClellan to Bailey, May 3, 1930, all in ACLU Archives. The ACLU and the ILD shared the cost of retaining McClellan, but the ILD let the ACLU handle the negotiations.

18. Walter Wilson to ACLU, May 27 and 30, 1930, and Wilson to Roger N. Baldwin, May 28, 1930, all *ibid*.

distaste for the prosecutions.[19] Wilson directed his major efforts toward the issuance of a public statement supporting free speech and civil liberties endorsed by numerous influential citizens. This, he hoped, would serve as a public rebuff to John H. Hudson's recent prosecutions. Sixty-one area residents signed this controversial declaration, which Wilson released to newspapers for their Sunday, August 3, editions. Included were Will W. Alexander, Mary Raoul Millis, the Reverend Edwin Poteat, the Reverend Adiel Jarrett Moncrief, Emory University Dean Comer M. Woodward, and Georgia Tech instructors Glenn Rainey and C. Vann Woodward. The document strongly endorsed basic constitutional rights and stressed the need to maintain freedom of thought during periods of economic change. Although those who signed specifically refused to endorse communism, they did urge that "Communists should be protected in their constitutional rights of free speech and free assemblage." The appeal further requested that the Six be tried for their alleged crimes and not for their political, social, economic, and religious beliefs.[20]

Public reaction to the statement was mixed. Several months passed before its restraining effect on the prosecution staff became clear. Meanwhile, the ACLU defended the move against criticism that it should remain quiet and let the law take its course. "We always take the position of pushing our propaganda even when trials are pending," Roger N. Baldwin, co-director of the union, explained to Wilson. "As a matter of fact, it's the best time. There is no use when the trials are all over."[21]

As the weeks went by, the state failed to take action against the Atlanta Six. With the passage of time it became apparent that the prosecution had become reluctant to bring them to trial. Former senator and governor Thomas W. Hardwick told the ACLU in mid-October that the situation in Atlanta "is not very serious and that it will readily yield to treatment." Later in the month, attorney Marvin Underwood summarized the situation, informing the national office that the cases would

19. Mary Raoul Millis to Roger N. Baldwin, July 1, 1930, *ibid*.
20. Atlanta *Constitution*, August 3, 1930; Atlanta *Journal*, August 3, 1930; New York *Times*, August 4, 1930, p. 4.
21. Roger N. Baldwin to Walter Wilson, August 6, 1930, in ACLU Archives.

not be called soon and that there would be no action on the matter unless there was public agitation. On the other hand, the charges would not be dismissed either. Matters would continue unresolved until the state finally took definite action, which it had no immediate desire to do.[22]

For the next sixteen months the Atlanta Six remained in this legal limbo. Although not in prison, they were not completely free either. In this intentionally confusing situation, the state held the upper hand, since the defendants were afraid to return to the state and resume their organizing work. Yet Atlanta authorities did not succeed in driving all six defendants completely out of the South. Joe Carr and Mary Dalton remained active in neighboring Alabama and Tennessee. But, because neither state possessed an insurrection statute, they were less successful in restraining such activities.

In July, 1930, Carr and Angelo Herndon, a young black activist, were arrested and indicted near Birmingham on vagrancy charges. The two had been seized as they attempted to talk about the National Miners' Union to coal miners at the Hamilton Slope Mines of the Tennessee Coal, Iron, and Railroad Company. Each was convicted and sentenced to a five-hundred-dollar fine and twelve months at hard labor. After sentencing the youthful Communists, the presiding judge was quoted as remarking, "I am only sorry that we haven't got an insurrection law here in Alabama as they have in Georgia." The convictions were thrown out, however, upon appeal.[23]

Another typical incident involving these radical organizers and local police occurred the following year in Chattanooga. In April, 1931, Mary Dalton and two other Communists were fined for inciting a "riot." They had been arrested the previous February when they tried to hold an unemployment demonstration and lead a march on the city hall. On April 18, 1931, a local judge overturned the convictions, stating that the evidence was insufficient to sustain the conviction. Although the defendants' actual activities had been similar to their previous efforts in

22. Thomas W. Hardwick to Forrest Bailey, October 14, 1930, and Marvin Underwood to Bailey, October 27, 1930, both *ibid.*

23. Fearful of reprisals, Herndon gave his name as Eugene Braxton, an alias he sometimes used when working on radical projects. New York *Times*, July 31, 1930, p. 22; Angelo Herndon, *Let Me Live* (New York: Arno Press, 1969), 96–97, 100–102.

Atlanta, the lack of an insurrection law prevented more serious charges from being pressed against them.[24]

The Atlanta Six's ambiguous legal status in Georgia ended in February, 1932, when the state announced a March 23 trial date. Defense attorney Oliver C. Hancock obtained a postponement while he and W. A. McClellan argued demurrers to the indictments before Judge E. E. Pomeroy. In gaining the delay the two defense attorneys clashed bitterly with prosecutor John H. Hudson. The controversial prosecutor, who personified the state's crusade against communism, angrily informed the attorneys that it did not make any difference to him if the courts accepted the demurrers and threw out the insurrection indictments, since he would still find some law under which to prosecute the Six. "You well know that this country cannot survive if people are allowed to go from one end to another of this country preaching, teaching, and working for its destruction," he warned ominously. "The Communists must be put down or civilization will fail. I see nothing but a death penalty rigidly enforced that will destroy communism."[25]

The *Daily Worker* promptly denounced Hudson's anti-Communist tirade, suggesting that only a death sentence "will satisfy the fury of the Georgia bosses, whose slave rule is threatened by the work of these six organizers in uniting the oppressed Negroes and whites for joint struggle." Referring to Hudson's remark about the death penalty, the newspaper charged that such demands were "an admission of the terrible conditions under which the southern masses and especially the Negro masses are forced by capitalism to exist." Moreover, the *Worker* asserted that these actions revealed the capitalists' fear of Communists as leaders of the "oppressed masses."[26]

While Judge Pomeroy conducted hearings on defense objections to the indictments, John Hudson went before the Fulton County Grand Jury seeking new indictments against Carr and Powers. The grand jury returned these more detailed indictments on March 29, 1932, and

24. New York *Times*, April 4, 1931, p. 29, April 5, 1931, Sec. 2, p. 1, and April 19, 1931, p. 27.
25. Atlanta *Daily World*, March 23 and 24, 1932; Abraham Isserman, report on Atlanta insurrection cases, June 25, 1932, and John Henry Hudson to Ansel W. Morrison, March 14, 1932, both in ACLU Archives.
26. *Daily Worker*, March 22, 1932.

extended them to the other four defendants in April. The wisdom of Hudson's move soon became clear when Judge Pomeroy unexpectedly upheld part of the defense's arguments. Pomeroy dismissed the indictments charging an attempt to incite insurrection on the grounds that they were not specific enough about the alleged violations. But he refused to throw out the accompanying indictments charging the Six with circulating insurrectionary literature. Despite this judicial rebuff, Hudson pressed on, obtaining a new trial date of June 13. The assistant solicitor general grumbled to reporters that the prosecution was being unduly maligned by Communists. "The communist press has jumped on the death penalty idea and have [*sic*] not shown the entire picture," Hudson explained, "when as a matter of fact the death penalty is not the only sentence possible under a conviction."[27]

It is not clear what happened next. Embittered by his poor relationship with the ILD, Oliver Hancock failed to keep either the organization or W. A. McClellan informed of day-to-day developments in Atlanta. As a result, Hancock and McClellan undertook contradictory legal maneuvers. Lucille Milner, secretary of the ACLU, blamed Hancock for erroneously scheduling the cases for trial on June 13 despite the fact that an appeal instigated by McClellan was still pending. The waspish Hancock apparently decided to punish the ILD for slighting him by not appearing in court on that date. Whatever his motivation, neither the defendants nor their lawyers appeared in court on June 13. Consequently Judge G. H. Howard, to whose court the cases had been moved, declared their bonds forfeited. Hudson promptly ordered their rearrest and announced that every effort would be made to locate them.[28]

These events disturbed the ILD and the ACLU. The ILD blamed Hancock for the mishap and launched an investigation. A resulting confidential memorandum, prepared by Abraham Isserman of Newark, New Jersey, a legal adviser for the ILD, concluded that Hancock had been primarily interested in the case as a source of income and that he was basically unconcerned with the welfare of the defendants. The

27. Atlanta *Constitution*, March 24 and April 2, 1932; New York *Times*, April 3, 1932, Sec. 3, p. 5; Atlanta *Daily World*, March 30 and April 20, 1932.

28. Lucille Milner to Joseph J. Soley, June 23, 1932, and Abraham Isserman, report on Atlanta insurrection cases, June 25, 1932, both in ACLU Archives; Atlanta *Constitution*, June 14, 1932; Atlanta *Daily World*, June 14, 1932.

report charged that Hancock had consistently distorted and exaggerated information in order to fabricate imagined crises. Moreover, he had even failed to inform McClellan of the bond forfeitures. Isserman's report cleared McClellan of any misconduct, observing that his reputation as a trial lawyer was unquestioned. But the Newark attorney charged that retaining Hancock had been "a very serious error." After adding that Hancock was not regarded locally as a particularly competent attorney, Isserman asserted that these "present difficulties in the cases . . . are due to the indifference and neglect of Mr. Hancock." [29]

The seriousness of the bond forfeitures was twofold. First, the loss of sixteen thousand dollars would be a heavy blow to the treasuries of the ILD and the ACLU. More serious was the problem of the ultimate freedom of the Six. John Hudson offered to revoke the forfeitures, but only if the bonds were transferred to the new indictments, which he had rewritten so as to withstand better a court challenge. This would in effect nullify the partial success of McClellan's demurrer to the original indictments. Normally the state would have been required to rearrest the defendants, a virtual impossibility since they had left the state. Consequently, they probably would be safe as long as they did not return to Georgia. However, the difficulty of recovering the bonds, particularly the cash bond of Ann Burlack, caused the defense reluctantly to consider Hudson's offer. Hudson thus cleverly used the bonds as a weapon with which to force defense lawyers to agree to the substitution of the new indictments. [30]

While continuing to work on the bond problem in July, Hancock reported a new round of prosecutions, centering on a young black Communist—Angelo Herndon. Hancock undertook legal action on his behalf but concentrated on the difficulties of the Atlanta Six. By late August, the defense despaired of regaining the bail money and accepted Hudson's proposal. New demurrers were to be filed to the new indictments, and Hudson agreed not to call the cases until all appeals had been settled. But when the Georgia Supreme Court denied the defense's

---

29. Abraham Isserman, confidential memorandum, June 25, 1932, in ACLU Archives.
30. Abraham Isserman, report on Atlanta insurrection cases, *ibid.*

challenge to the new indictments in December, 1932, the prosecution had already shifted its attention to Angelo Herndon.[31]

During the fall, as Hancock and McClellan worked to overturn the indictments, the ACLU tried to duplicate its earlier success in blocking the prosecution by organizing enlightened public opinion behind the Six. This time its efforts failed. Will W. Alexander of the Commission on Interracial Cooperation blamed the Communist party. He told Roger Baldwin that it was difficult to cooperate with the Communists because of their dogmatic and emotional attitudes in which they resembled political "holy rollers." Charging that the party remained primarily interested in propaganda, not in winning cases, he warned that little would be accomplished as long as it maintained that attitude.[32]

The arrest of Angelo Herndon during the summer of 1932 and the revived prosecution of the Atlanta Six indicated that Atlanta officials were increasingly worried about Communist activity. No doubt the country's dire economic situation made them very touchy about any public disturbance. But this fear of depression-related unrest hardly explains the scope and intensity of their anti-Communist campaign. What disturbed these officials most of all were Communist efforts among black southerners, which they feared would encourage blacks to attempt to obtain political, legal, and social equality through an aggressive assault on the Jim Crow system. These apprehensions contained a bit of truth, for during 1932 it did seem that black Atlantans were becoming more strident in their demands for equality, though not as a result of Communist encouragement. Some blacks were particularly unhappy with the legal system. One recent incident raised the question of whether controversial black defendants could receive unbiased justice in Georgia's white-dominated judicial system, an issue that the trial of Angelo Herndon in 1933 would emphasize.

31. Oliver C. Hancock to Abraham Isserman, August 25, 1932, Hancock to ACLU, August 29 and December 16, 1932, Isserman to Hancock, August 30, 1932, Roger N. Baldwin, memorandum, December 29, 1932, Baldwin to William L. Patterson, January 4, 1933, all *ibid*. The ILD finally released Hancock in December, paying him a terminal fee of one hundred dollars. But, since the ILD was as usual short of funds, the ACLU lent the money for his fee.

32. Will W. Alexander to Roger N. Baldwin, July 20, 1932, *ibid*.

The case of John Downer began on May 17, 1931, when a white woman was allegedly raped near Elberton, Georgia. Deputies arrested four black males the next day as suspects. A hostile mob of nearly fifteen hundred persons soon surrounded the jail, forcing county officials to remove the suspects to Athens for their safety. Angry citizens fired several shots at the hastily fleeing officers and their prisoners. On May 19, Downer, a black farmhand, and another black man were arrested and jailed at Elberton as additional suspects. Again a crowd gathered. This highly inflamed group repeatedly attacked the jail until it was finally repelled by national guardsmen wielding a machine gun. "For more than six hours the mob stormed and threatened, fired shots into the jail, smashed windows, threw dynamite [unsuccessfully], and threatened to blow up the jail." Only the arrival of additional guardsmen made it possible for the two blacks, disguised in guard uniforms, to be removed to Atlanta.[33]

Events moved rapidly. On May 25, six days after his arrest, a grand jury in Elberton indicted Downer. The next day he was speedily tried, convicted, and sentenced to death. His court-appointed attorney was not selected until one hour before the trial. Several hundred national guardsmen patrolled the courthouse area, barely controlling an unruly crowd in the town square. Without the guard's presence, the defendant probably would have been lynched. Understandably unnerved, Downer's lawyer so hesitantly defended his client that he even failed to request a change of venue, despite the open hostility and danger. The presiding judge set June 15, 1931, as the execution date.[34]

At this time, several liberal Georgia lawyers became concerned about the case. Black attorney A. T. Walden of Atlanta, president of the local branch of the NAACP, coordinated their efforts. Two days before the execution date, he petitioned Federal District Judge Bascom S. Deaver for a writ of habeas corpus, charging that Downer had been denied due process of law because mob hysteria had dominated the trial proceedings, eliminating the possibility of a fair trial. Although Judge

33. *Downer* v. *Dunaway*, 53 F.2d 586–89 (1931); *Daily Worker*, December 22, 1932; Atlanta *Constitution*, July 4 and 6, 1932; miscellaneous newspaper clippings in National Association for the Advancement of Colored People Papers, Library of Congress, hereinafter cited as NAACP Papers.
34. *Ibid.*

Deaver denied the petition, he signed an order of probable cause, which stayed the execution while the U.S. Circuit Court of Appeals reviewed his decision. On November 20, 1931, the circuit court overruled Deaver, ordering him to hear testimony on the petition. It instructed him to grant the petition should evidence support the allegations. The circuit court cited the milestone case of *Moore* v. *Dempsey*, which had resulted from the so-called Elaine, Arkansas, riot cases, as precedent for its ruling. In that decision, the U.S. Supreme Court had held that a trial dominated by a mob was invalid. The Downer ruling reaffirmed this vital earlier ruling, which has been cited by one civil rights historian as the turning point in relations between blacks and the federal courts.[35]

The hearing on the petition for the writ was held in July, 1932, in Macon. Attorneys Harry S. Strozier and Orville A. Park of Macon, assisted by W. A. Sutherland and Jerome Jones of Atlanta, represented Downer. Attorney Walden stayed discreetly in the background. Several defense witnesses testified to the disorderly state of affairs surrounding the trial. After hearing the evidence, Judge Deaver took the case under advisement. When he issued his decision in December, it upheld defense contentions and granted Downer a new trial. His action, coupled with that of the circuit court, marked a significant expansion of the power of the federal courts to review trial decisions from state courts.[36]

During 1932 the Atlanta branch of the NAACP, previously known more for its social functions than its protest efforts, became more outspoken. Efforts to reintroduce residential segregation by law and several sensational murders of blacks by white policemen stimulated the group to act. Although the early twentieth-century practice of requiring residential segregation by law had supposedly been abandoned by the 1930s, it enjoyed an attempted revival in Atlanta. On September 6, 1932, the city council passed an ordinance which prohibited blacks from moving into established white neighborhoods. The act empowered the city clerk to deny moving permits to members of one race intending to

35. *Downer* v. *Dunaway*, 53 F.2d 586–89 (1931); A. T. Walden to Walter White, May 26, 1933, in NAACP Papers; *Moore* v. *Dempsey*, 261 U.S. 86 (1924); author's interview with Howard N. Meyer, New York, N.Y., September 4, 1970.

36. Atlanta *Constitution*, July 4, 6, and 7, 1932; Atlanta *Daily World*, July 6 and 8, 1932; Atlanta *Journal*, December 23, 1932. The *Daily Worker*, December 22, 1932, credited the ILD's recent victory in the Scottsboro case (*Powell* v. *Alabama*) with heavily influencing the court's decision.

move into a district inhabited by members of another race, when "such moving may cause disorder, fighting, riots, etc." The resolution also aimed at restraining objectionable and "immoral" people from moving into a respectable neighborhood. The ordinance gave ultimate power to approve or reject a disputed application to the city council. This action evidently represented an effort to resurrect an earlier residential segregation ordinance which had been declared unconstitutional by a local judge in 1931.[37]

Attorney A. T. Walden announced that the national office of the NAACP would file suit against the plan. An NAACP press release denounced the statute as "plainly an effort to circumvent the Supreme Court's ban on segregated residential districts." Roger Baldwin of the ACLU also expressed an interest in the proposed legal action against the ordinance. When the city council failed to enforce the law because of its doubtful validity, the controversy subsided.[38]

A far more notorious incident occurred on October 17, 1932, when a white police officer fatally shot two black women in Newnan, Georgia, forty miles west of Atlanta. Dead were Dinah Strickland, fifty-two, and her daughter Oneta, twenty-three. The killings came at a time when black resentment concerning the shootings of black Atlantans by white policemen was running strong. It was reported that the two women were shot by a bailiff who became enraged when he could not locate Dinah Strickland's son, whom he had come to arrest.[39]

The normally complacent Atlanta *Daily World*, the only daily black newspaper in the South, broke its usual editorial silence on such matters with a front-page editorial entitled "Murdering Innocent, Defenseless Women." The editorial bitterly denounced the handling of the shooting by law enforcement officials. It urged blacks to "stand together and fight

---

37. Roger L. Rice, "Residential Segregation by Law, 1910–1917," *Journal of Southern History*, XXXIV (May, 1968), 179–99; copy of ordinance in NAACP Papers; Atlanta *Constitution*, February 14, 1931; Savannah *Tribune*, February 19, 1931. Atlanta's first municipal residential segregation ordinance was adopted in 1913. Others followed in 1916, 1924, and 1929. For details, see John M. Mathews, "Studies in Race Relations in Georgia, 1890–1930" (Ph.D. dissertation, Duke University, 1970), 133–35.

38. Atlanta *Daily World*, September 13 and November 8, 1932; *Daily Worker*, September 21, 1932; Walter White to A. T. Walden, September 8, 14, and October 28, 1932, Walden to White, September 14, 1932, Roger N. Baldwin to NAACP, September 9, 1932, and NAACP press release, September 9, 1932, all in NAACP Papers.

39. Atlanta *Daily World*, October 18, 1932.

through the courts these atrocities and wanton murders performed in the name of the law, or sit motionless and see still more slayings when it pleases the fancies of depraved men with official power." The newspaper continued to crusade for official action, seeking the assistance of whites as well as blacks. As the *World* explained, "Their death should awaken every decent white person and every Negro to the disgrace in official places to which this section of the nation is drifting." [40]

The Reverend J. Raymond Henderson, outspoken black Baptist minister, wrote Walter White of the NAACP on October 20 informing him of the shootings. After complaining that the NAACP's local branch had been inactive, Henderson urged the national office to prod it into action. News of the killings shocked the national office. Roy Wilkins, assistant secretary, promptly wrote A. T. Walden that the "killings are such outrageous and shameful ones that we believe our branch at Atlanta can find no better way to justify its existence than by launching an exhaustive and determined fight to see that this man is punished and that these repeated killings of Negroes by officers of the law in Georgia are checked." Wilkins suggested that the *Daily World*'s outspoken position had already prepared public opinion for such a campaign and urged prompt action. [41]

The Reverend Mr. Henderson carried his appeals for vigorous investigation of the Newnan deaths to the pages of the *Daily World*. Terming the slayings one of the "most dastardly crimes" ever committed, he exhorted blacks to stand up and fight for justice. He further suggested that the NAACP enter the case immediately. Although he praised Henderson's efforts, columnist Frank Marshall Davis of the *Daily World* warned that 98 percent of black Atlantans would say "ain't it a shame" and let matters drop. If the NAACP were ever going to do something, now was the time. Davis maintained that "as long as Negroes remain passive and scared, they can expect any kind of treatment any other race feels disposed to give at any particular time." Ultimately, he said, only political power wielded by blacks could prevent such abuses of justice. [42]

40. *Ibid.*, October 19 and 20, 1932.
41. J. Raymond Henderson to Walter White, October 20, 1932, and Roy Wilkins to A. T. Walden, October 21, 1932, both in NAACP Papers.
42. Atlanta *Daily World*, October 21 and 23, 1932.

By late October no action had been taken against the Newnan deputy. A. T. Walden explained publicly that the NAACP chapter chose not to press the matter at the moment because it did not wish to detract from the current Community Chest drive, which would help many needy people during the coming winter. As soon as the drive was finished, he promised, the organization would vigorously pursue the Newnan case. [43]

This delay worried the national office. Roy Wilkins requested further information from Walden on November 3. Although he expressed confidence in Walden's judgment, he warned that the emotional pitch of the community could not be maintained indefinitely. Wilkins labeled the slayings "the most shameless and outrageous reported in recent years." He added that most blacks "do not have much hope of any action being taken in dark and rural Mississippi, but they certainly expect that a city as large as Atlanta with its wealth of intelligent colored people will not sit idly by twiddling its thumbs while colored women are shot down in their own homes." [44] The always discreet Walden undertook private negotiations with the solicitor general of Coweta County, who promised to try to obtain an indictment from the grand jury in March, 1933. Walden told Daisy Lampkin, a field secretary for the association, that under the circumstances this was the best that could be done, since mass meetings would have prejudiced the case, not helped. [45]

It was against this background of rising racial tensions and legal assertiveness by middle-class blacks that the Angelo Herndon case moved toward trial. In late November, 1932, the ILD accepted the formal withdrawal of H. A. Allen from the defense, naming black attorneys Ben Davis and John Geer as replacements. These two young men announced that they would attack the constitutionality of the insurrection law and the exclusion of blacks from juries. The *Daily Worker* claimed that this would be the first time that the question of the systematic exclusion of blacks from juries had ever been raised in Georgia.

43. *Ibid.*, October 28, 1932.
44. Roy Wilkins to A. T. Walden, November 3, 1932, in NAACP Papers.
45. Daisy E. Lampkin to Roy Wilkins, February 4, 1933, *ibid.*

Davis and Geer first attempted to introduce this issue in December through a petition for habeas corpus but were overruled. They were successful, however, in getting Herndon's bond reduced from an exorbitant $25,000 to a more realistic figure of $2,500. When two prominent black druggists posted this amount in late December, Herndon was temporarily freed. Eager to hail any victory over the status quo, the *Daily Worker* labeled the bond reduction a triumph and attributed it to the influence of mass protest in support of legal action. [46]

On December 22, Geer and Davis filed a formal request for trial with the clerk of the Fulton County Superior Court. Since the work for the November–December term of this court had been completed, this assured that Herndon would get his long-anticipated day in court during the following month. The Atlanta Six also moved toward their often-postponed date in court. On December 31, their cases were formally remitted to Fulton County Superior Court by the Georgia Supreme Court, which had recently overruled demurrers to their latest indictments. Declaring that the court's action had in effect upheld the law, John H. Hudson announced that a trial date for the Six had been set for January 24, 1933, a week following the Herndon date. [47] Thus the long-awaited legal confrontation between radical organizers and the solicitor general's office was finally at hand.

46. Atlanta *Daily World*, November 27, 1932; *Daily Worker*, November 29, December 8, 14, 19, and 26, 1932; *State* v. *Angelo Herndon*, No. 37812, Fulton County Superior Court, in Miscellaneous Documents, Fulton County Courthouse, Atlanta, Ga.

47. Atlanta *Journal*, December 31, 1932.

CHAPTER THREE
In a Georgia Courtroom

AS THE trial date for Angelo Herndon drew near in early 1933, both prosecuting and defense attorneys hastened to complete their preparations. The prosecution initiated the only surprising pretrial move. Worried by reports that the defense planned to challenge the constitutionality of the exclusion of blacks from Fulton County juries, Assistant Solicitor General Hudson initiated a counterattack. He unveiled his plan on Tuesday, January 3, 1933, when two blacks were unexpectedly called for jury duty in the criminal division of Fulton County Superior Court. The two were John Moates, a fireman for the Southern Railroad, and Alex Carter, a businessman. Both were empaneled for a larceny case in which a white attorney was accused of defrauding a black woman.[1]

Their service proved brief, however, as defense counsel promptly struck them from the jury through peremptory challenges. Despite this setback, the city's black newspaper, the Atlanta *Daily World*, proudly credited Herndon's attorneys Ben Davis and John Geer with causing this significant advance toward full legal rights for blacks. But when *World* reporter Cliff W. Mackay interviewed Davis, he found him skeptical of any real progress. Instead, Davis dismissed the action as merely a "sham" designed to offset his coming attack on the lily-white jury system. Undaunted, the young attorney vowed to continue his fight "against the systematic exclusion of citizens from our juries on the basis of color, until names of Negroes are placed in the grand jury box, and not

1. Atlanta *Daily World*, January 4, 1933; *Daily Worker*, January 4, 1933. In Georgia the solicitor general was equivalent to a district attorney.

on pink slips either." Although the *Daily World* editorially complimented the International Labor Defense for its sponsorship of Geer and Davis, the newspaper caustically commented that this was the first time that the Communists had actually accomplished anything constructive in the South.[2] Despite the state's calling of Moates and Carter, Davis' planned attack was not really undermined, for his petition challenged the composition of the particular grand jury that had indicted Herndon in July, 1932, a time when no blacks had been called.

The long-awaited trial of Angelo Herndon, which the *Constitution* termed "unique in the annals of Georgia jurisprudence," opened promptly at 9:30 A.M. on Monday, January 16, 1933, in the Fulton County Courthouse in downtown Atlanta. The large courtroom overflowed with spectators, mostly white, but a few blacks, uneasy about their venture into what was then regarded as "enemy territory," huddled together at the back. Defense counsel sat at a table to the right of the judge, and the four prosecutors took their seats to his left nearest the jury box. Numerous lawyers were jammed inside the rail, some even standing because of the shortage of seats.[3] Presiding was Judge Lee B. Wyatt of La Grange, Georgia, who, it was said, had been imported specifically to provide a firm hand in the proceedings.

Benjamin J. Davis, Jr., served as chief spokesman for the defense. At first glance, Davis did not appear to be the type of person one might expect to find defending a black Communist in a southern court. Urbane and polished, he seemed more suited to be an educator or an insurance company executive. Yet his background had not left him completely unprepared for this new role. Born in 1903 in the sleepy little town of Dawson, in southwest Georgia, Davis came from a politically active family. His father Benjamin J. Davis, Sr., was a power in both the Grand United Order of Odd Fellows and the Republican party, serving for many years as Republican national committeeman from Georgia. Because of his success, the senior Davis moved to the capital city, where he also published a weekly newspaper, the Atlanta *Independent*. In Atlanta, Ben Davis enjoyed the advantages of a middle-class childhood,

2. Atlanta *Daily World*, January 8, 1933; Pittsburgh *Courier*, January 14, 1933; *Daily Worker*, January 10, 1933.

3. Benjamin J. Davis, *Communist Councilman from Harlem* (New York: International Publishers, 1969), 62.

including study at the high school operated by Morehouse College. Following graduation, he remained at Morehouse for an additional year's preparation before transferring to Amherst College. After receiving his bachelor's degree, Davis attended Harvard Law School, an opportunity offered few of his race. Graduating with an average record, he then worked for two years in the publishing business before returning to Atlanta and entering the practice of law.[4]

With the assistance of attorneys A. T. Walden and T. J. Henry, young Davis gained experience and valuable contacts. Soon a friendship developed with another young black lawyer, and eventually Davis asked John H. Geer, who came from almost the opposite social and economic background, to join him in establishing the firm of Geer and Davis. A native of Greenville, South Carolina, the twenty-six-year-old Geer had attended Morehouse College briefly and had studied law by correspondence before his admission to the Georgia bar in July, 1928. But the depression year of 1932 proved a poor time to open a law practice. Black clients were few in number. Then in July, 1932, Davis read in the Atlanta *Constitution* that a young black man had been jailed and charged with attempting to incite insurrection. Davis visited the prisoner in jail, asked to help represent him, and soon found himself caught up in a case which dramatically changed his life.[5]

Defense lawyers and Judge Wyatt immediately disliked each other. To Ben Davis, Wyatt was a real "humdinger," and he later asserted that the La Grange judge had been chosen to handle the case because of his heavy-handedness and unsophisticated nature. "He used the law with respect to Negroes like a butcher wielding a knife to kill a lamb," Davis subsequently charged. Wyatt's hostility played a major role in Davis' eventual disillusionment with American justice.[6]

John H. Hudson, assistant solicitor general, headed the prosecution in the absence of Solicitor General John A. Boykin, who apparently decided to stay out of the proceedings. To the defense, "Hudson was like a character out of a caricature." Deep-sunken eyes peered from

4. *Ibid.*, 21–44.

5. *Ibid.*, 45–58; Atlanta *Daily World*, April 15, 1932; Mrs. Mary V. Bennett [formerly Mrs. John Geer] to the author, March 14, 1975. Walden once saved an inexperienced Davis from being jailed on contempt charges for smoking in court.

6. Davis, *Communist Councilman from Harlem*, 62–63.

below his receding, short-cropped hair. Tall and sturdily built, Hudson radiated a commanding presence. Like many southern prosecutors, he also possessed considerable dramatic abilities, which he sharpened with occasional lay preaching. Hudson was particularly adept at using his lanky frame to emphasize and punctuate his comments. His intensity and hostility toward the defense clearly radiated throughout the courtroom. J. Walter LeCraw, an aggressive but diminutive man of pale complexion, assisted him. LeCraw, who handled most of the later appeals, frequently interjected his vigorous protests throughout the trial.[7]

The first day's activities centered primarily on legal maneuvers. As anticipated, the defense attacked the legality of the grand jury, offering four separate motions: a demurrer to the indictment, which Judge Wyatt quickly overruled; a motion to quash the indictment; a plea in abatement; and a motion to quash the traverse (petit) jury panel. Testimony was heard on the second and fourth proposals, although not until Davis strenuously attacked Wyatt's initial reluctance.[8]

The defense motion to quash the indictment argued that blacks were systematically and unlawfully excluded from the grand jury which indicted Herndon, that the evidence submitted to the grand jury did not warrant a true bill of indictment, and that the insurrection statute directly violated the state and federal constitutions. In the long run, the question of the insurrection law's constitutionality proved the defense's strongest point, but at the time Davis and Geer preferred to concentrate upon the jury issue. As part of their effort to establish a prima facie case of exclusion, Herndon's attorneys called several well-educated blacks to the stand to show that qualified Negroes not exempted from jury duty by law did exist and that some had served on juries in federal court.

David T. Howard, a successful Atlanta mortician and a wealthy property owner, testified that he had been a taxpayer for over forty years, that he was willing and able to serve on both grand and petit juries, but

---

7. *Ibid.*, 63–64; Angelo Herndon, *Let Me Live* (New York: Arno Press, 1969), 222–23; David Entin, "Angelo Herndon" (M.A. thesis, University of North Carolina, 1963), 26. Hudson had been a classmate of Judge Wyatt's at Mercer Law School.

8. Davis, *Communist Councilman from Harlem*, 65; *State* v. *Angelo Herndon*, No. 37812, Fulton County Superior Court, in Miscellaneous Documents, Fulton County Courthouse, Atlanta, Ga.

that he had never been called for duty. R. L. Craddock, a black college graduate, likewise testified that he was qualified for jury duty but had never been summoned. "Have you ever been called for jury service by the Federal Court of this district?" Ben Davis inquired. Before Craddock could answer yes, Hudson quickly protested that the question was irrelevant and immaterial. Judge Wyatt agreed. Although Davis explained that he sought to show that qualified blacks were called for jury duty by the federal district court, Wyatt refused to change his ruling.[9]

Expanding his probe of jury selection procedures, Davis called eleven county officials (all white) to the stand. Jury Commissioner Oscar Palmour testified first and explained the jury selection process. First, he said, the commissioners examined a list of all county taxpayers. If the officials were familiar with an individual and judged him acceptable, they entered his name on the petit jury list. If someone were felt to be especially well qualified, his name was starred and put on the double list for both petit and grand jury service. When pressed about the status of prospective black jurors, Palmour responded that none had been excluded from grand jury service because of race. Admitting that the tax rolls indicated the taxpayer's race, he stressed that usually two commissioners had to be familiar with a person before he could be put on the grand jury list. Palmour blamed the absence of names of blacks on their failure to meet the qualifications. Subsequently, he modified his statement by stipulating that he did know a few black professionals who were qualified but excused by law. Declaring that he knew "a good many names" of blacks who had been placed on the petit jury lists, he added that many taxpayers, including some of the wealthiest ones, could not

9. Davis, *Communist Councilman from Harlem*, 65; Herndon, *Let Me Live*, 224; printed transcript of *Herndon* v. *Georgia*, U.S. Supreme Court, October term, 1934, No. 665, pp. 27–28, copy in law office of Sutherland, Asbill, and Brennan, Atlanta, Ga. There is some confusion over Howard's and Craddock's testimony. The official transcript of testimony ignores their appearances because they took place at a pretrial hearing. But Davis and Herndon both describe the incident in their memoirs. The only reference to the two witnesses in the official proceedings is found as "Ground Thirteen" in the amended motion for a new trial. Because the press failed to report their appearance, historians have overlooked the matter. Nonetheless, this strategy of calling qualified blacks to establish a prima facie case later took on major significance. It was precisely these tactics which Samuel Leibowitz successfully used in the second and third Scottsboro trials. Through those efforts Leibowitz gained the momentous 1935 *Norris* v. *Alabama* decision, in which the Supreme Court declared unconstitutional the systematic exclusion of blacks from juries. Such a strategy had already been introduced two years earlier in Atlanta.

measure up to the qualifications for the grand jury. Palmour emphasized that it was difficult for him to remember if blacks had served on grand juries, because he did not normally pay attention to such incidentals as the race of a prospective grand juror.[10]

Jury Commissioner A. Steve Nance, a tall, muscular, outgoing man and a popular labor leader, proved no more helpful. He repeated much of what Palmour had said, explaining that the four thousand names for the grand jury list were selected from the petit jury list of approximately eighteen thousand names. He asserted that no juror was selected or excluded because of race, although he did concede that "no negro has ever been on the grand jury since I have been a member of the jury commission, to my knowledge." Denying the existence of any system designed to prevent blacks from serving on grand juries, Nance suggested that none had been recommended because the commissioners were not personally familiar with those qualified blacks who were not professional men or state or federal employees. A twenty-year veteran of the jury commission testified next. George H. Sims remarked that during his entire tenure he could "not recollect a negro serving on the grand jury." Although Sims admitted that the tax rolls and the petit jury lists divided blacks from whites, he hastily declared, "No negroes have ever been excluded from the grand jury list or kept off, because of their race." Jury Commissioner F. J. Paxon likewise denied that blacks were deliberately excluded from grand jury service. But he admitted that in his four years on the commission he had never seen a black grand juror.[11]

The next official questioned was A. Gordon Hardy, the chief deputy sheriff of the criminal division of superior court. Hardy stated that in his sixteen years of service he had never seen a Negro serve on a grand jury. He added, however, "I know of negroes being on the petit jury on a few occasions; it has been several years ago, I recollect one being called and he was excused; it has been three or four years ago." Furthermore, he recalled that one or two Negroes had been called since Christmas. R. B.

10. Brief of evidence of *Herndon* v. *Georgia*, 9–10, 41, 42–43, copy in law office of Sutherland, Asbill, and Brennan.
11. *Ibid.*, 43–47; Atlanta *Daily World*, January 17, 1933; Lucy Randolph Mason, *To Win These Rights* (New York: Harper and Brothers, 1952), 23. The original transcript does not capitalize *Negro*.

Gaines, deputy sheriff of Fulton County, offered similar testimony, asserting that he had not seen a black grand juror in the last fourteen years. Several other witnesses failed to provide any new information. But, when J. W. Simmons took the stand, the defense made some interesting discoveries. Simmons, the clerk of superior court since 1930, stated that no Negro had served on the grand jury during his service. To illustrate his certainty, Simmons revealed that the names of prospective jurors were printed on different colors of paper, according to their race. Simmons could not remember the exact colors, but he remained certain that he could tell the race of a prospective grand juror by the color of the slip on which his name appeared.[12]

Without further details on the colored slips, the hearing on the motion to quash the indictment concluded. The testimony had revealed that no black person had served on the grand jury for as long as any jury commissioner could remember. That this resulted from conscious discrimination against Negroes all witnesses denied. Intelligent blacks were all professional men or government employees and hence were excused. Judge Wyatt, who originally had displayed no interest in hearing evidence on the motion, took at face value the officials' statements that no discrimination was intended and overruled the motion. Defense attorneys duly took an exception to his action and moved to hear testimony on their motion to quash the traverse (petit) jury panel.

Ben Davis now directed his questioning to the matter of the colored slips and their racial classifications. Although Jury Commissioner Palmour confirmed the slips' existence, he denied responsibility for the process. He maintained that the names always arrived that way from the printer. Palmour added defensively that he could not even be positive that the different colors of slips did correctly distinguish blacks from whites, as he had never verified that assumption. Jury Commissioner Sims elaborated further on the dual slip system. He explained that the names of whites were printed on yellowish slips, and those of blacks were placed on pink slips. Then all the slips were put in the petit jury box and mixed together. About eighteen thousand names in all were put in the box. When asked to estimate the percentage of blacks included

12. Brief of evidence of *Herndon* v. *Georgia*, 44–49, copy in law office of Sutherland, Asbill, and Brennan.

among eighteen thousand, Sims declined to guess. He asserted that, since the jury commission had no system for selecting a certain proportion of blacks or whites, it would be impossible to speak accurately.[13]

In his testimony, Nance explained that the county tax-return lists were prepared on different colors of paper—white paper for whites and manila paper for blacks. From these lists the names of petit jurors were selected, making sure that the names of blacks and whites were kept on different-colored sheets. Although Nance claimed that he was unable to estimate the proportion of Negroes in the petit jury box, he did acknowledge that he had personally recommended eight or nine blacks for jury service and that his colleagues sometimes recommended blacks too. Another jury commissioner, F. J. Paxon, returned to the stand. Paxon charged that the printer, not county officials, determined the two colors for the petit jury slips—white and some distinctive color, pink or yellow—acting on official state policy. Which state agency required this policy he did not know. Paxon was unable to remember whether he had recommended any blacks for petit jury duty. He explained, "I don't remember anytime that I put John Smith's name in, whether he is white, colored or a Chinaman." Paxon did recall, however, that two colors of slips did distinguish between the races.[14]

As the day drew to a close, the defense summed up its arguments. Again it had demonstrated the virtual exclusion of blacks from petit jury duty in Fulton County. It had also uncovered a remarkable color blindness among county officials which prevented them from thinking in terms of race or noting the race of a prospective juror. All officials asserted that no conscious discrimination existed. Once more Judge Wyatt took their disclaimers at face value, contemptuously dismissing the motion. It had been a long and frustrating session for the defense, and the following day promised to be no better. But the day was not yet finished. As the young defense attorneys filed out through the half-empty courtroom and headed for the elevator, a hostile group of about eight white men closed in on them, glaring menacingly. At this moment, a powerfully built black minister, the Reverend J. A. Martin, and three friends joined Davis and Geer. When the whites grudgingly backed

13. *Ibid.*, 50–51.
14. *Ibid.*, 52–54; Atlanta *Journal*, January 17, 1933.

away, Martin and his group escorted the two lawyers back to their office in the Odd Fellows Building.[15]

There, Ben Davis later recalled, the Methodist preacher lectured the young attorneys on the historic significance of the case for the black community, warning them that many whites were unhappy over their efforts to challenge the lily-white jury system. During the conversation, Martin summed up the nondoctrinaire thoughts of many black Georgians on the Communist involvement in the case. "I don't know anything at all about communism," he said. "I've heard about the Scottsboro case, how the Communists kept the Alabama authorities from summarily executing those nine boys. But if communism has anything to do with what you're doing in this case for the freedom of my people, I'm with you one hundred per cent." [16] Davis remembered that Martin's talk inspired the two and partially compensated them for their frustrating day in court.

The following day, Tuesday, January 17, 1933, dawned cool and cloudy. As Davis prepared to leave for court that morning, he discovered that several unannounced callers had taken advantage of the relatively mild winter weather to leave him a message. In the middle of Davis' front lawn stood a four-foot white cross. A leaflet attached read: "The Klan Rides Again. Get out of the Herndon case. This is a white man's country." A startled Davis removed the cross and set it inside as a memento of the case. He then resumed his journey to court, meeting J. A. Martin and company en route. Arriving at the already overflowing courtroom, the group was helped by a bailiff to squeeze through the packed throng. Martin audaciously joined Davis and Geer at the defense table as the court prepared to convene at nine o'clock. Herndon joined them, sporting a red-striped tie.[17]

The second day in court witnessed no lessening of tensions between the defense on one hand and the prosecution and the presiding judge on the other. Repeatedly Davis and Geer objected to prejudicial statements by the prosecution or unfavorable rulings from the bench, but to no avail. First on the agenda was selection of a jury. Dissatisfied with the

15. Atlanta *Constitution*, January 17, 1933; Atlanta *Daily World*, January 17, 1933; Davis, *Communist Councilman from Harlem*, 68–70.

16. Davis, *Communist Councilman from Harlem*, 68–70.

17. *Ibid.*, 71–72.

prospective jurors, all white, the defense challenged fifteen of the first twenty-four examined. The state challenged one prospect during the entire process. Davis later recalled trapping one prospective juror into admitting membership in the Ku Klux Klan, but the man volunteered that this would not affect his rendering a fair verdict. He was stricken for cause. Eventually the defense became more lenient as its challenges neared exhaustion, and the twelve-man panel was finally completed.[18]

City policeman Frank B. Watson led off the state's case. He testified concerning the details of Herndon's arrest the previous summer. In July, 1932, recalled Watson, he and another officer had arrested the young Communist when he picked up mail from Box 339 at the post office. He had also seized from Herndon a pasteboard box containing numerous pamphlets and papers. The officers had then ordered Herndon to take them to his residence, where they "searched his room and all his papers and things that were in his room." The policemen confiscated a large box and a suitcase, which they claimed Herndon said had been mailed to him by Communist party headquarters in New York City. Watson also contended that Herndon had told him he had been sent to Atlanta by the party to work as an organizer.[19]

The material identified by Watson and introduced as evidence by the state was a curious collection of documents. It included Communist membership lists, circulars of the Unemployed Council, several books, and an article from the *Daily Worker* describing economic hardships in Georgia. For much of the morning, assistant prosecutor J. Walter LeCraw read numerous excerpts from the material to the jury. The membership and receipt books produced the names of only eleven local Communists, including Julius Klarin, who had been arrested originally with the Atlanta Six, Otto Hall, an area organizer, and Nannie Leah Young and Annie Mae Leathers, two sisters who were themselves charged in 1934 under the insurrection law.[20]

To the state, the Communist theory of "self-determination of the

18. *Ibid.*, 72; list of jurors of *State* v. *Angelo Herndon*, in Miscellaneous Documents, Fulton County Courthouse.

19. Brief of evidence of *Herndon* v. *Georgia*, 56–57, copy in law office of Sutherland, Asbill, and Brennan.

20. *Ibid.*, 92–116; Atlanta *Daily World*, January 18, 1933; author's interview with J. Walter LeCraw, Atlanta, Ga., August 25, 1970.

Black Belt" was a particularly incendiary doctrine.[21] While jurors viewed a map showing those areas of the South that would fall under black political control should the plan be implemented, LeCraw read lengthy passages explaining the theory, which he regarded as a serious threat to the state of Georgia. He also introduced a receipt pad for the William Z. Foster–James W. Ford campaign fund of 1932. Two books which further disturbed the prosecution were George Padmore's *The Life and Struggles of Negro Toilers* and Bishop William Montgomery Brown's *Communism and Christianism*. The prosecution stressed one particularly sensational passage from the Padmore book:

> In no other so-called civilized country in the world are human beings treated as badly as these 15 million negroes. . . . They are absolutely at the mercy of every fiendish mob incited by the white landlords and capitalists. Bands of business and professional men make periodical raids upon the black country-side, where they lynch negroes, burn homes and destroy the crops and other property belonging to the blacks. In most cases of lynching the negroes are burned to death after their bodies have been soaked in gasoline, while others are hanged from trees. On these occasions the entire white community turned out to witness the bloody spectacles, which were made 'Roman Holidays.'[22]

By far the most significant evidence came from the minutes of local sections of the Communist party and the Foster-Ford clubs. These records revealed that secret Communist discussions actually centered around such nonrevolutionary issues as recruitment of new members, popularizing the Scottsboro defense, paying dues, and adopting various political resolutions. The most frequent topic of discussion at these gatherings was the unemployment problem. Suggested remedies included a minimum subsidy of four dollars per week for families on relief, free coal during winter for such families, no discrimination against blacks in the distribution of relief funds, and free clothing and

21. According to this theory, blacks should exercise political control of those areas of the South where they constituted a majority. Contiguous areas of the Black Belt would be organized into an autonomous black republic, modeled on the Soviet Union's treatment of national minorities. See Wilson Record, *The Negro and the Communist Party* (Chapel Hill: University of North Carolina Press, 1951), 94; Theodore Draper, *American Communism and Soviet Russia* (New York: Viking, 1960), 319–52; James S. Allen, "The Black Belt: Area of Negro Majority," *Communist*, XIII (June, 1934), 581–99.

22. Brief of evidence of *Herndon* v. *Georgia*, 92–116, copy in law office of Sutherland, Asbill, and Brennan; Atlanta *Daily World*, January 18, 1933; author's interview with LeCraw.

carfare for the children of the unemployed.[23] Despite the enormous volume of material introduced as evidence, the state uncovered no secret plans for armed insurrection. The physical safety of Georgia officials had never been endangered, but the prosecution had discovered radical views on racial and economic matters. Subsequently, Hudson and LeCraw focused their arguments primarily on the defendant's radical ideology.

Once Detective Watson finished his analysis, "Young Ben" began a methodical cross-examination.[24] With tempers already short on both sides, it was not long before the prosecution and the defense clashed. At one point in identifying Herndon, Watson referred to him as "that nigger." Davis heatedly objected. Startled by the intensity of Davis' protest, Judge Wyatt grudgingly admonished Watson not to use the term. Wyatt's concession marked a major departure from normal courtroom practice in Atlanta. In fact, the novelty of the change remained evident as state witnesses repeatedly forgot Wyatt's suggestion and slurred their references to "the nigra."[25]

As Davis continued his cross-examination, it became apparent that the policeman had never witnessed Herndon commit anything vaguely resembling overt agitation. Watson conceded that he had never personally observed Herndon giving a speech or circulating radical periodicals. When pressed, he finally admitted, "I did not see Angelo Herndon attempt any combined resistance to the State government or any of its officers." Although the detective denied placing Herndon in a fake electric chair in order to extract a confession, he did admit searching Herndon's room without a warrant. In short, Davis had reduced

23. Brief of evidence of *Herndon* v. *Georgia*, 117–23, copy in law office of Sutherland, Asbill, and Brennan; Davis, *Communist Councilman from Harlem*, 58–59.

24. Hudson occasionally used this nickname to refer to Davis. The defense attorney in turn called the prosecutor "Preacher Hudson."

25. The trial transcript deleted references to "nigger" but allowed references to "darky" to remain. Nevertheless, several newspaper accounts confirmed the widespread use of both epithets. See Atlanta *Daily World*, January 18, 1933; Macon *Telegraph*, January 18, 1933; Savannah *Tribune*, January 19, 1933. In 1963, former *Daily World* reporter Cliff W. Mackay stated, "The term 'nigger' was repeatedly used during the trial not only by witnesses, but also by the prosecutor and Judge Lee B. Wyatt." Quoted in Entin, "Angelo Herndon," 29–30. Associated Press (AP) reporter James H. Street, a native white Mississippian, wrote later that defense objections to Herndon's being called a "niggah" convinced whites that he was "a smart aleck" and a danger to the community because he would not stay in his place. See James H. Street, *Look Away: A Dixie Notebook* (New York: Viking Press, 1936), 146.

Watson's testimony to the simple fact that Herndon had picked up mail from a post office box under surveillance and that he possessed materials—seized without a warrant—which contained allegedly insurrectionary passages.[26]

The next witness was another state employee, Assistant Solicitor General E. A. Stephens, who presented the heart of the prosecution's case. Like Hudson, Stephens, a short, slim man with "eyes like a hawk," had the reputation of being a "hard-nosed prosecutor." He testified that one of the county commissioners had complained about receiving "a certain scurrilous letter" which contained the return address of Box 339. Stephens asked the police department to watch the box. On that same day, a policeman "brought this darkey, Angelo Herndon, to the solicitor's office and I talked to him in the grand jury room."[27]

Ben Davis immediately jumped to his feet. Vociferously objecting to the use of the term "darkey," he indignantly warned the bench that "if they insist on using such opprobrious terms to the defendant, we will have to ask for a mistrial, because it is prejudicial to our case." Evading the main thrust of Davis' complaint, a perplexed Judge Wyatt cautioned, "I don't know whether it is or not; but suppose you refer to him as the defendant." From the witness stand Stephens in turn protested what he termed the "captious objections" of the defense, remarking that Herndon himself used "Negro" to refer to his race in their earlier conversation. Davis testily responded that the assistant solicitor general had nevertheless called the defendant a "darkey." Wyatt terminated the exchange by again urging Stephens to refer to Herndon as the defendant. Hudson resumed his questioning, only to have Stephens again slip, referring to Herndon as "the darkey with the glasses on, in the middle." In subsequent remarks, though, the witness successfully managed to follow the court's suggestion.[28]

26. Brief of evidence of *Herndon* v. *Georgia*, 57–58, copy in law office of Sutherland, Asbill, and Brennan; Atlanta *Daily World*, January 18, 1933.

27. Atlanta *Daily World*, January 18, 1933. The Reverend Vincent G. Burns gives a critical sketch of both Stephens and John A. Boykin in his introduction to Robert E. Burns, *I Am a Fugitive from a Georgia Chain Gang!* (New York: Grosset and Dunlap, 1932), 19–23.

28. Atlanta *Daily World*, January 18, 1933; Davis, *Communist Councilman from Harlem*, 73. Davis confuses the testimony of Watson with that of Stephens, but his general impressions are accurate. Neither the Atlanta *Constitution* nor the *Journal* mentioned the clash between him and Stephens, but the *Daily World* reported that Stephens substituted the word *Nigra*.

During his interrogation of Herndon, Stephens stated, the defendant revealed that he had joined the Communist party in Kentucky and had come to Atlanta as a party organizer. Stephens asserted that Herndon had told him that there were only five or six actual party members in the city. In describing the literature seized by police, the witness explained that Herndon claimed authorship for two of the circulars. Stephens accidentally admitted that part of the material had never been circulated when he pointed out that some of it had "never been taken out of the wrapper." But he quickly added that Herndon had said that the literature was to be distributed at meetings. Asked by Hudson if Herndon had discussed making speeches at Foster-Ford Club meetings, Stephens replied that the word *speech* had not been used. Although Davis subjected Stephens to a thorough cross-examination, the assistant solicitor proved a wily antagonist. He denied Davis' accusation that he was prejudiced against the defendant, asserting that he had been merely doing his job. When asked to itemize any specific violent actions Herndon had undertaken, Stephens remarked, "I have no personal knowledge of any of the acts that have been alleged to be committed in the indictment by the defendant." [29]

As Davis returned to his seat, having been unable to tear down Stephens' testimony, prosecutor Hudson moved to introduce as evidence the numerous papers contained in Herndon's pasteboard box. Davis quickly rose to object. He argued that Detective Watson had himself admitted obtaining the materials without a search warrant. Judge Wyatt informed Davis that state courts had ruled that a person might resist having his property taken from him but that, if he permitted it to be done, it was admissible as evidence. When Davis suggested that it had been impossible for Herndon to prevent the officers from searching his room while he was in jail or his person while he was under arrest, the judge remained unmoved. "Well, I have ruled on it," he declared characteristically. "I overrule the objection." To bolster its case, the state recalled Detective Watson, who described many of the seized documents. Watson identified various stacks of the *Daily Worker*, the *Southern Worker*, and the *Negro Liberator*, in addition to several copies

29. Brief of evidence of *Herndon* v. *Georgia*, 61–64, copy in law office of Sutherland, Asbill, and Brennan.

of local newspapers, as belonging to the defendant. He also identified a copy of Brown's book, *Communism and Christianism*, which contained several of the passages deemed most offensive by the prosecution.[30]

Attorney Davis again tried to offset the pamphlets' feared effect on the jury by repeatedly stressing that no witness had ever seen Herndon circulate the materials or make any overt act at revolt. Through careful questioning, he forced Watson to admit that he had "never seen Herndon distribute any of the material I identify in the box, and [had] never been to a meeting where I ever heard Herndon speak." The officer further stated that Herndon had not resisted arrest and that he had "never seen him combine with any others, whether white or black, in resistance of the State government." Following Watson's testimony, the state formally rested its case. Although Davis immediately moved for a directed verdict of acquittal, Judge Wyatt overruled the motion and ordered the defense to begin its case.[31]

Mercer G. Evans, professor of economics at Emory University, took the stand as the first defense witness. A well-known Atlanta liberal, Dr. Evans had signed the August, 1930, public statement urging a fair trial for the Atlanta Six. Evans stated that he was a native of Gulfport, Mississippi, and had attended Emory as an undergraduate. He had received an LL.D. degree from the University of Chicago. After establishing that Evans had studied the books cited in the indictment, Davis moved that he be qualified as an expert witness. Judge Wyatt denied the request, observing that it had not been proved that Evans was qualified as an expert to say whether the books were revolutionary.[32]

Undaunted, Davis continued to ask Evans about his professional qualifications. The Emory professor stated that he had published articles in the *Annals of the American Academy of Social and Political Science* and in the *American Federationist*, the official monthly publication of the American Federation of Labor (AFL). Davis again took exception to

30. *Ibid.*, 65–68; Atlanta *Daily World*, January 18, 1933. The exchange over the admission of evidence was stricken from the record. It may be found in typed transcript of record, *Herndon* v. *Georgia*, No. 9871, in Georgia Supreme Court, Atlanta.
31. *Ibid.*
32. Brief of evidence of *Herndon* v. *Georgia*, 68–69, copy in law office of Sutherland, Asbill, and Brennan. See also typed transcript of record, *Herndon* v. *Georgia*, in Georgia Supreme Court.

the judge's refusal to qualify Evans as an expert witness. He then asked Professor Evans about a survey taken in an Emory University class comparing the revolutionary nature of one of the books cited by the prosecution and certain writings by Thomas Jefferson. Assistant prosecutor LeCraw bobbed up to object that the questioning was immaterial and irrelevant. When Wyatt upheld the protest, Davis complained, "I intend to prove that the students of Emory University voted Thomas Jefferson was more radical than that [book]." Wyatt again upheld the prosecution's objection.[33]

Professor Evans continued his testimony. When Davis asked if he had found any Communist literature readily available in area libraries, Evans replied that the Emory library contained one book by Nikolai Lenin, another by Karl Marx, and a copy of Marx's and Friedrich Engels' *The Communist Manifesto*. As Davis tried to make the point that Emory encouraged students to read and think freely, Hudson interjected that such an observation was, in the prosecution's favorite phrase, irrelevant and immaterial. Upholding the objection, Judge Wyatt blandly commented, "If Emory University is guilty of anything, we will try them; I think even if Emory University had actually attempted to incite riot, it wouldn't be material in this case; it is a question of what the defendant has done." Davis then asked Evans about a radical book he had found in the Carnegie Library. Again Hudson objected. Once more the judge sustained him, observing that "the Carnegie Library isn't on trial."[34]

Prosecutor Hudson's vigorous cross-examination failed to produce the anticipated fireworks. His questioning revealed that Evans was a Congregationalist, not a Communist. He quizzed the Emory professor carefully about the Russian Revolution and the assassination of the czar, trying to show that these developments were inherent in Communist activity, but with little success. Hudson's chief accomplishment was to force Evans into admitting that he had spent two weeks in the Soviet Union during the previous summer.[35]

33. *Ibid*.
34. Brief of evidence of *Herndon* v. *Georgia*, 69, copy in law office of Sutherland, Asbill, and Brennan.
35. *Ibid*., 69–70. Hudson's questioning of Evans was not without comic overtones. "The prosecutor and judge attempted to question him about the Soviet Government," wrote James H.

Herndon himself was the next witness. According to Georgia procedure, the defendant could make only an unsworn statement and was exempt from questioning by either prosecution or defense. The jury alone determined the credibility of the statement. As the crowd leaned forward, the slender, brown-skinned youth boldly rose and walked to the stand. Here on public display at last was the obscure young man who had caused such a furor among local officials. A hush settled over the audience as the trial's "dramatic climax" commenced. Herndon opened his remarks by describing the relief crisis in Fulton County during June, 1932, and the reaction of the Unemployed Council. Explaining that the council organized both black and white workers together on the same basis because of common problems and interests, he urged both races to put behind them "this question of the white skin and the black skin, because both are starving and the capitalistic class will continue to prey on this tune of racial discrimination . . . in order to keep the negro and white divided." [36]

To dramatize the widespread suffering in Atlanta, the Unemployed Council scheduled the original relief demonstration at the county courthouse. County Commissioner Walter Hendrix, who had previously denied the existence of hunger, was conveniently absent when they arrived. Had he been present, Herndon declared, he would have seen "unemployed white women with their babies almost naked and without any shoes to go upon their feet," as well as "negro women with their little babies, actually starving for the need of proper nourishment . . . which had been denied them by the county of Fulton and the State of Georgia and city of Atlanta as a whole." Commissioner Walter Steward had talked to the white workers only, recalled Herndon, but this gesture failed to help them, for "they had just about as much results as the negroes did—only a lot of hot air blowed over them by the commission-

---

Street, "but they got all mixed up. They didn't know as much about the governments and organizations of the Soviets as the professor. They kept confusing the president of the U.S.S.R. with the secretary of the Communist Party." See Street, *Look Away!*, 148.

36. Code of Georgia, cited in Cullen B. Gosnell, *Government and Politics of Georgia* (New York: Thomas Nelson and Sons, 1936), 156; brief of evidence of *Herndon v. Georgia*, 70–72, copy in law office of Sutherland, Asbill, and Brennan. The Atlanta *Constitution* repeatedly identified Herndon as a native of Cincinnati, *i.e.*, an "outsider." Several black newspapers copied this identification, too.

ers, which didn't put any shoes on their little babies' feet and no milk in their stomach to give their babies proper nourishment."[37]

Herndon recounted next the details of his arrest, stressing that he was held incommunicado for eleven days. He also emphasized the "horrible conditions" in the Atlanta jail. "I was placed in a little cell there with a dead body and forced to live in there with this dead body," he stated. Furthermore, the defendant charged that the dead prisoner, who had "fought in the Spanish-American war for the American principles," had been ill for three days but had been denied proper medical treatment. Herndon declared that he was occasionally ill himself "because of the fact that the food they gave me in there, I couldn't agree with it," and neither could other prisoners.[38]

Despite these difficulties, Herndon remained resolved to press on with his work. He warned that the city could lock him up but that "there will be more Angelo Herndons to come in the future." He blamed the "capitalistic class" for creating racial bias and charged that capitalists would still exploit the racial issue even if there were no blacks in the United States; "probably it would be the Jews, or the Greeks, or something like that, because it is in their interest to bring up all of these things, so that they can get a good profit out of the working people." Observing that the frustrations of unemployment were strong enough sometimes to cause a person to contemplate suicide, Herndon said that the Unemployed Council urged workers not to despair but to organize to fight for better conditions. Reaching the climax of his speech, he ominously predicted that the capitalistic system was on the verge of collapse.[39]

It had been a dramatic twenty-minute oration, one not forgotten in Georgia for many years. Certainly it was a courageous act. The young Communist categorically refused to disguise or apologize for his beliefs. But his undiplomatic and inexpedient speech, with its simplistic Marxist

37. Brief of evidence of *Herndon* v. *Georgia*, 72–73, copy in law office of Sutherland, Asbill, and Brennan.

38. *Ibid.*, 73–75. I am indebted to Henry Cobb, clerk of the Georgia Supreme Court, for calling Herndon's phrasing to my attention.

39. *Ibid.*, 75–78; Atlanta *Constitution*, January 18, 1933. The *Daily Worker*, January 20, 1933, reported that Herndon used the courtroom as "a tribunal" to attack capitalism and to defend the Communist party's role "in the struggles against starvation, Negro national oppression and imperialist war."

interpretations, did little to aid his cause. Not surprisingly, the jury remained unmoved. Apparently neither Ben Davis nor John Geer had encouraged Herndon to soften his remarks, though it is unclear whether they fully realized what he had planned to say. Associated Press reporter James H. Street commented that the defendant had "really talked himself into jail. It seemed to me that he wanted to make a martyr of himself, and he did." Nevertheless, Street admired Herndon for his honesty and fearlessness.[40]

Tension remained high in the packed courtroom as the defense called its next witness, T. J. Corley, an assistant professor of economics at Emory.[41] Corley testified that he was a native of Comanche, Texas, that he had never visited Russia, and that he was not a Communist. When pressed by Hudson he did concede that he found "elements within Communism with which I agree." However, he hastily added that it depended on how one defined communism. Defense efforts to qualify Corley as an expert witness failed. The prosecution's hostility toward the defense reached its zenith during Corley's testimony. The emotional Hudson demanded to know if there were not a little Communist party at Emory. Corley strenuously denied this allegation. Hudson then asked a series of questions concerning the Communist party platform. The distasteful phrases "self-determination" and "equal rights for Negroes" especially troubled him. After Corley explained that "equal rights" meant equal rights for all people under the law, Hudson suddenly pounced on the most sensational implications of the remark. "You understand that to mean the right of a colored boy to marry your daughter, if you have one?" he demanded. A shocked Ben Davis loudly protested this inflammatory question to no avail. The flustered Corley managed to respond in a restrained manner that a black man "doesn't happen to have the right to marry my daughter, under the laws of this State." Undaunted, Hudson then asked if he knew how many states permitted intermarriage. Corley replied that he did not, and Hudson eventually dropped the issue.[42]

40. Street, *Look Away!*, 149.

41. The fact that two Emory professors testified for the defense did not sit well with some Atlanta residents. "There were a lot of mumblings against Emory for having teachers of that type," commented AP reporter James Street. See *ibid.*, 148.

42. Brief of evidence of *Herndon* v. *Georgia*, 78–82, copy in law office of Sutherland, Asbill, and Brennan.

But the excited prosecutor continued to badger Corley about various controversial Communist positions. The Emory professor admitted being unaware that one Communist pamphlet advocated seizing land in the South from whites and giving it to blacks. He also expressed ignorance of the Communist demand for the establishment of a Black Belt government which would be free to secede from the rest of the country if it so desired. At the conclusion of Corley's testimony, the defense rested.[43] Although Hudson did not trick Corley into any incriminating remarks, he accomplished a great deal in his cross-examination. Through his skillfully worded questions, the prosecutor had given the jury the impression that the Communist party advocated racial miscegenation, seizure of white-owned property, and (ironically, in light of Georgia's role in the Confederacy) secession from the United States. The implication was clear. As a member of the Communist party and a firm believer in its tenets, Angelo Herndon constituted a serious threat to the state of Georgia.

Herndon's accusations about prison conditions had angered the prosecution. John Hudson called three rebuttal witnesses to challenge Herndon's comments concerning the jail. W. T. Turner, engineer and steward at the jail, took the stand first. His lengthy testimony primarily revealed the primitive facilities available to all prisoners, not just to Herndon. Turner stressed that decent food was served at Fulton Tower Prison; certainly there was no record that anyone had ever died from it. Denying Herndon's allegations, he argued that the defendant "was not subjected to any inhuman treatment whatever, he was not subjected to any rotten food." In response to Davis' charge that black prisoners were treated more harshly than whites, Turner retorted that in his "jail there is no discrimination whatever between negro and white prisoners; as to treatment, of course, they are segregated . . . and the negroes get the same treatment." In fact, commented Turner, it was the white prisoners who complained most often about the food, especially when collards had been served for two consecutive days.[44]

Turner further disputed Herndon's charges that a corpse had been allowed to remain in his cell. He stated that all corpses were promptly

43. *Ibid.*, 82.
44. *Ibid.*, 82–86.

removed by an undertaker. Davis did uncover some evidence that ailing black prisoners were given inferior treatment. All inmates could be treated in the prison clinic, but the hospital ward was reserved exclusively for whites. "As to the places they are kept, the white prisoners and the colored prisoners are kept in two different types of places," said the witness, "the colored in the cage and the white in what we call the white hospital ward." However, Turner maintained that occasionally black prisoners were admitted to the ward and that "there has never been a colored man in that jail that suffered for want of attention if we knew it; he gets as good treatment as the white man does." [45]

Jailer R. N. Holland supplied additional information about the death of Herndon's cell mate William Wilson, asserting that his body had been promptly removed. Like previous witnesses, Holland maintained that "Herndon was treated just like any other colored prisoner in the Fulton County Jail." During his testimony, the jailer succeeded in painting the picture of an unhappy prisoner who was a chronic complainer. For example, Herndon had been audacious enough to request ham and eggs for breakfast instead of grits. "That's a jailhouse, not a hotel," Holland snorted. It was late afternoon when the last state witness, Dr. J. C. Blalock, the county physician, took the stand. Blalock told the court that Wilson had died of heart disease, having suffered from hypertension and arteriosclerosis. Although he had been treating Wilson for several weeks, Blalock denied that the prisoner's condition had warranted hospitalization. He added that Wilson's body was removed from the jail as quickly as possible. [46] The day's session ended with Blalock's testimony.

For defense lawyers, it had been another long and grueling day. Davis found it especially frustrating. Much of his previous life now appeared irrelevant. His exclusive schooling at Amherst and Harvard seemed useless in a Georgia courtroom where racial prejudice overrode law and justice. As he later explained, "What I had not found at Morehouse, Amherst and Harvard I had discovered in a dingy Georgia courtroom whose realities were far more penetrating than the abstractions of classical scholarship." The rush of events had convinced Davis

45. *Ibid.*
46. *Ibid.*, 86–92; Atlanta *Constitution*, January 18, 1933.

that something more than polite requests for equal rights was needed. The greater his involvement in the case, the greater became his sympathy for radical solutions to the racial dilemma. Now, a "grim joke" on Judge Wyatt and Hudson loomed in his mind. He had contemplated the idea previously, but the farcical trial now persuaded him to take immediate action. That night Benjamin J. Davis, Jr., secretly joined the Communist party.[47]

Closing arguments for both sides occupied Wednesday morning. Wyatt allotted each side two hours. The prosecution chose to divide its time into two portions, with Hudson speaking first. The continuing mild weather and the sensational nature of the case again produced a full courtroom of some six hundred black and white spectators. Showing the strain of the case, Hudson began in a low, husky voice stemming from a sore throat. Warming quickly to his subject, however, he soon rose to intense emotionalism in what was termed a "fiery" address. His experience as a lay preacher served him well that morning, as he appeared to one observer to be an "avenging angel" of the Lord, slaying his enemies left and right. In an initial attack on Emory University, he labeled the school "a hotbed of iniquity." Professors Mercer G. Evans and T. J. Corley he contemptuously dismissed as "renegades."[48]

As his tirade progressed, Hudson swayed from side to side, flapping his arms like a windmill, daring the Communist party to do its worst. "Must the State of Georgia sit idly by while you organize and mobilize your Red Army?" he exclaimed. "No, you lay down your defy [*sic*] and I as a representative of the State of Georgia accept the challenge." Stressing the difference between "philosophic discussion and rank treason," he charged that Herndon's activities fell into the latter category. With tears in his eyes, the emotional Hudson pleaded with the jury to "send this damnable anarchistic Bolsheviki to his death by electrocu-

47. See Davis, *Communist Councilman from Harlem*, 75–76, for a full account. See also Benjamin J. Davis, "Why I Am a Communist," *Phylon*, VIII (Spring, 1947), 105–16. Historian C. Vann Woodward, then an instructor at Georgia Tech, suspected that Davis might have become a Communist by the time of the trial, but John H. Hudson later asserted that Davis joined the party well in advance of the trial. See Entin, "Angelo Herndon," 37. I am inclined to take Davis' statement at face value. However, it should be noted that Davis disclaimed membership in the party while he remained in Atlanta.

48. Davis, *Communist Councilman from Harlem*, 76; Herndon, *Let Me Live*, 237–38; Atlanta *Daily World*, January 19, 1933; Atlanta *Constitution*, January 19, 1933; Atlanta *Journal*, January 18, 1933; Macon *Telegraph*, January 19, 1933.

tion, and God will be satisfied that justice has been done and the daughters of the state officials can walk the streets safely. Stamp this thing out now with a conviction." [49]

John Geer spoke first for the defense. Short and of medium build, with gray eyes and a medium brown complexion, he stressed the legality of the Communist party, reminding jurors in a soft, deep voice that the Georgia secretary of state had permitted it a spot on the official presidential ballot in 1932. Quiet, intense, and hardworking, the unassuming Geer had been overshadowed by his more articulate partner during the trial. His forte was legal maneuvers and procedures, not public speaking, and he concluded his remarks far short of the hour he had planned to talk. [50]

Ben Davis rose hastily. The strain and pressures of the trial had affected him so deeply that he no longer feigned respect for the court. He began "in the heat of anger." Caution, discretion, moderation—all of these virtues Davis cast aside in an emotional challenge to the southern Jim Crow system. The intensity of his words shocked the crowd. All the frustrations and resentments of the black middle class poured from his lips in a torrent. To those blacks present, his rousing speech evoked a deep, personal response. Who among them had not suffered similar frustrations, but in silence? Now, one of their own, a product of the best schooling, challenged the system in uncompromising language. They thrilled to his words, words they had all felt but had never dared to utter publicly. Davis depicted the prosecution as fundamentally hostile to constitutional rights. "Don't try to organize for better conditions . . . don't try to fight for bread for yourselves and starving families," for the state might charge you with insurrection, he warned. The only charge against Herndon was his race, he asserted, and the state had responded by waving "the bloody flag of racial prejudice" and shouting "nigger, nigger, nigger." The chief prosecutor he labeled a "hypocrite" and charged, "Mr. Hudson's vaunted piety is only a cloak for his evil deeds." Davis argued that, instead of sending Herndon to the electric

49. *Ibid.*

50. Davis, *Communist Councilman from Harlem*, 76; Atlanta *Daily World*, January 19, 1933; Floyd W. Crawford to the author, November 21, 1973. Crawford was related by marriage to John Geer and graciously supplied information about him.

chair, he "should be hailed for his courage" and his interracial efforts.[51]

Davis' words provoked a hostile reaction from whites in the packed courtroom. Several members of the jury became visibly angry. Three of them turned their backs on him as he paced near the jury box, but Davis plunged ahead undaunted. "Mr. Hudson knows as much about communism as a pig knows about a full-dress suit," he declared contemptuously. Next the fiery attorney picked up one of the radical pamphlets and read aloud several passages. One particularly graphic excerpt described the lynching and burning of a pregnant black woman. As Davis paused dramatically, a spectator fainted. After a momentary lull, Davis proclaimed that this "case is a blot upon an American civilization which boasts of liberty, democracy, freedom of speech and press." Not the Communist party but the Ku Klux Klan was the real insurrectionary force in the state, he charged. Reminding the court that not a single witness had testified to any violent act by the defendant, he asked, "Would you call a peaceful demonstration for relief an attempt at insurrection?" Davis issued an eloquent plea for a verdict of not guilty: "Any other verdict will be a mockery of justice; any other verdict will be catering to the basest passion of race prejudice which the Reverend Hudson has sought to conjure up in you all; any other verdict will be making a scrap of paper out of the Bill of Rights, the Constitution of the United States and the State of Georgia, out of the democratic rights which are the property of every citizen whether his skin is black or white."[52]

While the shaken audience absorbed Davis' words, the diminutive J. Walter LeCraw began his presentation. Although one local newspaper merely noted that the assistant prosecutor restricted his remarks to the legal issues involved, LeCraw himself struck an emotional tone on several occasions. He stressed that the Communists wanted to create a Negro republic out of the Black Belt, a suggestion which LeCraw found revolting. He warned that the state could not sit idly by and allow a Red army to come "into this country and destroy our civilization." He

51. *Ibid.* This version of Davis' speech is taken from the St. Louis *Post-Dispatch*, January 18, 1933. Davis, *Communist Councilman from Harlem*, 76–77; Herndon, *Let Me Live*, 351; Atlanta *Constitution*, January 19, 1933.

52. Davis, *Communist Councilman from Harlem*, 77–79; Herndon, *Let Me Live*, 351–54.

added, "Do we have to wait until they get their Red 'Rooshian' army together to attack our homes, take our property, rape our women, and murder our children? Do we have to sit until they perfect their schemes of insurrection and violence?" His answer was a ringing no. In closing, LeCraw declared that not only Herndon but also the principles of communism were on trial.[53]

It was early afternoon when Judge Wyatt formally charged the jury. Apparently hostile to the defense throughout the trial, Wyatt rendered a surprisingly judicious charge. Despite numerous defense objections, his interpretation of the insurrection law proved in the long run more flexible than that later placed upon it by the Georgia Supreme Court. In sober tones, the judge reminded the jury that the defendant had entered the court with the legal presumption of innocence until proved guilty beyond a reasonable doubt. After reading the indictment, he instructed the jury that, if they possessed reasonable doubt that the state had proved those allegations, then the defendant should be given the benefit of that doubt and be acquitted. He cautioned that advocacy of insurrection, "however reprehensible morally," was not sufficient for a conviction without evidence that the advocacy would be acted upon immediately. "In order to convict the defendant, gentlemen," stated Wyatt, "it must appear clearly by the evidence that *immediate serious violence* against the State of Georgia was to be expected or was advocated." He added that the "mere possession of radical literature" was not sufficient for a conviction. After hearing the mechanics of the three possible verdicts (guilty, guilty with mercy, and not guilty) explained, the jury withdrew to deliberate.[54]

Given the resentment shown toward the defense throughout the proceedings, Davis and many observers were surprised when the jury did not immediately return a verdict. Shortly before six o'clock, how-

53. Since in a criminal case the burden of proof lies upon the prosecution, it makes the last presentation to the jury. Davis, *Communist Councilman from Harlem*, 79–80; Atlanta *Daily World*, January 19, 1933; Atlanta *Constitution*, January 19, 1933; Atlanta *Journal*, January 18, 1933; author's interview with LeCraw. LeCraw regarded Communist activities in Atlanta as a "probing action," hoping to find a fertile field among southern blacks. Despite these efforts, the assistant prosecutor felt that there was no significant interest in party doctrine among black Georgians.

54. Brief of evidence of *Herndon* v. *Georgia*, 126–37, copy in law office of Sutherland, Asbill, and Brennan.

ever, word came that a decision had been reached. The courtroom rapidly filled with eager spectators who had remained nearby in the hope of a speedy verdict. Prior to admitting the jury, Judge Wyatt cautioned the tense crowd against any outburst or demonstration following the verdict. He stationed "a corps of sheriff's officers" around the room to guarantee order. The jurors filed in and handed a note to the bailiff, who read: "We the jury find the Defendant Angelo Herndon = Guilty= and recommend him to Mercy, and fix his Penalty at from 18 years to 20 years." Despite Wyatt's admonitions, an uproar momentarily broke out among the spectators before officials restored calm. After the judge formally pronounced sentence, a stoic Herndon was led away.[55]

So ended "one of the most spectacular trials in the annals of Fulton Superior Court," acknowledged the Atlanta *Constitution*.[56] But the paper was only partially correct. The state of Georgia had not heard the last of Angelo Herndon. In fact, it would take four long years of legal and political debate before the Herndon case would finally be resolved.

55. Atlanta *Constitution*, January 19, 1933; Atlanta *Daily World*, January 19, 1933; Atlanta *Georgian*, January 19, 1933; Atlanta *Journal*, January 19, 1933; Davis, *Communist Councilman from Harlem*, 81; Herndon, *Let Me Live*, 238–39. Actually, the first quick poll of the jury revealed that all twelve jurors favored a guilty verdict. On the first four ballots, two insisted on the death penalty. On the fifth ballot one changed his mind, but not until the sixth ballot, after nearly three hours' deliberation, did the twelfth juror accept the recommendation of mercy. Following the verdict, J. Walter LeCraw announced that trial dates would soon be set for the Atlanta Six. What appears to be the jury's original note stating the guilty verdict can be found in *State* v. *Angelo Herndon*, in Miscellaneous Documents, Fulton County Courthouse. It should be noted that the *Constitution*, the *Journal*, and the *Georgian* failed to provide adequate coverage of this "spectacular" trial and acknowledged its importance only in retrospect. Street, *Look Away!*, 150, observes that Atlanta newspapers were afraid to "play" racial troubles because of past criticism of the role of the press in the 1906 race riot and the Leo Frank case.

56. Atlanta *Constitution*, January 19, 1933.

CHAPTER FOUR

"A Shameful Verdict"

THE HARSH "justice" meted out to Angelo Herndon in a crowded Georgia courtroom did not immediately stir the souls of white Americans. Most whites remained unaware of the tragic chain of events in Georgia. Not until 1935, when the case finally reached the United States Supreme Court, did the affair become widely known. The emergence of the Herndon case as a *cause célèbre* was not foreordained. Only the tireless publicity efforts of the ILD and liberal and leftist sympathizers brought the case to national attention. Meanwhile, in Atlanta, the hope of county and state officials that such vigorous prosecution would halt radical activity in Georgia proved false. In fact, additional efforts at repression only heightened tensions between law enforcement agencies and the black community, providing a fertile field for radical propaganda.

Despite widespread ignorance of the Herndon case, a small but articulate minority carefully monitored the proceedings. Officials of the NAACP, the ACLU, and the Commission on Interracial Cooperation, assorted radicals, the black press, and the Communist party all followed developments. This was not an easy task, though, because few newspapers outside the Atlanta and New York City areas, except for the St. Louis *Post-Dispatch*, provided any coverage. Even the New York *Times*, which announced Herndon's conviction on page one, carried only two brief articles on the case during the remainder of the year.[1] The New York *World-Telegram* and the *Herald-Tribune* published slightly

1. New York *Times*, January 19, 1933, p. 1.

more information, but, throughout the rest of the East and the Midwest, only scattered newspapers mentioned the case.

Probably the best coverage appeared in the St. Louis *Post-Dispatch*, which printed the unabridged wire service accounts in full. Following the conviction, the newspaper editorially denounced the trial as "a shameful proceeding, masquerading under the forms of law" and the setting as "an atmosphere of intense racial prejudice." The *Post-Dispatch* surmised, "We do not know what success Herndon had as an organizer, but the Judge, the jury and the prosecutor in this medieval court are far more potent organizers of insurrection than the poor Negro they had before them. It is just this sort of stupid tyranny upon which subversive movements thrive." [2]

Most national magazines exhibited little curiosity about the case. *Time* briefly noted the conviction but took no further interest during the year. [3] The liberal-leftist press displayed considerably more concern, but only after the conviction, not before, when national publicity might have embarrassed Atlanta officials and forced them to modify the prosecution. The *New Republic* termed the sentence an "outrageous injustice" which tended "to prove what the Communists have long charged about capitalist-ruled courts in the Deep South and elsewhere." The *Nation* asserted that the verdict was as fantastic as it was cruel and partisan. The real issue, it said, was that a black Communist had dared to organize the unemployed on an integrated basis. The magazine added that the sentence stood as "a dramatic example of class and race [in]justice." [4]

In contrast to most white periodicals, the national Negro press showed considerable interest in the Herndon case. In general, black newspapers strongly condemned the actions of Georgia authorities and displayed ambivalent feelings toward Communist involvement. This response, typical of the 1930s, had been foreshadowed in the magazine *Crisis* the previous summer, when a symposium on communism by black editors had been printed. Although the editors polled exhibited a

2. St. Louis *Post-Dispatch*, January 18–20, 1933. See also Milwaukee *Leader*, February 8, 1933, and Indianapolis *Times*, February 6, 1933, both in American Civil Liberties Union Archives, Princeton University Library, hereinafter cited as ACLU Archives.

3. "Red, Black, and Georgia," *Time*, January 30, 1933, p. 14.

4. "The Week," *New Republic*, February 1, 1933, pp. 308–309; *Nation*, February 15, 1933, p. 162.

wide range of attitudes, few were bitterly anti-Communist. Only Frank Marshall Davis of the Atlanta *Daily World* and Robert L. Vann of the Pittsburgh *Courier* seemed completely skeptical of the party's efforts.[5]

Most other black editors proved more open-minded, with a few offering outright support. Carl Murphey of the Baltimore *Afro-American* went so far as to argue that the Communist party was the heir of the abolitionists and the only party going the Negro's way. The contributors repeatedly listed as the chief cause for black dissatisfaction the failure of the American system to afford blacks full equality. Given these disabilities, most editors observed that it was only natural for black people to take help from whoever offered it. As E. Washington Rhodes of the Philadelphia *Tribune* pointed out, a "drowning man will grab at a straw." In fact, much like later scholars, Rhodes admitted surprise that more blacks had not joined the party's ranks, given its efforts to obtain equal rights. This hesitancy some ascribed to the innate conservatism of the race, to blacks' deep patriotism, or to radical attacks on religion. The revolutionary role of the white working class remained questionable to the editors, who seemed skeptical over that class's racial views. Although the wide range of views expressed in the symposium precluded a unanimous conclusion, it appeared evident that the party's involvement in the Scottsboro case, in the struggle for equal legal rights for blacks, and in other related causes was bringing approval from a modest but growing segment of the black community.[6]

The immediate reaction of the black press to Herndon's conviction in January, 1933, was highly critical. "Not even the infamous Scottsboro cases surpass in hideousness and barbarity the judgment entered by a Georgia Court sentencing Angelo Herndon, 19-year-old Negro, to twenty years in the living hell of a Georgia chain gang," exclaimed the Richmond *Planet*. The Philadelphia *Tribune* similarly castigated the strained quality of Georgia justice: "In Georgia lynchers and mob murderers go unpunished, but a young man distributing 'red' literature

5. "Negro Editors on Communism: A Symposium of the American Negro Press," *Crisis*, XXXIX (April, 1932), 117–19, and (May, 1932), 154–56.

6. *Ibid*. For a black Communist's bitter rejoinder, see James W. Ford, "Communism and the Negro," *Daily Worker*, April 28–30, May 2–4, 1932. This hostile description of black editors, in a later article, was typical: "Shamelessly grovelling and boot-licking before their white masters, they pick up the slimiest excretions of the white bourgeoisie." See *Daily Worker*, June 4, 1932.

gets twenty years. Another black eye for the sovereign State of Georgia." A "savage and inhumane" verdict, trumpeted the Washington, D.C., *Tribune*. The Norfolk *Journal and Guide* labeled the decision "an atrocious verdict," and the New York *Amsterdam News* asserted that the conviction "tears away the last shred of Georgia's claim to decency and exposes her foul body to the world." [7] Other black newspapers, including the Chicago *Defender*, Savannah *Tribune*, New York *Age, Louisiana Weekly* (New Orleans), and St. Louis *Argus*, denounced the conviction with equal indignation. [8]

The role of the Communist party in the case proved more difficult to evaluate. Several writers strongly sympathized with Communist efforts. Columnist Fred Frenwick of the *Amsterdam News* charged that Georgia and Alabama "have created in the minds of thousands of young colored men like myself a complex which closely resembles affection for the Communist Party. It seems to stand out more conspicuously than ever, that almost any doctrine which is hostile to Southern fancy, ought to be friendly to mine." William D. Kelley, editor of the *Amsterdam News*, likewise praised party efforts. Apologizing for his earlier suspicions, he observed that party actions in the Scottsboro, Euel Lee, and Herndon cases illustrated its determination to expose the fundamental injustices suffered by black Americans. He praised Ben Davis and John Geer's success in forcing Judge Wyatt to rule out such references as "nigger" and "darky" as a significant advance. The willingness of two white southern professors to testify in Herndon's behalf further encouraged Kelley. "The spotlight Communists have turned upon the South's crimes is a service to humanity in general and the Negro in particular," he concluded. [9]

7. Richmond *Planet*, January 28, 1933, Philadelphia *Tribune*, January 26, 1933, Washington, D.C., *Tribune*, January 27, 1933, Norfolk *Journal and Guide*, January 28, 1933, New York *Amsterdam News*, January 25, 1933, all in clippings file, International Labor Defense Papers, Schomburg Collection, New York Public Library, hereinafter cited as ILD Papers.

8. Pittsburgh *Courier*, February 4, 1933; *Louisiana Weekly* (New Orleans), January 28, 1933; Chicago *Defender*, February 4, 1933; Savannah *Tribune*, January 19, 1933. See also New York *Age*, January 28, 1933, St. Louis *Argus*, January 27, 1933, and *California Eagle*, February 3, 1933, all *ibid.*

9. New York *Amsterdam News*, January 25 and February 4, 1933, and Richmond *Planet*, January 28, 1933, all in clippings file, ILD Papers. See also James B. LaFourche, "The South in Arms," *Louisiana Weekly* (New Orleans), February 18, 1933.

Other black journalists blamed short-sighted Georgia officials for ironically abetting Communist efforts through their own bigotry and stupidity. Noting that the Herndon affair would give a "tremendous impetus" to Communist efforts in the United States, the Norfolk *Journal and Guide* remarked that "if it had been treated as it deserved to be treated it would have no particularly stimulating effect upon a movement that is so distasteful to Georgia." The Savannah *Tribune* and the Cincinnati *Union* agreed with that sentiment. Declared the *Union*, "Only the stupidity of southern officials furnishes the Communists with material for propaganda among the Negroes."[10]

The Pittsburgh *Courier*, which had earlier tangled with the party over the Scottsboro case, expressed outright hostility to Communist activities. Although the newspaper denounced Georgia as "the most savage state" in the nation, it hastened to indict the Communists as well. Contending that "Red" tactics had failed in the South, it suggested that more experienced "agitators" stayed clear of Dixie but that inexperienced, idealistic youths were being sent there to suffer. "If Herndon dies, the responsibility for his death will rest not only upon the planter-manufacturer dictatorship of Georgia, but upon the Communist Party, which persists in callously sending these youngsters down to certain imprisonment and death," it charged. Yet eventually, the *Courier* asserted, the Communist party always found it necessary to fall back on the courts just like the NAACP and the Commission on Interracial Cooperation, organizations whose tactics it constantly maligned. The newspaper sarcastically concluded that the party's chief accomplishment among blacks "has been to draw into its folds a few scatter-brained 'intellectuals,' sincere and otherwise, who, surrounded by worshipful whites, can preen themselves as 'champions of the proletariat' in the comfort and safety of Northern urban centers." Journalist George S. Schuyler, a regular columnist in the *Courier*, also lambasted the Communists on several occasions.[11]

10. Norfolk *Journal and Guide*, January 28, 1933, and Cincinnati *Union*, quoted in New York *Age*, February 18, 1933, both in clippings file, ILD Papers; Savannah *Tribune*, January 19, 1933; Chicago *Defender*, February 4, 1933.

11. Pittsburgh *Courier*, February 4, 1933; George S. Schuyler, "Views and Reviews," Pittsburgh *Courier*, January 21 and February 18, 1933; Reminiscences of George S. Schuyler, 226, in Oral History Collection, Nicholas M. Butler Library, Columbia University. In response, the

The Communist party and its major newspaper, the *Daily Worker*, followed the Herndon affair closely and with mounting indignation. Ever since the Communists had aroused national interest in the Scottsboro rape case, party leaders had been alert for cases involving blacks and the courts. Despite initial slowness in grasping the significance of Scottsboro, the party had energetically plunged into the defense campaign and raised it to international notoriety.[12] This time the Communists were better prepared, especially since the defendant was a black man, a Communist, and a yankee! Moreover, the ILD, the Communist-influenced legal defense organization, already had full custody of the case, thereby eliminating any potential struggle with the NAACP.

On January 20, 1933, the *Daily Worker* carried a front-page banner headline announcing the conviction. The accompanying story, the *Worker*'s first major report on the trial, was written by Robert H. Hart, an Atlanta activist, who indignantly declared that the "sentence is clearly a class verdict aimed at the suppression of the struggles of the white and Negro masses against starvation and for Negro liberation." The article further asserted that black and white workers jammed the courtroom and "hung on Herndon's words" during his address. Judge Lee B. Wyatt, Hart charged, overruled defense objections "with machine-like regularity," although he was forced to prohibit the use of opprobrious terms to describe blacks. Hart concluded that a sizable local protest movement was under way, as "many Negroes, liberals and intellectuals already have come forward with promises of support."[13]

In an editorial the following day, the *Daily Worker* denounced the conviction as a futile effort to halt the growing black liberation movement by resurrecting the ancient slave code. Herndon's real crime, it claimed, had been to work for unity between blacks and whites. Linking the case with those of the Scottsboro boys, the Atlanta Six, and the Tallapoosa, Alabama, sharecroppers, the newspaper urged the creation

---

Daily Worker, February 7, 1933, denounced the *Courier*'s attack as a typical slander by Negro "reformists" and blasted the newspaper for remaining "persistent in the defense of its white ruling-class masters."

12. Dan T. Carter, *Scottsboro: A Tragedy of the American South* (Baton Rouge: Louisiana State University Press, 1969), 49–52.

13. *Daily Worker*, January 20 and 21, 1933.

of a broad-based mass defense movement that would stress such issues as the immediate release of Herndon, abolition of the chain gang system, the right of free speech, and the right of the Communist party to a legal existence. Readers were further urged to contribute to an emergency fund-raising drive for the newspaper in order to guarantee the continued dissemination of the truth about Herndon and other working-class prisoners.[14]

There were additional attacks on the Herndon conviction in the following weeks. Viola Montgomery, mother of Olen Montgomery, one of the Scottsboro boys, denounced Judge Wyatt for encouraging attacks on the Communist party. An outraged William L. Patterson, the black national secretary of the ILD, called on workers and intellectuals of all races to rally to Herndon's defense. Patterson vowed to develop the case into national and even international prominence. He pledged that the entire forces of the ILD would be devoted to organizing a mass defense movement in support of appropriate legal action. In turn the ILD announced that it would open an office in Atlanta to serve as headquarters for the Herndon fight.[15]

Herndon himself proved a more cooperative and articulate symbol than the Scottsboro boys. From Fulton Tower Prison he penned a letter urging blacks and whites to fight his sentence to the chain gang, the harassment of black and white workers, and the national oppression of the Negro people. In simplified Marxist language he stridently declared, "Now is the time for all workers of Georgia and the United States, Negro and white, to organize ourselves in a united and solid bond and be prepared to give the bloody damnable system of capitalism the final blow and take over the power that the capitalists now possess and turn it into the power of the proletariat, the class that produces everything and keeps the machinery of life turning."[16]

Meanwhile, Walter White, executive secretary of the NAACP, observed the case with growing concern. The bitter fight between the NAACP and the ILD for control of the Scottsboro case had left deep

---

14. *Ibid.*, January 21, 1933. In 1931 Communist efforts to form a sharecroppers' union in Tallapoosa County, Alabama, resulted in white hysteria and widespread violence against blacks. Another outbreak in the same county occurred in 1933. See Carter, *Scottsboro*, 123–29, 174–78.

15. *Daily Worker*, January 23, 26, and 30, 1933.

16. *Ibid.*, January 26, 1933.

scars. As a consequence, White believed that the Communists were deliberately waging a vicious campaign to destroy the NAACP. As he had explained to Will W. Alexander the previous summer, "Back of this also are orders from Moscow to destroy public confidence in non-Communist organizations that are working for justice to the Negro on the ground that as long as such organizations as the NAACP can continue to win victories, just so long will it be impossible for the Communists to convince the Negro that his only hope lies in revolution and in complete destruction of the capitalist system." [17]

Convinced that the intrusion of communism into a sensitive racial case only made matters worse, White moved discreetly. On January 24, 1933, six days after the conviction, he wrote A. T. Walden, president of the Atlanta chapter, requesting him to contact Herndon and his lawyers about the appeal. He asked Walden to ascertain "the possibilities of the Association gaining exclusive control of the case to fight the matter out on the legal and human principle involved, and not having it distorted by injection of the Communist angle." White warned that, if the insurrection law could be used against the Communist party, it could be used against the NAACP and other organizations as well. [18] White's inquiry elicited no response but it did indicate the NAACP's desire to challenge the conviction. However, as in the Scottsboro case, the association preferred to move cautiously and clarify details before plunging into the defense of an unpopular figure.

Daisy E. Lampkin, regional field secretary for the organization, visited Atlanta during February, 1933. She optimistically reported to Roy Wilkins that intelligent blacks were now more favorably inclined toward the association than before, because they realized "that the Angelo Herndon case stirred up more racial discord than anything else." Whites too were said to be more inclined toward "the saner program of the NAACP." In fact, Lampkin revealed that several white lawyers had assured Walden that he personally could have won an acquittal in the case. Although noting that there was "a great admiration" for the

17. Walter White to Will W. Alexander, August 16, 1932, in Commission on Interracial Cooperation Papers, Trevor Arnett Library, Atlanta University. For a fuller statement of White's views, see his "The Negro and the Communists," *Harper's*, CLXIV (December, 1931), 62–72.

18. Walter White to A. T. Walden, January 24, 1933, in National Association for the Advancement of Colored People Papers, Library of Congress, hereinafter cited as NAACP Papers.

courage shown by Geer and Davis, she observed that "sensible" blacks could not afford to be associated with communism.[19]

William Pickens, another field secretary for the association, took a characteristically outspoken position. Two years earlier, his public comments supporting the ILD's Scottsboro activities had embarrassed the NAACP and earned him a reprimand. In February the volatile Pickens denounced the state of Georgia as a "grim and beastly joke." Labeling the entire proceeding an "outrage" and describing the insurrection law as "a dead and discredited agency of tyranny," he urged that the conviction be reversed. In time, though, Pickens toned down his comments until the NAACP was ready to take a more active role.[20]

Roger N. Baldwin of the American Civil Liberties Union likewise followed developments in Atlanta. Unlike the NAACP, however, the ACLU was well acquainted with prosecutor John H. Hudson, having previously worked with the ILD in defending the Atlanta Six against his efforts. But new developments threatened to divide the ACLU and the ILD. The day following the Herndon conviction, Patterson notified Baldwin that John Geer and Ben Davis had been placed in complete charge of the Atlanta Six cases, replacing Oliver C. Hancock. Taken by surprise, Baldwin quickly wrote Will Alexander of the Commission on Interracial Cooperation about the two black attorneys. "You can appreciate the reasons which move the ILD to employ Negro lawyers," he told Alexander, "even though you may not agree with that course." Baldwin also hastily wrote attorney W. A. McClellan to assure him that the ILD had acted without consulting the ACLU and in ignorance of the earlier agreement between the two groups over counsel for the Six. Since Patterson was not working with the ILD at the time of the earlier agreement, he had not been familiar with its terms. Baldwin strongly urged the Macon attorney to remain in the case.[21] The ACLU leader next volunteered the union's services to the ILD for the Herndon case. Specifically, he offered the assistance of the group's distinguished legal

19. Daisy E. Lampkin to Roy Wilkins, February 4, 1933, *ibid.*

20. Norfolk *Journal and Guide*, February 11, 1933, in clippings file, ILD Papers; Carter, *Scottsboro*, 60–61.

21. William L. Patterson to Roger N. Baldwin, January 19, 1933, Baldwin to Will W. Alexander, January 20, 1933, and Baldwin to W. A. McClellan, January 20 and 23, 1933, all in ACLU Archives.

counsel, Arthur Garfield Hays, to help with the appeal "and to be associated with the Negro lawyers in a *subordinate* capacity." Patterson thanked the group for its "generous offer" but declined. The ILD expressed brief interest in the ACLU's subsequent recommendation of a liberal white southern lawyer, but it later dropped the plan.[22]

In his efforts to retain McClellan as counsel for the Atlanta Six, Baldwin ultimately failed. The Macon attorney quickly indicated his displeasure over the addition of Geer and Davis. Although stressing that he had "no animosity" toward the two, he nevertheless charged that the ILD had committed "the biggest tactical blunder that could have been made by them." Baldwin defended the action, explaining that the ILD was "interested in establishing the equality of races before the law and believes that the employment of Negro lawyers will help their campaign to that end, even though it may somewhat jeopardize the interests of the defendants." Despite Baldwin's efforts to soothe McClellan's feelings, the lawyer regretfully announced "that the ILD, by their present arrangements, has placed the Atlanta Cases . . . beyond the pale of my help in the approaching trials."[23]

In response to Baldwin's request, Alexander supplied the ACLU with a critical appraisal of the ILD's role in the Herndon case. His evaluation depicted Davis as "a young man of good appearance" and "native ability." Geer, he stated, had qualified for the state bar examination through self-study and a correspondence course. According to his research, though, neither lawyer possessed much practical experience in criminal cases. The actual trial, he reported, had degenerated into an argument between the defense and "an ignorant, fanatical prosecutor as to the merits and demerits of communism." Since Herndon and his attorneys had lent themselves quite willingly to this confrontation, Alexander feared that subsequent appeals would merely involve "further agitation on behalf of communism." If an experienced lawyer took charge of the appeal, Alexander confidently maintained, he should have no trouble getting the verdict set aside. Yet, he held little hope for

22. Roger N. Baldwin to William L. Patterson, January 24 and 26, 1933, and memorandum, February 14, 1933, all *ibid*.
23. W. A. McClellan to ACLU, January 24 and February 2, 1933, and Roger N. Baldwin to McClellan, January 26, 1933, all *ibid*.

this eventuality.[24] In reply, Baldwin reassured Alexander that the case would be handled according to proper legal procedure. "I have no doubt that the ILD will on appeal stress the issues of law and subordinate the issue of Communism," he remarked.[25]

When informed of Alexander's complaints against the ILD, Patterson penned a vigorous denial. The main controversy, he argued, was precisely the issue of communism. He explained that "no attorney could have held the prosecution from a discussion of 'the merits and demerits of Communism.'" Denying that different counsel might have won the case, he asked why such experienced lawyers never seemed to win "any cases of this kind in the Southern courts." Instead of being a weakness, the presence of Davis and Geer was "our strength," he declared. The ILD's chief failure in the case, he maintained, was the absence of a mass movement. Patterson went on to blast Alexander as a pseudoprogressive, asserting that he stood for "reformism of a character that tends to stabilize the position of the landlords and their henchmen at the expense of the Negro and white toilers."[26] Two weeks later, Patterson also attacked Walter White and the NAACP, alleging that they were attempting to sabotage ILD defense efforts, just as they had done in the Scottsboro case. To avoid further such clashes, the NAACP left the case entirely in the hands of the ILD.[27]

While the NAACP, the ILD, and the ACLU reviewed the Herndon case, most white southerners remained only vaguely aware of the affair. But those whites who had followed events in Atlanta despite the limited newspaper coverage strongly supported the jury's decision. The Sons of the Revolution in Georgia, a patriotic organization, adopted a resolution at its annual meeting in early February petitioning Congress to force "all vicious red, radical and revolutionary agitators" to leave the country. Likewise endorsing the conviction, one southern newspaper warned that communism had an intoxicating effect upon Negroes and predicted that

24. Will W. Alexander to Roger N. Baldwin, January 24, 1933, *ibid*.
25. Roger N. Baldwin to Will W. Alexander, January 26, 1933, *ibid*; Alexander to Baldwin, January 31, 1933, in Commission on Interracial Cooperation Papers.
26. William L. Patterson to Roger N. Baldwin, February 7, 1933, in ACLU Archives.
27. ILD press release, February 23, 1933, in ILD Papers.

the harsh judgment would halt "the culprit's teachings." [28] Practically all public officials in Georgia approved of the decision. Like most white southerners, these officials were quite sensitive to "outside" criticism. Since several recent exposés of the Peach State's notorious chain gang system had produced unfavorable national publicity, the authorities were quite touchy, the more so when several northern governors subsequently refused to extradite escaped prisoners to Georgia. [29] The most recent such incident had occurred just one week before the Herndon trial. [30]

But not all white southerners adopted this conservative position. Although dissenters were few, several courageously voiced their dissatisfaction. Immediately prior to the trial, the tiny remnant of the Socialist party in Atlanta, numbering about a dozen members, adopted a statement demanding Herndon's release. Labor leaders in the city likewise criticized the heavy-handed persecution of Communists. The best way to handle communism, pronounced the *Journal of Labor*, "is to forget the Communist and begin thinking about our fellow-man, thinking about his difficulties and his problems." [31]

W. T. Anderson, outspoken editor of the Macon *Telegraph*, emerged as the most prominent white Georgian critical of the harsh sentence. In fact, he was the only prestigious journalist in the state to decry the sentence. A southern liberal on race relations and at the same time a close political ally of newly elected Governor Eugene Talmadge, Anderson commanded influence far beyond the Macon city limits. On Thursday, January 19, 1933, the day following the verdict, Anderson blasted the conviction as both a tragedy and a farce. He chastised the prosecution's fears of communism, contending that "it is highly absurd now for state attorneys to be protecting us from the Red Menace by urging the death sentence for such men as Herndon and for others whose

28. Atlanta *Constitution*, February 8, 1933; Meridian *Star*, quoted in Angelo Herndon, *Let Me Live* (New York: Arno Press, 1969), 242–43. The major Atlanta dailies maintained their editorial silence on the affair.

29. For a conservative view of the case, see E. Merton Coulter, *Georgia: A Short History* (Chapel Hill: University of North Carolina Press, 1947), 446–47.

30. Atlanta *Constitution*, January 14, 1933. See also Robert E. Burns, *I Am a Fugitive from a Georgia Chain Gang!* (New York: Grosset and Dunlap, 1932).

31. Atlanta *Constitution*, January 15, 1933; *Journal of Labor*, January 6, 1933. The labor movement had been sympathetic to the Atlanta Six two years earlier.

chief crime is possession of Communist literature of the sort which may be found in any library." [32] The next day, Anderson reiterated his indignation. In an editorial entitled "Shameful Verdict," he suggested that white people should be ashamed to find the courts used for such a "farcical purpose." He ridiculed the idea that a nineteen-year-old boy had endangered the state of Georgia. Urging readers to remember that the ultimate purpose of communism was to feed and clothe people, Anderson voiced the conviction that the real danger to America came from tired fathers looking "into the faces of pinched and hungry children and mothers." He concluded with the hope "that the supreme court of this state will substitute common sense for the Bourbonism of the jury that tried Herndon." [33]

Although no other prominent journalist raised his voice within the state, Anderson's views were echoed by Virginius Dabney, a young editorial writer with the Richmond *Times-Dispatch*. Dabney criticized Georgia's political leadership for tolerating such abuses of justice as the Herndon verdict and the chain gang system. He repeated the familiar warning that the persecution of Communists only strengthened their cause. [34]

Inside Georgia, Anderson continued to stand virtually alone in his outspoken public position. Even though the trial and the resulting controversy distressed local liberals, they feared to speak out. In addition to public hostility, the emotion-laden issue of communism served as the chief barrier to their action. Leaders of the Commission on Interracial Cooperation had already been alienated by the tactics of the Atlanta Six. In addition, the rejection of Will Alexander's advice prior to the actual trial engendered more mistrust and suspicion. According to Alexander, Clarina Michelson, a representative of the ILD, visited his office shortly after Herndon's arrest, "giving the name of some alphabetical organization which did more to conceal than to reveal what sort of organization it was." Alexander suggested "that Herndon

---

32. Macon *Telegraph*, January 19, 1933.
33. *Ibid.*, January 20, 1933.
34. Quoted in Richmond *Planet*, February 4, 1933, in clippings file, ILD Papers. Dabney became editor of the *Times-Dispatch* in 1936 and won a Pulitzer Prize for his editorials in 1948. Most other major southern dailies, even the Raleigh *News and Observer*, neither reported nor editorialized about the case.

needed, more than anything else, an able lawyer who understood constitutional questions and who would lay a basis in the trial court for a case that could be carried to the Supreme Court." He recommended W. A. Sutherland, a brilliant young white attorney who had graduated from the Harvard Law School. But, after consulting him, Michelson came away dissatisfied because "he was not interested in the class struggle and wanted to take the case simply as a civil liberties case."[35] This incident only solidified Alexander's opinion that the "Reds'" excessive emotionalism and desire for propaganda, rather than for winning cases on points of law, made it impossible to work with them in such matters.[36]

In his opposition to cooperation with Communist groups, Alexander had been consistent since 1930, when he had been first approached about the Atlanta Six. To him, the concepts of procedure and due process were dear, and, quite naturally, Communist views on publicity and mass protest offended these values. Moreover, the Scottsboro episode had deeply embittered him. "Perhaps no single experience in the history of the commission contradicted Alexander's sense of due process more completely than the famous Scottsboro case," write his biographers.[37] Given these views and the Communists' sectarianism and lack of propriety, it is understandable, though unfortunate, that the ILD and the Commission on Interracial Cooperation could not work together. Eventually, in 1934 and 1935, when the party changed its stance on such issues, cooperation became possible. In the meantime, Alexander remained willing to work with the ACLU, but that organization had no voice in policy-making decisions about the Herndon case.

Many middle-class blacks in Atlanta did not see the affair in the same light as did Alexander. To them, Herndon was another outspoken black man whose complaints against injustice had resulted in punitive action by authorities. Shortly after the conviction, a large group of black ministers issued a statement denouncing the decision as "the type of

35. Will W. Alexander to Roger N. Baldwin, July 30, 1933, Alexander to Ruth Scandrett, August 15, 1932, Alexander to Katherine Gardner, October 26, 1935, and Walter White to Alexander, August 16, 1932, all in Commission on Interracial Cooperation Papers.
36. Wilma Dykeman and James Stokely, *Seeds of Southern Change: The Life of Will W. Alexander* (Chicago: University of Chicago Press, 1962), 153. This is a laudatory but useful biography.
37. *Ibid.*

injustice which indicates we live in a maze of corruption wherever the courts and public sentiment must deal with black people." The resolution decried the fact that the convicted murderers of Dennis Hubert[38] were given shorter sentences than Herndon, "to say nothing of the thousands of lynchers who roam at will throughout the nation." The Reverend J. A. Martin, editor of Sunday school periodicals for the Colored Methodist Episcopal (C.M.E.) church, the Reverend A. F. Bailey, pastor of Butler Street C.M.E. Church, and the Reverend I. C. Nicholson of West Mitchell C.M.E. Church were some of the more prominent persons who signed.[39]

Such protest by black ministers during the months following Herndon's conviction was not atypical. In May the general board of the C.M.E. church condemned the Herndon, Scottsboro, and Willie Peterson "convictions as indicating the rankest type of race prejudice against a minority group." [40] Members of Atlanta's 27 Club, an organization of socially prominent black educators, businessmen, and professionals, adopted a resolution criticizing the handling of the Herndon case. The Atlanta *Daily World* reported that club members were quite concerned about the matter. The *World* also commented that it had been the only Atlanta newspaper to report the full details of the trial, thus proving that only a black newspaper would tell the full story about black affairs.[41]

In late January, 1933, ILD attorney Irving Schwab came to Atlanta and established a local office, naming Ben Davis as the branch attorney. Through the ILD chapter, several area radicals campaigned for Herndon's release, circulated information on the case, and attempted to raise funds. Bess Schwarz served temporarily as secretary of the group, assisted by E. E. Fields, who had helped Herndon organize the June, 1932, unemployment demonstration, and Robert H. Hart, an Atlanta

38. Hubert had been murdered in 1930 by a white man who was convicted and given a twelve-year prison term.

39. Atlanta *Daily World*, January 25, 1933; Savannah *Tribune*, January 26, 1933; Pittsburgh *Courier*, February 4, 1933.

40. Willie Peterson was a black resident of Birmingham, Alabama, who was apparently unjustly convicted in 1932 for rape and murder. See Carter, *Scottsboro*, 129–35.

41. *Daily Worker*, May 13, 1933; Atlanta *Daily World*, January 29, 1933. Jesse O. Thomas, southern field director of the Urban League, was instrumental in the club's creation. It held monthly public forums to discuss current events. See Jesse O. Thomas, *My Story in Black and White* (New York: Exposition Press, 1967), 114–15.

native and a brilliant undergraduate at Emory. Despite the national organization's attacks on moderates and liberals, the Atlanta branch of the ILD made overtures to local liberals, such as Professor Glenn W. Rainey of Georgia Tech. It also urged mass pressure and a "united front to force the frame-up courts and the class which controls them to free Angelo Herndon." [42]

By far the most influential local organization, however, was a loosely knit, interracial group known as the Provisional Committee for the Defense of Angelo Herndon. Formed in late January, the committee had made itself well known by the summer, primarily in the black community, and served as a "united front from below" organization. According to this strategy, overtures should be made to the mass membership but not to the so-called reactionary leadership of groups such as the NAACP and the National Urban League. One advantage of such committees was their ability to recruit sympathizers for the defense movement who might otherwise have been alienated by more direct ties with Communists. [43]

The Herndon defense committee worked successfully with ministers and other leaders of Atlanta's black community. At first, a few sympathetic whites, usually intellectuals but also several manual workers, cooperated with the committee. No formal political requirements were made for association with the defense group, save a desire to free Herndon. Walter Washburn, a white electrician, served as chairman of the committee for most of 1933 and the Reverend J. A. Martin as vice-chairman. Other prominent Atlantans affiliated with the group included the Reverend J. Raymond Henderson, well-known black Baptist minister; Sarah Ginsberg and Mrs. Benjamin E. Mays of the Atlanta University School of Social Work; J. B. Blayton, a certified public accountant and member of the Atlanta University faculty; Ben Ronin, a merchant; Mrs. C. H. Connally, a member of the NAACP; R. Ricarno of the ILD; and Clarence Weaver, a black trade union leader. Mary Raoul Millis, a Socialist and the first chairman of the committee, and Professor C. Vann Woodward, then an English instructor at Georgia

42. Atlanta *Daily World*, January 22, 1933; Benjamin J. Davis, *Communist Councilman from Harlem* (New York: International Publishers, 1969), 85; Bess Schwarz to Glenn Rainey, February 9, 1933, and miscellaneous circulars, all in possession of Glenn W. Rainey, Atlanta, Ga.
43. Carter, *Scottsboro*, 67–68.

Tech, were briefly active. The defense committee attempted to raise funds to pay for court costs, to publicize the facts in the case, and to recruit sympathizers. [44] The number of prominent blacks associated with it testified to the success of the ILD's strategy.

Woodward's involvement in the case caused some consternation in his friend and mentor Will Alexander, who pursued a more cautious course. To the idealistic young instructor, Alexander was too timid and conservative. In a personal letter to a New York lawyer, Woodward voiced some of these complaints. To his surprise and dismay, the letter was published. Alexander sent the clipping to the young teacher with a note to the effect that "the unkindest cut of all is the cut of a friend." "Dr. Will" eventually took the affair in stride, though, and forgave his friend. "I learned a good deal in that particular episode, you can be sure," Woodward later said. Subsequently, Woodward drifted away from the committee and eventually moved to Chapel Hill, North Carolina, to work on his doctorate. [45]

The *Daily Worker* closely reported the ILD and the provisional committee's activities in Atlanta, as well as printing various Communist writings about possible strategies for the Herndon campaign. In March, 1933, Syd Benson explained the concept of the "united front from below." Benson urged that workers in "reformist" organizations and liberals with honest sympathy for Herndon be won to the defense effort. Since Atlanta was an educational center containing many liberals, excellent possibilities existed there for a broad united front. The first step had already been achieved through the creation of the provisional committee with its diverse membership. Although noting that the ILD would continue its own independent efforts, Benson warned that, within

44. Benjamin J. Davis to Will W. Alexander, September 9, 1933, in Commission on Interracial Cooperation Papers. One rally sponsored by the committee in May listed Millis, Woodward, Martin, and Ben Davis as speakers. See handbill in Glenn W. Rainey Papers, Emory University Library. Walter Washburn, the committee chairman, later married Nannie Leah Young, a white textile worker also indicted under the insurrection law.

45. Dykeman and Stokely, *Seeds of Southern Change*, 155–56; author's interview with C. Vann Woodward, Atlanta, Ga., November 8, 1973. Woodward came under fire from Georgia Tech's president for his work with the committee and was terminated along with two dozen other professors that summer as part of an austerity move by the administration. David M. Potter, "C. Vann Woodward," in Marcus Cunliffe and Robin Winks (eds.), *Pastmasters: Some Essays on American Historians* (New York: Harper and Row, 1969), 376–77, briefly mentions the affair.

the provisional committee, ILD members "must work with the view of showing without the shadow of a doubt to any honest worker or intellectual that the ILD is sincerely interested in forming a real front, and not in dominating the whole action merely because we are the International Labor Defense." He added, though, that the full ILD program concerning Scottsboro, Tom Mooney, and other controversial cases could later be carefully explained.[46]

William L. Patterson, head of the ILD, elaborated on the organization's strategy in April. His article, specifically designed to defend the ILD's Scottsboro tactics from charges of "opportunism" by a Trotskyist newspaper, the *Militant*, served also to illuminate similar policies in the Herndon defense. Patterson affirmed the ILD's recognition of the class struggle as the basis for all bourgeois "legal" action. Because of this "class essence of capitalist justice," the ILD steadfastly maintained "that only mass pressure can bring about the release of a class war prisoner; that pressure must be supplemented by legal defense," preferably of the highest expertise. Basically, the attorney served as a "court-room technician," and the defendant himself exposed the bias inherent in class justice. In several formal statements from prison, Herndon echoed this official Communist refrain, agreeing with Patterson that "the fight to obtain the elementary rights for the whole Negro people does not lie in the channels of the capitalist courts alone but through mass struggle of both white and Negro workers."[47]

Although the ACLU did not share all the ILD's views about the American judicial process, it lent moral support to the Herndon defense campaign. More important, it also provided badly needed funds, contributing $234 during 1933 toward Herndon's legal expenses. In the same period the Provisional Committee for the Defense of Angelo Herndon raised only a meager $100. Despite frequent rumors of "Moscow gold," the ILD remained chronically short of funds during the year, with receipts coming to a standstill on several occasions. This created a serious problem when premiums for the bonds on the Atlanta

46. *Daily Worker*, February 8 and March 21, 1933. Mooney was a California labor leader convicted of the 1916 San Francisco Preparedness Day bombing. His case became an international *cause célèbre* for liberals and leftists. He received a full pardon in 1939.
47. *Ibid.*, April 7 and May 6, 1933.

Six fell due midway through the summer. Ever since the flight to Russia of Fred Beal and several other defendants in the controversial Gastonia, North Carolina, textile strike, which resulted in forfeiture of their bonds, the ILD had experienced difficulty in finding bonding companies willing to provide bail for their clients. In response to public pressure, the ACLU publicly announced it would no longer supply bail money in cases involving Communists.[48] In private, though, the organization proved more flexible. Apparently the ACLU agreed to contract with the David L. Roston Agency to provide bonds for the Six, with the understanding that the ILD would actually pay the premiums. ILD tardiness in meeting premium deadlines, allegedly due to lack of funds, proved a constant irritant to the ACLU. In order to avoid withdrawal of the bonds, the ACLU covered for the ILD and paid the fees. Subsequently, Baldwin lectured Patterson on the need for improved fiscal practices within the ILD.[49]

Despite these complaints about sloppy bookkeeping, Baldwin and the ACLU remained loyal to the ILD defense. In a letter to Mary Raoul Millis in November, 1933, Baldwin elaborated on his reasons. "But when issues arise such as the Scottsboro case, the Herndon case and the Tuscaloosa lynchings," he said, "violent extremes are thrown into conflict. We are then facing problems of passion with the Klan on one side and the negroes and their new left wing allies on the other." In light of these developments, the ACLU saw no way of escaping the inevitable conflict. "We confront a practical situation in which we are forced to stand for legal defense in any form it is organized," Baldwin explained, "whatever we may think of the wisdom of selection of counsel or of tactics in court." Defending the introduction of the lily-white jury issue into the proceedings, he declared, "Raising the issue of negro jury service and of negro lawyers may only inflame feelings but it is obvious that it has to be done and the only question remains is how most

48. Benjamin J. Davis to Roger N. Baldwin, September 6 and October 12, 1933, Carol Weiss King to Lucille Milner, October 2, 1933, Baldwin to Davis, October 23, 1933, and statement on expense accounts, September 6, 1933, all in ACLU Archives. William Z. Foster resigned from the ACLU as a result of the union's refusal to continue posting bond for Communists. See Lucille Milner, *The Education of an American Liberal* (New York: Horizon Press, 1954), 180.

49. David L. Roston Agency to Lucille Milner, April 21, 1933, Milner to William L. Patterson, May 23, June 30, and August 4, 1933, and Roger N. Baldwin to Patterson, July 17, 1933, all in ACLU Archives.

effectively to do it. We do not create these issues. We merely aid after they are created." [50]

While publicity efforts were being developed, Ben Davis and John Geer continued their legal efforts. Immediately following the conviction, they filed a motion for a new trial and an application for bond with Judge Lee B. Wyatt, who denied the request for bail but scheduled a formal hearing on the new trial motion. Later that same day, Wyatt used the occasion of the sentencing of a black murderer to life imprisonment to defend the Georgia chain gang system. Citing his personal familiarity with conditions on the chain gangs, Wyatt declared that "these reports of brutalities are false, from beginning to end," even when they came from northern governors. Perhaps feeling uneasy about the future of the Herndon case in the higher courts, he also complained that appeals courts too frequently overturned rulings from lower courts on "mere technicalities." [51]

Apparently Davis and Geer decided not to wait until the scheduled hearing to try to free Herndon. In early February, 1933, they filed a habeas corpus petition contending that jailer R. N. Holland had refused to accept a one-thousand-dollar bond in exchange for Herndon's freedom. Judge E. D. Thomas presided over a hearing on the petition on February 4. Herndon sat quietly throughout the proceedings, having been temporarily removed from jail for the inquiry. After listening to John Geer's arguments, Judge Thomas dismissed the request. Ansel W. Morrison, a young white lawyer who had volunteered his services to the ILD, assisted Geer and Davis. Through his presence the ILD hoped to demonstrate interracial support for the Herndon defense. [52]

---

50. Roger N. Baldwin to Mary Raoul Millis, November 21, 1933, *ibid*. For a partial defense of Communist legal tactics by another ACLU spokesman, see Arthur Garfield Hays, *Trial by Prejudice* (New York: Convici and Friede, 1933), 84.

51. Atlanta *Journal*, January 19, 1933; Atlanta *Georgian*, January 19, 1933; Atlanta *Constitution*, January 20, 1933.

52. Atlanta *Journal*, February 4, 1933; *Daily Worker*, February 6, 1933; Chicago *Defender*, February 11, 1933. The St. Louis *Argus* termed this recent development "epoch making." See St. Louis *Argus*, February 24, 1933, in clippings file, ILD Papers. On February 17, 1933, the Atlanta *Constitution* reported that Herndon and three convicted murderers, Richard Morris, Richard Sims, and Mose White, had made an unsuccessful attempt to escape from Fulton Tower Prison during the previous night. Herndon and the three others promptly denied the charge, and local officials did not press charges. See Atlanta *Daily World*, February 19, 1933; *Daily Worker*, February 27, 1933; Herndon, *Let Me Live*, 245–46. Morris, Sims, and White were all black teenagers who, many black

Eventually, in late June, Judge Wyatt held a formal hearing on the petition for a new trial, as well as another request for bail. He promptly overruled the bond request and later denied the motion for a new trial. Defense lawyers immediately vowed to appeal the case to the United States Supreme Court, if necessary, and began work on the bill of exceptions to the decision. Geer denounced Wyatt's rulings as "those of a prejudiced judge." He promised that the legal fight had only begun. "We will not give back one iota of an inch in the fight for Negro liberation until fifteen million black Americans are given their equal rights under the law as their white brothers," he declared.[53] Thus, within the court system and outside it too, the ILD had given notice in early 1933 that it would vigorously defend Herndon's innocence, as well as confront the southern Jim Crow system. Not only Herndon but "southern justice" would be on trial.

Atlantans felt, did not deserve their sentences of death by the electric chair. See Roy Wilkins to A. T. Walden, April 27, 1932, and Walden to Wilkins, May 7, 1932, both in NAACP Papers; Atlanta *Daily World*, June 20, 1932.

53. Atlanta *Daily World*, July 7, 1933.

CHAPTER FIVE

Building a Local Defense Movement

DURING the remainder of 1933, members of the International Labor Defense worked not only to build up public support for Angelo Herndon but especially to dramatize injustices suffered by black Atlantans. The ILD gained considerable respect from blacks when it joined them in protesting the treatment of black residents by Atlanta police. Worried by this growing merger of radical activity with black protest, Atlanta authorities watched such developments closely, reaffirming their determination to prevent the growth of any radical sentiment, serious discussion of racial problems, and, indeed, virtually any change in the conservative status quo of their city.

As part of its program to inform Atlantans more fully about the Herndon case and other radical issues, the Provisional Committee for the Defense of Angelo Herndon sponsored in May, 1933, a rally at Taft Hall in the city auditorium. Approximately four hundred blacks and whites gathered there on Sunday afternoon, May 7, to hear about the Herndon, Scottsboro, and Atlanta Six cases. Although the committee particularly wished to attract blacks, it prudently adhered to local segregation ordinances on this occasion, with blacks sitting on one side of the room and whites on the other. Ben Davis, C. Vann Woodward, the Reverend J. A. Martin, the Reverend J. Raymond Henderson, W. G. Binkley, southern district organizer for the ILD, and Allan Taub, attorney for the Scottsboro boys, all spoke. Mary Raoul Millis, prominent local Socialist leader, presided over the "stormy session." She had previously threatened to resign over Taub's attacks on "social fascists."

When Taub renewed his criticism of Socialists and liberals at this time, she became infuriated. Protesting his remarks, as well as the wording of the proposed Herndon resolution, which she said endorsed the principles of the Communist party, Millis dramatically resigned her position and stormed from the meeting, leaving a startled and confused C. Vann Woodward in charge. In spite of the resulting uproar, many members of the audience remained. They adopted several resolutions supporting vigorous defense efforts in behalf of Herndon and the Scottsboro boys, demanding repeal of the Georgia insurrection law, and attacking both the exclusion of blacks from southern juries and segregated seating on city streetcars.[1]

The furor ignited by Millis' resignation created the first split in the ranks of the emerging local defense movement. As a result of the ILD attacks on non-Communist liberals and leftists and her withdrawal, several other white liberals, Socialists, and labor leaders defected from the provisional committee. They apparently felt that ILD representatives did not genuinely seek a united, cooperative effort but rather wished to dominate the movement in behalf of the Communist party.[2] Such inflexible actions by Communists were quite common in the early 1930s, when they arrogantly spurned cooperation with groups lacking ideological purity. These sectarian attitudes nearly rendered the local Herndon defense movement stillborn. But black Atlantans did not at this time fully share the fears of white liberals; hence they remained loyal to the provisional committee and saved it from oblivion. Later events would strain their confidence in the ILD and the committee, but in May local blacks were willing to trust the two groups.

A few days following the May 7 meeting, the ILD sponsored its own rally and musical in a black theater. The *Daily Worker* boasted that over eight hundred blacks and whites mixed freely at the gathering, allegedly the first integrated indoor meeting held in Atlanta for many years. Attorney John Geer explained details of the case to the sympathetic audience, and Viola Montgomery, a "Scottsboro mother," exhorted the

---

1. *Daily Worker*, May 11, 1933; Atlanta *Constitution*, May 8, 1933; author's interview with C. Vann Woodward, Atlanta, Ga., November 8, 1973.
2. Author's interview with Woodward.

crowd to fight for Herndon's freedom, comparing his case to that of the Scottsboro boys.[3]

The efforts of the provisional committee drew praise from the southern field director of the Urban League, Jesse O. Thomas. In the July 14 Atlanta *Daily World*, he pleaded for contributions to defray the cost of appealing the case. Thomas reminded readers that Herndon was a normal person whose innocence had been obscured by the widespread hysteria over communism. According to Thomas, Herndon's sole crime had been to tell black and white workers that their economic interests were identical. He observed, "It is not a question of socialism or communism, it is purely a question of whether this dead, reactionary, antiquated law, the product of the slave regime, shall be resurrected . . . for the purpose of restraining underpaid, under-employed and unemployed would-be wage earners from engaging in collective bargaining, regardless of race." Thomas earnestly asked for financial support, dismissing "moral support" as practically worthless.[4]

The provisional committee remained active during the summer. It designated Sunday, July 23, Herndon Day in Atlanta. Special collections were planned in black churches with a mass meeting concluding the day's affairs. The ILD also scheduled activities for that weekend, organizing a midnight vaudeville show at a black theater to raise funds for the Scottsboro and Herndon cases.[5] A large crowd turned out for the rally in the Butler Street C.M.E. Church on Sunday afternoon. Wheat Street Baptist Church, whose pastor was J. Raymond Henderson, reported the day's largest offering—a modest twenty-six dollars. Jesse O. Thomas told the audience that the controversy over communism had distracted blacks from the true issues in the case. He also urged blacks to follow the example of Jews and organize to protect themselves. Attorney Irving Schwab likewise stressed the need for blacks to organize and demand their full legal rights, particularly that of jury service.[6] In subsequent months the provisional committee kept busy, holding meetings periodically to drum up support for Herndon and other radical causes.

3. *Daily Worker*, May 13, 1933.
4. Atlanta *Daily World*, July 14, 1933.
5. *Ibid.*, July 6, 12, 16, and 19, 1933.
6. *Ibid.*, July 24, 1933.

Perhaps the most bizarre sidelight in the Herndon case came in June, when the Atlanta *Constitution* and the New York *Times* reported that seven national guardsmen had been assigned to guard the Georgia state capitol after several bomb threats were allegedly received. The guardsmen carried pistols, rifles, and eventually machine guns.[7] Tom Linder, executive secretary to Governor Eugene Talmadge, and George B. Hamilton, state treasurer, told newsmen that Herndon's sentence had spawned numerous threats to blow up the building. But the officials' story proved a hoax. It was soon discovered that the placing of the guards had nothing to do with Angelo Herndon. Instead their real purpose was to protect over two million dollars in cash which the governor had ordered stored in capitol vaults pending settlement of a financial squabble with the highway department.[8]

Meanwhile, tensions between local officials and Atlanta blacks increased during the hot summer months. In mid-June the local NAACP chapter sent a telegram to Mayor James L. Key protesting several recent shootings of blacks by white policemen. The wire provoked a stinging rebuttal from Police Chief T. O. Sturdivant. He complained that, despite frequent accusations of police brutality from "so-called advancement and uplift associations," he had yet to learn of a case in which those groups criticized a black person for shooting a policeman. Sturdivant specifically cited the recent murders of two detectives. "Did you take any notice of them in your meetings, except perhaps to cut another notch in your gun stocks?" he indignantly demanded.[9] His comments hardly improved the image of the police force among members of the black community.

When August arrived, additional incidents further strained the shaky relationship between blacks and local police. On Tuesday night, August

7. New York *Times*, June 14, 1933, p. 6; Atlanta *Constitution*, June 13 and 14, 1933.

8. New York *Amsterdam News*, June 21, 1933, in clippings file, International Labor Defense Papers, Schomburg Collection, New York Public Library; Atlanta *Constitution*, June 14 and 15, 1933.

9. The Atlanta *Daily World*, July 2, 1933, pointed out that both of the police chief's examples demonstrated the prompt, severe punishment handed out to blacks who killed policemen. In the first case, the murderer had been killed on the spot by police, and his accomplices, Richard Morris, Richard Sims, and Mose White, had been sentenced to the electric chair. In the second, the convicted murderer had been sentenced to twenty years on the chain gang for shooting a police officer who was illegally breaking into the defendant's home.

1, police raided a party at the home of C. L. Harper, principal of all-black Washington High School. They arrested thirteen juveniles. The next morning after a lengthy hearing, the magistrate, John L. Cone, concluded that no serious breach of the peace had occurred and dismissed disorderly conduct charges against the entire group. But black Atlantans did not quickly forget the incident. The Atlanta *Daily World* suggested that such outrages provided yet another reason for supporting the voter registration campaign currently being sponsored by the Negro Chamber of Commerce. "The only way to make over-zealous and prejudiced city policemen conscious of at least some rights justly due Negro citizens is to register at once and vote," it said.[10] The *Daily World* reaffirmed this stand later in the month, admonishing city fathers that discriminatory law enforcement hampered Atlanta's progress. Arguing that black Atlantans felt singled out as special targets by police, the newspaper suggested that policemen themselves set an example of respect for the law. "We are sick and tired of policemen pumping, without cause, bullets in black victims," the *Daily World* complained.[11]

Into these troubled waters strode William L. Patterson, the controversial national secretary of the ILD. On Thursday night, August 24, Patterson spoke to an enthusiastic audience of three hundred blacks and whites in Atlanta's Elks Hall. In his dynamic address he asserted that the condition of black people was worse now than before emancipation, because the white ruling class ("silk hat lynchers") no longer had an economic interest in blacks. Launching a stinging attack on the NAACP, Patterson charged that the association concerned itself solely with the "talented tenth" of the race to the neglect of the black masses. Not only were "do-nothing" NAACP leaders indifferent to the needs of the masses, they were even so callous as to pocket the money from fundraising drives. Portraying Herndon as a "martyr," he assured the audience that the only way to secure Herndon's release was through mass pressure, supplemented by support for the local ILD branch and Herndon's attorneys, Geer and Davis.[12]

Events in Atlanta heightened the impact of Patterson's words. On

---

10. Atlanta *Daily World*, August 3, 1933.
11. *Ibid.*, August 20, 1933.
12. *Ibid.*, August 25, 1933.

each of the two days immediately preceding his address, an Atlanta policeman shot a black suspect. Early Friday morning, one of these men, forty-year-old Glover Davis, died in Grady Hospital. What made his death seem particularly shocking was the fact that he was blind. Patrolman O. W. Allen, who had shot Davis twice, justified his action by claiming that Davis had advanced on him with an ice pick.[13] On the following Monday, the *Daily World* issued a plea for "visible protest" against the police department. "We have written, we have preached, and we have sung about these things, now let's come out in the open and do something about the whole outfit," it urged. The Davis family announced that it had given the ILD responsibility for the funeral. The ILD in turn revealed that it planned to stage a "mass protest funeral" as a symbol of united protest against further outrages.[14]

On Monday afternoon, representatives of the Urban League, local black churches, the Fulton County Civic League, and the ILD met in the Auburn Avenue branch of the Carnegie Library to discuss proposed action on these recent incidents. The group drew up a list of three demands to present to the police department: the removal of an unpopular white patrolman, I. B. ("Babyface") Jones, from black neighborhoods, the suspension and prosecution of O. W. Allen, who had shot Davis, and the installation of black policemen in black neighborhoods.[15] Another meeting four days later pursued the idea of legal action against Patrolman Allen. Those present formed a special committee to try to influence the solicitor general's office to prosecute Allen. Invited to serve on the committee were Jesse Thomas of the Urban League, Nathan Yagol, an Emory University student, Ben Davis, John Geer, the Reverend J. Raymond Henderson, A. T. Walden of the NAACP, R. B. Eleazer of the Commission on Interracial Cooperation, attorney T. J. Henry, and Forrester B. Washington. The Reverend J. A. Martin, rapidly acquiring a reputation as a local activist, headed the committee.[16]

13. *Ibid.*, August 26, 1933.
14. *Ibid.*, August 28 and 29, 1933. For a description of a similar ILD funeral for murdered blacks in Birmingham, see John Williams, "Struggles of the Thirties in the South," in Bernard Sternsher (ed.), *The Negro in Depression and War* (Chicago: Quadrangle, 1969), 172–73.
15. Atlanta *Daily World*, August 29, 1933.
16. *Ibid.*, September 2, 1933.

As promised, the ILD held its mass protest funeral for Glover Davis on Labor Day, September 4, in the Mount Zion Baptist Church. Despite heavy pressure from local officials, neither the ILD nor the church pastor would cancel the funeral. Upset by the refusal, Chief Sturdivant personally led a contingent of fifty uniformed officers which surrounded the church during the service. The police prevented most whites from entering the building and arrested one white Communist who attempted to pass out literature denouncing the murder. Sturdivant himself warned whites to keep "away from Negro funerals in the future." In spite of such intimidation, several thousand mourners still attended, spilling over into church aisles and even outside into the streets. Although emotions ran high within the packed church, both the speakers and the audience retained their self-control. No doubt Chief Sturdivant's legions prompted this discretion and contributed to the relatively mild tone of the gathering.[17]

The Reverend J. T. Dorsey, pastor of Mount Zion, nervously opened the service by cautioning the scheduled speakers to refrain from "any insurrectionary remarks" and warned that he would terminate the meeting if anything besides religion were discussed. He criticized the ILD for terming the meeting a "protest funeral," suggesting that the controversial phrase had caused much misunderstanding. Ben Davis, representing the ILD, then took the floor and agreed that the service was technically not a protest funeral. He explained that the ILD planned a mass meeting elsewhere later in the day. Although he spoke only briefly, Davis received a thundering ovation when he passionately declared, "The funeral of Glover Davis, whose body lies down there, is the funeral of every Negro in this city unless the murderous brutality of the Atlanta police is stopped."[18]

As Davis finished, Dorsey hastily rose and quieted the crowd, repeating his earlier threat to dismiss the gathering if another speaker

17. *Ibid.*, September 5, 1933; Atlanta *Constitution*, September 5, 1933; *Daily Worker*, September 6, 1933. A sign reading End Police Murders, which was to have been placed on the coffin, never appeared after Chief Sturdivant visited the Hanley Funeral Home and conferred with the owners. See Atlanta *Daily World*, September 16, 1933. Benjamin J. Davis, *Communist Councilman from Harlem* (New York: International Publishers, 1969), 84–85, recalls that there were fifty policemen inside the church and another two hundred outside.
18. Atlanta *Daily World*, September 5, 1933.

departed from purely religious subjects. Martin next offered a prayer and spoke briefly. "If the pulpit cannot denounce tyranny," he prayed, "to whom are our oppressed people going to turn?" When called upon to talk, the normally outspoken Henderson declined to make any formal remarks, hoping to avoid trouble. "If I tried to speak," he explained, "I'd tear this thing to pieces." Without further incident the funeral concluded, and the crowd dispersed.[19]

Convinced that firm action was needed to halt the merger of radical and black protest in Atlanta, John H. Hudson led a raid on the International Labor Defense office at 141½ Auburn Avenue later in the week. Pamphlets, records, receipts, and practically every piece of material within the room were seized. While the raid was in progress, Ben Davis entered the office. When he asked Hudson if he had a search warrant, the two quickly became embroiled in an argument. Although the two white ILD representatives present, Ruth Mulkey and Martin Walker, denied being Communists, Hudson questioned them carefully and threatened them with arrest. After Davis apparently vouched for their appearance in court should it be required, Hudson angrily stalked away. The prosecutor seemed particularly upset at the audacity of Davis in daring to speak for Mulkey, a southern white woman. Hudson later claimed that he had received complaints that the office served as the center of Communist activities in Atlanta.[20]

Hudson's testy disposition worsened the following day when he discovered, much to his dismay, that the two ILD workers had hastily left town. The prosecutor blamed Davis personally for their disappearance, admonishing him that his failure to produce the two would hurt his standing before the bar. Hudson announced to the press that he would seek indictments against all ILD activists in the city for circulating insurrectionary literature. He dramatically claimed that Mulkey and Walker were secretly en route to Cuba. Defending his conduct, Davis denied that the two organizers had actually been arrested or that bond

19. *Ibid.*
20. *Ibid.*, September 8, 1933; *Daily Worker*, September 8, 1933; Davis, *Communist Councilman from Harlem*, 86–87; R. B. Eleazer to Mary Raoul Millis, September 18, 1933, in American Civil Liberties Union Archives, Princeton University Library, hereinafter cited as ACLU Archives.

had been discussed. For once it seemed that John H. Hudson had been outsmarted.[21]

A week later, Police Chief Sturdivant promised further punitive measures against communism. In an address to a group of policemen, he instructed officers to seek out and break up meetings of Communist sympathizers. "The distribution of Communist literature has got to stop," he insisted. Since Communists spread this propaganda among "the ignorant classes and the unemployed," Sturdivant labeled them a serious threat to the city. Asserting that "Communism has no place in the life of a city like Atlanta," he vowed prompt action against any radical activity. Chief Sturdivant's words found support from one well-known organization. The official magazine of the Ku Klux Klan, the *Kourier*, warned that Communist efforts in Dixie were causing blacks to become more troublesome. Only a strong detail of officers at the Glover Davis funeral had prevented violence, it claimed. The magazine strongly urged Klansmen to assist law officers and concluded, "Remember, Communism must go and White Supremacy must be maintained at all costs!"[22]

Behind-the-scene efforts in the Glover Davis shooting appeared to bring results in mid-September when Municipal Judge L. Z. Rosser issued a bench warrant calling for the arrest of Patrolman Allen on murder charges. Ollis Davis, brother of the dead man, filed the complaint; John Geer and Ben Davis represented him. Judge Rosser set Monday, September 18, as the date for a preliminary hearing to determine if Allen should be bound over to the grand jury. The *Daily World* reported that the warrant had been obtained only after much difficulty, as the solicitor general's office and several judges had refused to investigate. The newspaper also announced that Glover Davis had made a deathbed statement to its reporters, in which he admitted holding an ice pick when confronted by Patrolman Allen but maintained that he had his hands in the air when he was shot.[23]

21. Atlanta *Daily World*, September 8 and 9, 1933; *Daily Worker*, September 8, 1933; R. B. Eleazer to Mary Raoul Millis, September 18, 1933, in ACLU Archives.

22. Atlanta *Daily World*, September 16, 1933; *Kourier*, IX (October, 1933), 19–20.

23. Atlanta *Daily World*, September 17, 1933. Ben Davis tried unsuccessfully to have this deathbed statement entered into the record.

Testimony at the subsequent hearing confirmed that Davis had frequently carried an ice pick which he used to weave cane bottoms in chairs. However, two neighbors who had entered the scene immediately after the shooting said that they had seen nothing in his hand. At this time the defense produced its key witness. Maggie Dyer, at whose home Davis was killed, testified that she and Davis had been fighting. When Patrolman Allen arrived, she said, Davis grabbed the ice pick and lunged at the policeman. Upon close questioning by a skeptical Ben Davis, Dyer admitted that she had signed a statement to this effect at police headquarters only after several days had passed, not immediately following the shooting.[24]

Defending his conduct, Allen said that when he had entered the Dyer house he had seen a man advancing on him with an ice pick. "I didn't know Davis was blind," he declared. Ben Davis argued that the evidence indicated that Allen should be bound over, but despite his plea Judge Rosser dismissed the charges, terming the shooting justifiable homicide. The prosecution committee felt dejected, even though the dismissal had been anticipated. But the effort was not a total failure. It nonetheless did mark one of the few times during the 1930s when a white law enforcement official in the South was charged, even though temporarily, with murder for shooting a black person. Subsequently a group of Negro residents drew up a petition calling for black policemen in black neighborhoods. Attorney A. T. Walden and J. B. Blayton, president of the Negro Chamber of Commerce, presented the request to the city council, which filed the statement without discussion.[25]

William L. Patterson of the ILD wired Chief Sturdivant to protest Allen's exoneration, demanding the arrest and vigorous prosecution of the officer. Angered by the telegram, Sturdivant replied that, "in all instances where Negroes are felled by police bullets, police officers are forced in self-defense to kill Negro hoodlums." He reiterated his willingness to use tear gas, machine guns, and every available man in order to defeat communism in Atlanta. Sturdivant challenged the ILD head to

24. *Ibid.*, September 19, 1933; *Daily Worker*, September 21, 1933; Atlanta *Constitution*, September 19, 1933.
25. Atlanta *Daily World*, September 19 and October 21, 1933; *Daily Worker*, September 21, 1933; Atlanta *Constitution*, September 19, 1933.

come to Atlanta to make a personal investigation. The police chief added that he had no hard feelings toward blacks, as he treated all lawbreakers alike.[26]

In this highly charged atmosphere, the arrest of Effie Cox soon revealed the extremes to which these Atlanta officials would go in their pursuit of communism. Several policemen arrested Effie Cox, a forty-year-old white woman, on Sunday afternoon, October 9, as she attempted to make what one officer termed "a soap-box 'Red' oration" to a crowd near the Ringling Brothers and Barnum & Bailey Circus. The prisoner, who said she came from Detroit, Michigan, and Birmingham, Alabama, contended that she had merely urged white southerners to improve their treatment of blacks. Although authorities initially charged her with vagrancy, Hudson indicated that he would seek an indictment under the insurrection law, even though a raid on her room had failed to produce any radical literature. While in jail, Cox denied being a Communist and told reporters that she was a Christian woman who wanted to see all people treated fairly.[27]

In spite of the flimsiness of the charges, she remained in jail for the rest of the month. Had not a brief article in a local newspaper mentioning the arrest caught the eye of Mrs. S. D. Halley, an Atlanta Socialist, there is no way to estimate how long Cox might have remained confined. Halley mailed the newspaper clipping about the arrest to Roger N. Baldwin of the ACLU and then contacted a local attorney, Hewitt W. Chambers. After investigating, Chambers reported that Cox had been arrested for "making announcements to the general public that she was going to teach the southern people how to treat the colored race." Even though he found the charges "on the verge of being ridiculous," he feared that a writ of habeas corpus might be needed to free her.[28]

When informed of the arrest, the ILD undertook its own investigation. An ILD spokesman informed the ACLU of its findings in November. S. Horwatt reported that Effie Cox, far from being a Communist, was really "an eccentric middle-aged woman" and a religious

26. Atlanta *Daily World*, September 24 and October 5, 1933. Although Patterson responded that he would be delighted to return to Atlanta, his proposed visit never developed.

27. *Ibid.*, October 10, 1933; Atlanta *Constitution*, October 9, 1933.

28. Hewitt W. Chambers to Mrs. S. D. Halley, October 27, 1933, and Halley to Roger N. Baldwin, October 28, 1933, both in ACLU Archives.

fanatic. Despite what alarmists had said, she preached at best a mild "reformist" tolerance for blacks. She told the ILD investigator that she was "first, last, and always a seven-day [*sic*] adventist, and she thought that Negroes were mistreated children and had souls just like white people and should be given more political and economic opportunities." She added that blacks should stay in their place "until the Lord Jesus Christ came to earth and straightened the whole world out." In early November, Chambers finally succeeded in gaining her release, apparently on his own initiative, since he received no compensation from the ACLU or the ILD. Nonetheless, the fear of communism had led Atlanta officials to imprison an innocent woman for nearly a month under the threat of the dreaded insurrection law. The serious extremes to which the statute could be used could hardly have been better illustrated.[29]

Activities of the ILD and the Provisional Committee for the Defense of Angelo Herndon did not go unchallenged. In August, members of the Ku Klux Klan burned a cross in front of the home of Mr. and Mrs. Walter Washburn, active members of the provisional committee. But by far the most important clash between the KKK and Herndon activists came several months later. On Sunday evening, December 10, the ILD sponsored a rally for the Scottsboro boys in the Holsey Temple C.M.E. Church. As early arrivals filtered into the church, they were suddenly startled to discover a band of twenty-two white-robed Klansmen picketing in front of the church. Dressed in full regalia, they handed out leaflets, printed on cheap yellow paper, carrying the message: "Communism will not be tolerated. Ku Klux Klan Rides Again." In spite of the Klan's intimidating presence, the church gradually filled. Across the street, a group of irritated area residents slowly gathered. An occasional breeze blew open their coats to reveal pistols and sawed-off shotguns.[30]

When police arrived, they quickly explained to the angry blacks that nothing could be done as long as the picketing remained peaceful. Officers did enter the church to inquire about the meeting's purpose.

29. S. Horwatt to ACLU, November 13, 1933, and Mrs. S. D. Halley to Mary Raoul Millis, November 11, 1933, both *ibid*.

30. *Daily Worker*, August 4, 1933; Atlanta *Daily World*, December 11, 1933; Atlanta *Constitution*, December 11, 1933.

They then attempted to remove whites from the audience and to prevent others from entering the building. After mistaking several light-skinned Negroes for whites and several Jewish persons for mulattoes, the police finally gave up, allowing several whites to remain in the church. The officers did succeed, however, in preventing several whites, including the two scheduled ILD speakers, from attending the rally. In their absence, the Reverend J. Raymond Henderson delivered the main address. "I'm not a member of the International Labor Defense and do not believe in some of its principles," he declared, "but I am ready to give up my life here and now to fight for my rights." Attorneys Ben Davis and John Geer, their legal assistant Edward D'Antignac, and the Reverend E. B. McNair also spoke. Afterwards, a collection of fifteen dollars was taken.[31]

Outside the church, a prominent white minister who was a member of the Commission on Interracial Cooperation stopped to speak with both police and Klan leaders. Evidently he convinced the KKK to depart, and the Klansmen silently marched away, "their long robes flowing in the breeze." Police did arrest one white man, Nathan Yagol, the Emory University student, charging him with disorderly conduct and inciting a riot. The charges came as a shock to Yagol, who had been quietly entering the church when arrested. At first, authorities denied him bail, but late Sunday night he gained release on a three-hundred-dollar bond. The following day, Yagol told the magistrate John L. Cone that he was not a Communist and that he had gone to the meeting to learn about current events. He explained that he majored in political science at Emory and was president of a student organization. After delivering a stern lecture, Cone dismissed the charges, generously noting that Yagol had committed no overt act.[32]

The Atlanta *Daily World* decried the Klan picketing, protesting that peaceful assembly was a fundamental American right. The newspaper asserted that, given the unrest in the country, the United States "can least afford lawlessness and public intimidation against peaceful citizens in their churches." Although the editorial demanded that someone

31. Atlanta *Daily World*, December 11, 1933; Atlanta *Constitution*, December 11, 1933.
32. Atlanta *Daily World*, December 11 and 12, 1933; Atlanta *Constitution*, December 11 and 12, 1933.

accept responsibility for the Holsey Temple incident, public officials and the major white newspapers declined comment on the affair.[33] Apparently they regarded Klan activity as less threatening than interracial meetings.

As the year ended in Atlanta, Angelo Herndon remained behind bars, his appeal still pending in the state courts. Although its legal efforts had been unable to free Herndon, the ILD had formed a viable local protest movement. Despite the early defections of white liberals and labor leaders from the provisional committee, black members remained loyal. The ILD gained further respect from black Atlantans by its forceful denunciation of police brutality. Hence, the growing appeal of the ILD to black Atlantans rested not so much on its Communist ideology but on its vigorous action against specific local injustices. Consequently, Georgia officials discovered that Herndon's conviction, rather than quieting radical and black protest, had actually stimulated its growth.

33. Atlanta *Daily World*, December 13, 1933.

Angelo Herndon at press
conference, 1936

Benjamin J. Davis, Jr.

John Geer

Angelo Herndon and
an attorney

W. T. Anderson

William L. Patterson

Angelo Herndon, 1935

Courtesy Schomburg Center for Research in Black Culture
The New York Public Library—Astor, Lenox and Tilden Foundations

Angelo Herndon, *third from left*

Crowd greets Herndon upon his arrival at Penn Central Station in New York, August 7, 1934, after his release from prison.

Courtesy United Press International

From left: Milton Herndon, Angelo Herndon, and Ruby Bates, a witness in the Scottsboro case.

Courtesy Schomburg Center for Research in Black Culture
The New York Public Library—Astor, Lenox and Tilden Foundations

The Process Server! by Phil Bard
Daily Worker, June 17, 1936

CHAPTER SIX
Free
on Bail

DURING the first few months of 1934, the continued national rivalry between the International Labor Defense and the National Association for the Advancement of Colored People threatened to destroy the shaky unity of radical and black protest movements in Atlanta. From 1929 until 1935, American Communists followed the directives of the Sixth World Congress of the Communist International and spurned cooperation with bourgeois organizations. For the ILD this meant refusing to work with the NAACP in legal controversies involving black defendants. Instead, the ILD and other Communist groups viciously denounced the "reformist" NAACP for its allegedly feeble efforts to fight racial discrimination and asserted that they, not the association, really represented the interests of black Americans. Several bitter clashes in 1931 and 1932 over the Scottsboro rape case had demonstrated ILD antagonism, if not contempt, for the NAACP and had convinced Walter White that Communists actually sought to destroy the association.[1] But in Atlanta the ILD played down this conflict in order to forge a local united front with blacks, liberals, and Socialists. Although the last two groups had left the alliance in May, 1933, because of ILD attacks on them as "social fascists," the ILD had gotten along reasonably well with black Atlantans. But the ILD destroyed this unity in April, 1934, with a slashing attack on NAACP legal efforts in Georgia.

1. Dan T. Carter, *Scottsboro: A Tragedy of the American South* (Baton Rouge: Louisiana State University Press, 1969), 51–103; Wilson Record, *The Negro and the Communist Party* (Chapel Hill: University of North Carolina Press, 1951), 60–65; Walter White, "The Negro and the Communists," *Harper's*, CLXIV (December, 1931), 66–67.

The split between ILD supporters and Atlanta's black middle class developed from the controversial case of another black defendant, John Downer. In May, 1932, an all-white jury in Elberton, Georgia, convicted Downer, a field hand, of raping a white woman. He narrowly missed being lynched by a large mob following his arrest, and another mob gathered menacingly during his brief trial. Through the efforts of attorney A. T. Walden, president of the local chapter of the NAACP, and several liberal white Atlanta attorneys, Downer's conviction was overturned on grounds that the trial setting had been dominated by a mob.[2] The Commission on Interracial Cooperation provided Downer with counsel at his second trial, hiring attorney Henry C. Hammond of Augusta, a former judge. Harry S. Strozier, a lawyer from Macon, assisted him. Despite their vigorous efforts, another all-white jury convicted Downer and sentenced him to death. Following Governor Eugene Talmadge's refusal to grant a last-minute request for executive clemency, Downer was executed on March 16, 1934, protesting his innocence until the end.[3]

His death severely distressed many blacks and liberal whites. Strozier, who had been especially diligent in Downer's defense, felt greatly disheartened. "I am firmly convinced that the State of Georgia put to death this morning an innocent man," he wrote a fellow lawyer. To Will Alexander he confided that if Downer "had been a white man he never would have been convicted on any such evidence." The Atlanta *Daily World* likewise voiced "emphatic doubt" concerning Downer's guilt and warned that there would be similar "black Fridays" in the future until blacks were finally granted the right to a jury trial by their peers.[4]

Ramifications of the Downer case soon provoked an acrimonious split within the ranks of the Herndon defense movement in Atlanta. To be sure, relations between ILD radicals and some of the more conservative black professionals had not always been smooth. Yet most involved

2. *Downer* v. *Dunaway*, 53 F.2d 586 (1931).
3. Atlanta *Daily World*, March 16, 1934.
4. Harry S. Strozier to Elbert P. Tuttle, March 16, 1934, Strozier to Will W. Alexander, March 22, 1934, Tuttle to Alexander, March 20, 1934, all in Commission on Interracial Cooperation Papers, Trevor Arnett Library, Atlanta University; Atlanta *Daily World*, March 18 and August 13, 1934.

blacks, feeling the two groups shared a common cause, had been willing to cooperate with the radicals. However, inaccurate ILD attacks on the local NAACP chapter for its alleged role in Downer's death sparked a sharp reaction. About the time of Downer's execution, the ILD issued a pamphlet accusing the NAACP of mishandling the defense and in effect contributing to his death. The reality was quite different; the NAACP had had no connection with Downer's defense at his second trial. What apparently confused the ILD was A. T. Walden's role in the appeal of Downer's first conviction. But the always discreet Walden had had nothing to do with the second trial, and even his actions during the first appeal were taken on his own initiative and not on behalf of the association. Walter White of the NAACP had explained these facts to columnist Sender Garlin of the *Daily Worker* in May, 1933, so the association's position should have been known to other Communist leaders. Yet the *Worker* printed the ILD charges in full without questioning their accuracy.[5]

The allegations were quickly answered in late March by the Reverend J. Raymond Henderson, "one of the most fiery, militant speakers in the city." Henderson explained that in the past he had opened his church to ILD meetings and had even served on the Herndon defense committee, in spite of the ILD's godlessness and hostility to religion. But no longer. Henderson announced that, instead, he would henceforth oppose the efforts of ILD members, declaring, "They are the most ungrateful lot I know in America." After defending the NAACP and the Commission on Interracial Cooperation, the indignant minister charged that the ILD sought to cripple the association during its annual membership drive and urged all black churches to close their doors to these "ingrates." Because of Henderson's influence, his blast at the ILD immediately hurt the Provisional Committee for the Defense of Angelo Herndon. A mass meeting previously scheduled for the Central C.M.E. Church was canceled when the pastor, the Reverend J. A. Baxter, withdrew permission for the rally.[6]

5. *Daily Worker*, April 3, 1934; Walter White to Roy Wilkins, May 4, 1933, in National Association for the Advancement of Colored People Papers, Library of Congress, hereinafter cited as NAACP Papers. Garlin said he had been told by Herndon that the NAACP had won the new trial for Downer.

6. Atlanta *Daily World*, January 14 and March 24, 1934.

The controversy became even more heated when Ben Davis and Henderson traded insults in a bitter exchange of open letters in the *Daily World*. Infuriated by the minister's "vicious and treacherous attack," Davis issued several counterblasts aimed at both Henderson and the NAACP, even reviving the charge concerning John Downer. Asserting that Henderson had secretly played the role of the "typical Negro selfish demagogue," the black attorney repeated the frequent Communist accusation of those years that one could not serve both the Negro people and the "misleaders" of the NAACP and the Commission on Interracial Cooperation. Although he jabbed at the NAACP leadership, Davis praised the efforts of the association's rank-and-file members, expressing regret that they had been deceived by their leaders. In a subsequent statement, Davis chastised Henderson for failing to distinguish between the ILD and the Herndon defense committee. "This is unmitigated deception," he proclaimed in exaggerated rhetoric, "designed to confuse the public, designed to throw a 'red scare' into the Negro people, designed to crush the mass struggle for Herndon's freedom, the Scottsboro Boys' freedom, and the liberation of the Negro race." [7]

Henderson responded acidly to Davis' "tirade." Dismissing the allegations of opportunism, he declared that he had actually lost friendships and endangered contributions to his church by his erstwhile support of radical causes. He criticized Davis as irresponsible for repeating the accusation that the NAACP was to blame for Downer's death and warned the ILD that it could not retain the support of blacks while denouncing the ideas and institutions in which they believed. Although Henderson conceded that the Herndon defense committee was not the same as the ILD, he pointed out that there could never have been a provisional committee if the ILD had not desired one. Citing financial contributions to the defense and his own personal efforts, such as participation in the Klan-picketed Scottsboro rally at the Holsey Temple C.M.E. Church, he vigorously defended his record. The Reverend J. A. Martin, also active in the Herndon committee, publicly took a middle-of-the-road position in the dispute at first. Later, though, he adopted the orthodox Communist position on several issues and came over fully to the ILD. [8] Despite Martin's continued support, the Herndon defense

7. *Ibid.*, March 31, 1934.
8. *Ibid.*, March 31, 1934, and April 21, 1934.

committee's effectiveness had been seriously damaged. No longer did it enjoy the support of many members of Atlanta's black middle class. Other than Ben Davis, John Geer, and Martin, no prominent black leader would be publicly identified with either the ILD or the provisional committee. Although both groups continued their work, the membership of the two increasingly became the same.[9]

This split between Communist and non-Communist Herndon sympathizers strongly resembled the earlier rupture in May, 1933. At that time, white liberals and labor leaders defected from the defense coalition; now black leaders did likewise. The chief reason for the collapse of the local united protest movement was the ILD's inability to cooperate successfully with other groups. Unable to restrain its narrow sectarianism and to avoid quarrels of the national office which had little application to the local level, the ILD repeatedly alienated its natural allies. This was a fatal error. By the middle of 1935, when the organization underwent a change of heart, the ILD would be virtually nonexistent in Atlanta.

At the same time that the local defense movement was falling apart, the ILD expanded its national publicity about Herndon, warning that continued imprisonment would seriously jeopardize his failing health. At his original trial, he had denounced the primitive living conditions in Fulton Tower Prison. Local officials felt that Herndon's conviction had ended these complaints. But they were mistaken. While in prison Herndon continued to protest substandard conditions. In several letters to northern comrades, he charged that prison officials were using "savage" and "criminal" treatment in order to break his spirit and undermine his health. Herndon further alleged that he was fed dog meat and that human excrement dripped into his cell. Noting President Franklin D. Roosevelt's frequent trips to the health resort at Warm Springs, Georgia, he suggested that public attention be drawn to the differences

9. This by no means implies that there were no grounds for criticism of the Atlanta branch of the NAACP. Columnist Frank Marshall Davis of the *World* received several letters critical of the chapter's inactivity, and even Henderson himself had previously complained that the branch was not aggressive enough. Davis concurred, observing that the local chapter "has done little but stage annual drives and conduct citizenship schools." The NAACP's national office frequently encountered difficulty in obtaining information from the branch, which was more noted locally for its social activities than its protest activity. These were not the points stressed by the ILD, however. See Frank Marshall Davis, "Touring the World," *ibid.*, July 29, 1934.

between treatment accorded a capitalist leader and a working-class leader.[10]

In early March, 1934, a national protest campaign over Herndon's treatment was launched. The ILD specifically charged that the young Communist suffered from stomach pains, failing eyesight, and generally poor health as a result of his imprisonment. The organization also decried his assignment to a death cell. On March 14, in a public letter to Governor Talmadge and other state officials, the ILD asserted that Herndon was being subjected to "barbaric cruelties." Because of the wretched prison conditions, the ILD communiqué charged Georgia officials "with the attempted murder of Angelo Herndon." Stating that the spirit of a "militant fighter" could not be broken, the ILD urged workers and intellectuals to rush protests to the governor. *New Masses* also deplored prison conditions in Atlanta, charging that debased officials were even plotting to assign sexual perverts to Herndon's cell.[11]

The ILD informed the ACLU on March 3 that "Angelo Herndon is dying by inches in Fulton Tower" and urged the ACLU to assist in the publicity campaign. A week later, the ILD reported that local efforts had resulted in a slight improvement in the treatment accorded Herndon but that he was still ill. Disturbed by these reports, Roger Baldwin asked Mary Raoul Millis, the Atlanta Socialist, to verify the allegations, particularly regarding the death cell. She in turn asked Edgar Watkins, Sr., a conservative but open-minded attorney, to visit Herndon and inspect conditions in Fulton Tower. Despite initial skepticism, Watkins agreed to investigate. His subsequent report denied most of Herndon's charges, pointing out that there was no death house in Fulton Tower, since prisoners sentenced to be executed were taken to the state prison at Milledgeville. Although Watkins denied that the jail was as bad as alleged, he conceded that in one sense the complaints were partially justified. "It is not a nice place to be in and the county has begun the construction of a new jail, or rather, the remodeling of this jail with additions," he commented. Herndon told Watkins that he had not been

10. Angelo Herndon to Comrade Freida, October 12, 1933, and Herndon to William L. Patterson, undated, both in American Civil Liberties Union Archives, Princeton University Library, hereinafter cited as ACLU Archives; Sender Garlin, "Change the World!" *Daily Worker*, March 13, 1934.

11. *Daily Worker*, March 7 and 14, 1934; *New Masses*, March 27, 1934, p. 4.

well, having suffered for several months from sharp pains in his side, which he feared might be appendicitis. Much to his relief, though, the pains had now almost completely subsided. Although the situation in jail was not pleasant, Watkins found Herndon apparently treated like other prisoners. He concluded his account by repeating that Herndon's health appeared good.[12]

If Watkins' report did not fully satisfy the ACLU, it did convince Millis. In June she wrote *Opportunity*, the monthly magazine of the Urban League, criticizing an account of Herndon's health based on ILD complaints. Discounting this report, she stated that in reality his health was satisfactory. But the ILD refused to retract its statement. Ben Davis attempted to refute several of Watkins' findings in a lengthy memorandum. Denying that Herndon exhibited a morbid attitude or sought martyrdom, he also challenged Watkins' favorable evaluation of Herndon's health. "He suffers from vomiting which could be due to ulcers of the stomach caused by the bad food," Davis wrote, "and he has lung trouble which *may be* tuberculosis." He added that prison conditions were quite primitive and that the young Communist had been mistreated. Watkins' complaints of excess publicity Davis dismissed as a crude attack on the ILD policy of mass protest.[13]

Not satisfied with its previous efforts, the ILD announced a national Save Angelo Herndon campaign in mid-March. It sought to force Herndon's release, charging that he was slowly dying in jail. Even though the ILD reported that Herndon was receiving somewhat better treatment as a result of recent protests, the organization warned that these slight concessions could be quickly withdrawn at any time. Hence a stronger mass movement was sorely needed. Other Communist spokesmen likewise challenged workers and intellectuals to build a successful campaign for Herndon's release. Ann Burlack, one of the Atlanta Six, urged Herndon sympathizers everywhere to work to free

12. Lawrence Emery to Roger N. Baldwin, March 3 and 9, 1934, Baldwin to Mary Raoul Millis, March 5, 1934, Edgar Watkins, Sr., to Millis, March 10, 1934, and Watkins to Baldwin, March 22, 1934, all in ACLU Archives. Watkins did report that the prosecution first raised the issue of communism at Herndon's trial, although he noted that the defense willingly accepted the topic.

13. *Opportunity*, XII (August, 1934), 253, 256; Ben Davis to Lawrence Emery, April 13, 1934, in International Labor Defense Papers, Schomburg Collection, New York Public Library, hereinafter cited as ILD Papers. Despite her criticism of the ILD, Millis voiced disappointment that the communism furor had obscured Herndon's innocence.

him from Fulton Tower, which she described as an "old stone, damp, filthy dungeon of the type that existed in the medieval days." Crediting her release in 1930 from the same jail to mass protest, she appealed for similar action in Herndon's behalf.[14]

As a result of these claims about Herndon's health, a delegation of four Atlanta liberals visited Dr. J. C. Blalock, the county physician, on April 18 and requested that Herndon be taken to a hospital for a complete examination. Dr. Blalock promised to have X rays taken of Herndon to investigate possible tuberculosis symptoms. The ILD soon revealed that one member of the group, a white female doctor, had conducted an unannounced examination of the prisoner which had revealed possible stomach trouble and complications in the lungs. Not content with Blalock's promises, the ILD obtained an order from Fulton County Superior Court Judge James M. Maddox transferring Herndon to Grady Hospital. On Friday afternoon, April 27, Herndon was moved to Grady under heavy guard. Though weakened, the courageous young Communist still possessed "the same spirited gleam in his eyes," the *Daily Worker* declared. Before X rays could be taken, however, prison guards became suspicious of several unidentified persons awaiting treatment and, fearing a possible rescue attempt, returned Herndon to jail.[15]

These efforts to obtain a medical examination for Herndon quickly degenerated into a farce. When deputy sheriffs returned with him the following Monday, Grady officials refused to examine him, contending that the hospital was a city institution and hence unaffected by the superior court ruling. L. R. Weatherwax, the white supervisor of the separate X-ray department used for Negroes, explained that it was not the custom to examine county prisoners who were not emergency cases. He also denied that the court order specified anything about giving an X ray. When reporters contacted the director of the hospital, he declared that Grady would be happy to render the county any technical assistance necessary and signed an order authorizing an X ray for Herndon. Finally, on Wednesday, May 2, hospital authorities examined Herndon's chest. According to a hospital spokesman, the results revealed no evidence of tuberculosis. "Herndon's chest, though not exactly normal,

14. *Daily Worker*, March 13, 17, 21, and April 24, 1934. For similar appeals, see *Nation*, May 2, 1934, p. 508, and *New Republic*, April 4, 1934, p. 218.
15. Atlanta *Daily World*, April 19, 26, and 28, 1934; *Daily Worker*, May 1, 1934.

is all right," announced Weatherwax. When the prisoner was again taken to Grady for a medical examination later in the month, officials once more pronounced his health to be satisfactory.[16]

This optimistic report did not quiet the suspicions of the ILD, which charged that the X rays were so unclear that it was impossible to evaluate the true state of Herndon's lungs. ILD apprehensions were further aroused when an anonymous hospital worker called Ben Davis to tell him that Herndon's lungs were really in bad condition and that the hospital account had been incorrectly given. In a letter to the ILD, a weary Herndon reported that he was still not feeling well. Despondent after sixteen months behind bars, he complained that he had not received mail or other items from local sympathizers in several weeks. Uneasy over unfulfilled ILD promises, he pointedly asked what had happened to a proposed committee which was to have investigated conditions at the jail. "It is also imperative that this be done as quickly as possible, for these fascist dogs are certainly determined to get my blood," he bitterly charged.[17]

To check on prison conditions and to focus national attention on Herndon's imprisonment, the Communist-influenced National Committee for the Defense of Political Prisoners, along with the ILD and ACLU, organized a committee of northern liberals to visit Atlanta. This delegation hoped to determine the precise nature of Herndon's imprisonment and to examine the state of civil liberties in Atlanta. The group also planned to visit the Scottsboro boys in Alabama. John Howard Lawson, author of the play *They Shall Not Die*, based on the Scottsboro case, served as unofficial chairman. Other members included novelist William Rollins, Jr.; Winifred Chappell of the Methodist Federation for Social Service; Martin Russak, the Communist editor of the *Textile Workers' Voice*; Herbert Abrons, southern field representative of the ACLU; and William Serber, a Yale University student.

The delegation, accompanied by Ben Davis and the Reverend J. A. Martin, visited Georgia officials on July 2, commencing with assistant prosecutor John H. Hudson. After giving the representatives a curt

16. Atlanta *Daily World*, May 1–3, 1934; Atlanta *Constitution*, May 26, 1934.
17. John Howard Lawson, *A Southern Welcome* (New York: National Committee for the Defense of Political Prisoners, 1934), 4; Angelo Herndon to Comrade Freida, June 1, 1934, in ILD Papers.

reception, Hudson examined them as if they were on the witness stand. His first words to Chappell were, "Tell me, Winifred, how many times have you been arrested?" When the delegates explained that they represented liberal opinion, Hudson exploded, "You're all too liberal for the good of this country." The enraged prosecutor next accused the ACLU's Abrons of representing a "Communistic, Anarchistic organization" and the group in general of being "part of the red set-up." Then Hudson picked up from his desk a copy of a booklet entitled *The Communist Position on the Negro Question* and began to read aloud. According to Lawson, "In reading this he transposed the word 'nigger' for Negro whenever the word occurred in the text. As Hudson read, he became increasingly apoplectic; the reading of the passage evidently having the effect of driving him into a helpless rage. At the conclusion of the reading, he trembled with excitement. He rose and rushed out of the room, at the same time ordering us to get out of his office." [18] Hudson's conduct shocked and angered the committee. An unsmiling Lawson characterized the encounter to reporters as an "amazing experience." Labeling the assistant prosecutor a "hysterical fanatic," he emphatically declared that it was "a disgrace to have such men in public office." When contacted by the press, a much calmer Hudson explained that he had been misled concerning the committee's political views. "I don't care to have any discussion with criminals or people with criminal records," he snorted. [19]

Governor Eugene Talmadge proved a far more tolerant and cooperative host. The chief executive skillfully mixed graciousness with evasiveness. He greeted the delegates cordially, although he carefully avoided shaking hands with Davis and Martin. He artfully dodged most of their questions, explaining that the current political campaign necessitated his avoiding controversial issues. When called upon for a report, the state adjutant general, Lindley Camp, said that Herndon was "uppity" and had a "chip on his shoulder." After Talmadge blandly asserted that conditions were satisfactory in Georgia, he turned to Davis and Martin for expected confirmation. To his surprise, Martin denied

18. Lawson, *A Southern Welcome*, 10; *Daily Worker*, July 5, 1934; Pittsburgh *Courier*, July 14, 1934; Atlanta *Constitution*, July 3, 1934; Atlanta *Daily World*, July 3, 1934; New York *Post*, July 3, 1934, in ILD Papers; Herbert Abrons to ACLU, July 4, 1934, in ACLU Archives.
19. Atlanta *Constitution*, July 3, 1934.

this, saying that many blacks were unhappy. He added that he personally would vote the Communist ticket before supporting some local officials who permitted intimidation of black citizens.[20]

Startled by Martin's audacity, Talmadge protested that he was a friend of the Negro. He said that he knew a black lawyer who, though successful, "is as humble as the lowest farmer," adding, "I love that nigger." Then Talmadge cut short the interview, thanking the group for its visit. After departing, committee members stopped at Fulton Tower Prison to visit Herndon. While suspicious officials looked on, they spoke with him about his imprisonment. Herndon explained that one chronic problem was censorship of his mail. At his request, they urged jail officials not to interfere with his mail or reading matter. Supervisor R. N. Holland assured the committee that they treated Herndon no differently than other prisoners and that he could receive any non-Communist publication he desired.[21]

Committee members next journeyed to Alabama to investigate the treatment of the Scottsboro boys, which they found to be harsher than that of Herndon. Alabama officials proved equally inhospitable to the group. Birmingham police arrested John Howard Lawson and charged him with criminal libel, stemming from critical remarks he had written about an Alabama judge while reporting the first Scottsboro trial. He was released on a three-hundred-dollar bond.[22]

To no one's surprise, the committee's report took a dim view of conditions in Georgia and Alabama. The report declared, "The delegation stated categorically that the *facts* in regard to violations of civil rights in these states were far more serious and more threatening than was generally realized." It charged that normal constitutional safeguards had been abandoned and that the rights of free speech, free assembly, and free association were blatantly ignored by local officials. The report further warned that these abuses were not restricted to blacks and professed Communists alone but applied to poor whites and liberals as well. The group singled out the conduct of John H. Hudson for

20. Lawson, *A Southern Welcome*, 12; *Daily Worker*, July 5, 1934; Atlanta *Daily World*, July 3, 1934; Angelo Herndon, *Let Me Live* (New York: Arno Press, 1969), 276–77; Benjamin J. Davis, *Communist Councilman from Harlem* (New York: International Publishers, 1969), 88–89.

21. Atlanta *Constitution*, July 3, 1934; Herndon, *Let Me Live*, 277–79.

22. Lawson, *A Southern Welcome*, 12–13, 6–9.

criticism and called for his removal from office. Warning that a small group of politicians sought to "hitlerize" Georgia and Alabama, the committee urged widespread national publicity on the problem and the formation of strong local organizations of liberals and intellectuals in both states to protect civil liberties and civil rights.[23] These incidents had little apparent effect on Georgia authorities, except to make prison officials more cautious in their treatment of Herndon. But, in other sections of the country, the publicity gradually awakened people to conditions in Georgia, and Herndon's name and his cause slowly acquired notoriety.

While the ILD began its publicity campaign over Herndon's alleged mistreatment, the Georgia Supreme Court finally considered his appeal. On May 24, 1934, the court announced its long-awaited decision, affirming the earlier conviction. The judgment came as a bitter but not unexpected defeat for Herndon and his attorneys. The lengthy opinion dismissed all the defense claims, frequently on errors of procedure resulting from the inexperience of Geer and Davis. Defense objections concerning the pretrial hearings (which attacked the lily-white jury and the insurrection statute's constitutionality) were thrown out because they had not been raised at the proper time. The court overruled the defense objection that Communist literature introduced as evidence had been illegally obtained. According to Georgia law, the justices declared, "evidence discovered by the search of a person while he was under an illegal arrest, if relevant, is not inadmissible as contravening the constitutional provision against compelling a person to give testimony against himself." As long as the evidence was produced by another and not by the defendant through coercion, it was admissible. Additional defense complaints were likewise summarily dismissed. Davis and Geer had objected to Hudson's inflammatory questioning of the Emory professor T. J. Corley about racial intermarriage. The court denied this contention, reasoning that other material introduced at the trial, to which the defense did not object, illustrated that "the Communist Party did advocate racial and social equality for the negro." Therefore no proper objection could be made to the exchange in question. The ruling further

23. *Ibid.*, 10–14.

dismissed the defense allegations concerning the use of the word *darky* to describe Herndon. The court denied that the use of the word was prejudicial, observing, "The term 'darky,' as applied in this state to a person of color, is not opprobrious." [24]

The last section of the opinion dealt with the issue of whether the evidence had been sufficient to support the verdict. In so doing the Georgia Supreme Court explained its own interpretation of the insurrection law and constitutional limits on free speech. After citing its previous decisions in *Carr* v. *State*, the court concluded by quoting from the classic free speech case of *Gitlow* v. *New York*. The passage, which reaffirmed the danger resulting from such material as Carr and Herndon possessed, said: "The State cannot reasonably be required to measure the danger from every such utterance in the nice balance of a jeweler's scale. A single revolutionary spark may kindle a fire that, smouldering for a time, may burst into a sweeping and destructive conflagration." [25] The Georgia court thus expressed its acceptance and rather loose application of the "dangerous tendency" test developed by the U.S. Supreme Court in the 1920s. By doing so the court gave a broader interpretation of the insurrection law than had Lee B. Wyatt, the original presiding judge. Wyatt had charged the jury that *immediate* serious action must have been anticipated against the state in order for the defendant to be found guilty. [26]

The court's ruling disappointed sympathizers who had followed the case. The New York *Amsterdam News* warned that if the ruling were not reversed "we may not be entirely wrong in predicting that some day the conservative Interracial Commission will be brought on the carpet for advocating the end of racial discrimination and lynching." [27] Defense

24. *Herndon* v. *State*, 174 S.E. 597–615 (1934). In one place Geer and Davis had in their zeal actually objected to a portion of one charge which they had originally suggested to Judge Wyatt.

25. *Ibid.*, 615–16.

26. The court echoed a frequent worry of assistant prosecutor J. Walter LeCraw when it declared that the Communist plan for creation "of the 'Black Belt' by peaceful and through lawful processes could not have been reasonably anticipated." The so-called dangerous tendency test was developed in the early 1920s by the United States Supreme Court. It meant that the state could curtail the constitutional right to free speech if there was the possibility that an utterance might tend to stir up serious disorder in the long run. Legal historian Zechariah Chafee, Jr., argued that this approach was too broad and sweeping, unnecessarily restricting free speech and open discussion. See Zechariah Chafee, Jr., *Free Speech in the United States* (Cambridge: Harvard University Press, 1941), 23–35, 91–92, 322–25, 392.

27. New York *Amsterdam News*, June 2, 1934, in clippings file, ILD Papers.

attorneys were especially irritated at the court's refusal to consider the unconstitutionality of the statute. Worse yet, the court had actually broadened the scope of the insurrection law.

This legal rebuff forced the ILD to consider carefully the next logical step—an appeal to the U.S. Supreme Court—and the selection of veteran attorneys to handle it. John Geer and Benjamin Davis had already stretched their legal experience rather far and were not qualified to argue before the Supreme Court. Their earlier direction of the case, including the attack on the insurrection law's constitutionality, had already been questioned by some observers. Since it now appeared that this issue might be the one most likely to find favor with the high court, it became vital that the issue be raised properly so that the justices would be confronted with a clear-cut choice.[28]

While the ILD pondered these questions, Atlanta authorities interpreted the Georgia Supreme Court action as a vindication of their antiradical activities. Hudson responded with a reinvigorated crusade against communism. On Monday, May 28, 1934, just four days after the court's ruling, he launched another series of "Red raids." Acting on a tip from Birmingham police, the so-called Red squad swooped down on the suspected secret headquarters of local Communist activity, the City View Realty Company on Auburn Avenue. Officers broke down the door to the office only to find the room deserted. Inside, police found numerous copies of the *Daily Worker* and confiscated two burlap bags full of Communist literature. After reading through office files, Hudson announced that he had discovered material which might warrant an indictment under the insurrection law against Don West, a young white Georgian who was said to have been in charge of the office. But raids on several suspected locations failed to turn up the elusive West. Undaunted, Hudson subsequently secured warrants for the arrest of West and Martha Stafford, another worker for the Herndon defense committee, on charges of "circulating insurrectionary literature."[29]

Once again Hudson warned the public that Communist agitators posed a serious danger to the state. But he reassured citizens that

28. William L. Patterson to Roger N. Baldwin, June 1, 1934, in ACLU Archives.
29. Atlanta *Daily World*, May 29, 1934; Atlanta *Constitution*, June 3, 1934; *Daily Worker*, May 30 and June 4, 1934.

"Georgia has a law for these people which has teeth in it, and we intend to use those teeth." The assistant prosecutor claimed that literally thousands of names and addresses of local Communists had been seized. This inflated figure was a far cry from the dozen or so actual members mentioned in the minutes of Communist meetings introduced as evidence at Herndon's trial. Hudson charged that intellectuals, along with "bums, imbeciles, ex-convicts, fugitives from justice, people who are insane or partly insane, and those who are down and out," were responsible for much Communist agitation. Furthermore, he announced that his office would request that Herndon be transferred to the chain gang since his current "illness" was feigned.[30]

During the following week, Hudson continued to raid the homes of blacks and whites thought to be involved in radical activity. It soon became clear that he was acting on the basis of inside information. The *Daily Worker* publicly revealed his confidential source on June 5, when it announced that Ansel W. Morrison, a former legal assistant to Ben Davis, and Willie Leathers, formerly a member of the Communist party, had delivered secret information to Hudson. Morrison was a valuable catch for the prosecutor. The young white lawyer had come to Atlanta shortly after Herndon's conviction, apparently with the aim of infiltrating radical activities, and had done some legal paperwork for Geer and Davis. After disappearing for several months, he returned in March, 1934. His earlier work, coupled with the fact that he had attended high school with Don West, helped him gain acceptance. More important, he lived in a respectable, middle-class neighborhood, an asset to the ILD and the Herndon committee, who needed a "safe" location for their headquarters because of frequent police surveillance. Both groups moved most of their records to Morrison's home, only to see them fall into the hands of police. The embarrassing loss of these materials placed the membership of both groups on the defensive.[31]

Don West soon became the principal target of Hudson's raids. A native of northern Georgia, West had been educated at the Mount Berry School for mountain children at Mount Berry, Georgia. Ordained a

30. Atlanta *Constitution*, June 3, 1934.
31. Atlanta *Daily World*, June 5, 1934; *Daily Worker*, June 5 and 11, 1934; author's interview with Don West, Pipestem, W. Va., September 13, 1970; A. W. Morrison to Don West, May 29, 1934, in ACLU Archives.

Congregationalist minister, he studied religion briefly at Vanderbilt University. Like many other activist southern ministers of the decade, such as Claude Williams, Howard Kester, and Ward Rogers, West took his Christian ethics seriously and applied them to contemporary situations in a manner not always appreciated by local power structures.[32] After leaving Vanderbilt and preaching for several years, West assisted Miles Horton in founding the Highlander Folk School in Monteagle, Tennessee. This controversial school attracted the wrath of many conservative politicians for its radical economic and racial views. In early 1933, West noticed an article in a Chattanooga newspaper describing Herndon's trial and conviction. Impressed by the description of Herndon's efforts to help the unemployed, he hitchhiked to Atlanta seeking more information. There he quickly became involved in the Herndon defense movement. Though he rejoined Highlander briefly, he soon returned to Atlanta as head of the defense committee.[33]

West found defense work in Herndon's behalf rather difficult. Heavy police surveillance made it unwise to circulate handbills except under cover of darkness. Meanwhile, rumors grew that the police had orders to get West "dead or alive." Such pressure forced him to abandon his work and go into hiding with sympathetic families. Once police raided the home of the Reverend J. A. Martin while West was there, and the minister's quick-thinking wife grabbed him and pushed him down into a cellar under the kitchen, covering the trapdoor with a rug. Although officers carefully searched the house, they failed to discover West. On another occasion, he beat a hasty retreat to bushes behind the home of Walter Washburn, a white electrician active in the Herndon defense committee, when officers descended unexpectedly. His effectiveness destroyed, West reluctantly decided to leave the city. Fearing that authorities were watching the Atlanta train and bus stations, Ben Davis put West in the back of a Ford, covered him with sacks, and drove out to suburban Decatur. From there West caught a bus to North Carolina and then another one to New York City. Also under heavy pressure, Davis

32. For a fascinating glimpse into Williams' life, see his interview in Studs Terkel, *Hard Times: An Oral History of the Great Depression* (New York: Pantheon Books, 1970), 328–32.

33. See H. Glyn Thomas, "The Highlander Folk School: The Depression Years," *Tennessee Historical Quarterly*, XXII (December, 1964), 358–71; author's interview with West; *Daily Worker*, June 11, 1934.

himself departed several weeks later for New York, where he became editor of the Communist publication *Negro Liberator* and openly identified with Communist causes.[34]

Ansel Morrison's actions became more understandable when West received a letter from him defending his undercover role. This fascinating document exposed Morrison as an extreme anti-Semite who believed that "Communism is a child of the Jewish race." In the letter he begged West to examine the facts objectively, suggesting that if he did he would realize that the Jews were behind communism and that he should leave the "contemptable [*sic*] Jewish Communist bunch." Asserting that such revolutionaries as Marx, Lenin, Engels, Leon Trotsky, and Grigori Zinoviev were Jews, he added "that Trotsky was sent to Russia before the revolution by Jacob Shift [*sic*] of the Jewish Wall Street firm of Kuhn, Loeb, and Co., who helped finance the Russian Revolution." Morrison disclosed his belief that communism had helped destroy the Roman and Persian empires and that the "Civil War was a Jewish plot to divide the United States." After these "revelations," Morrison again pleaded with West to abandon his Communist activities.[35]

When ACLU leaders tried to verify West's account of his Atlanta experiences through Mary Raoul Millis, they were disappointed. She reported that nothing out of the ordinary was occurring and that West had not been seen recently. Within a month, though, Millis informed the ACLU that the situation was more serious than she had originally thought. She explained that a group of area residents were ready to form a liberal organization, probably affiliated with the League for Industrial Democracy (LID), the Socialist counterpart of the ILD. But, since they feared that too much publicity would only encourage more anti-

34. Author's interview with Glenn W. Rainey, Atlanta, Ga., August 26, 1970; author's interview with West; Don West, "The Atlanta Situation and the Recent Herndon Decision," memorandum dated June 24, 1934, in ACLU Archives; *Daily Worker*, June 15, 1934. Although virtually unknown to the general public, West played a key role in the Herndon defense movement because of his Georgia background and his dynamic personality. Despite charges made at the time and again in the late 1940s, West never officially joined the Communist party. Although a communist in spirit, his passionate commitment to social justice led him on his own independent path. Literally burned out of Georgia in the 1940s, West now resides near Pipestem, West Virginia, where he coordinates the Appalachian Folklife Center.

35. A. W. Morrison to Don West, May 29, 1934, in ACLU Archives.

Communist hysteria, they were proceeding very cautiously. Millis felt this necessary because the visit by John Howard Lawson's committee had only inflamed local prejudices.[36]

Acting on the belief that Hudson was the chief force behind these persecutions, Millis and several of her friends visited Solicitor General John A. Boykin to ask that the charges against the Atlanta Six be dropped. But the group quickly realized that he was as obsessed with communism as Hudson. "His state of mind was a revelation to me," she declared. "We found him rabid, fanatically rabid, on the subject of the 'reds,'" she explained, comparing his intolerant attitude to that of the notoriously anti-Communist Fish Committee, a special investigating committee set up by the House of Representatives. Boykin seriously warned his visitors that Communist propaganda and "Moscow gold" were undermining the tranquillity of the state. After reaffirming his dedication to stamping out this "evil in our midst," the solicitor general indicated that he felt that the Ku Klux Klan would do Georgia a service by putting blacks in their place. Millis concluded that the situation was "very serious." Editor W. T. Anderson of the Macon *Telegraph*, who was a close political ally of Governor Talmadge, confided to her that charges against the Atlanta Six should be dropped but that the issue could not safely be brought up during the governor's race. Millis added that in her opinion future legal action should not be undertaken by black or northern lawyers.[37]

Communist spokesmen never doubted West's account of the situation in Atlanta. The *Daily Worker* protested Hudson's latest raids by editorially blasting Georgia officials for attempting to "burn Communism out of Georgia" and accused authorities of reviving terrorism aimed at workers and working-class organizers such as Don West and Angelo Herndon. Disturbed by reports that Hudson planned to charge every ILD member in Georgia with "inciting to insurrection," William L. Patterson publicly announced that the ILD would refuse to be driven underground.[38] During the summer of 1934, the *New Republic* and the

36. Lucille Milner to Mary Raoul Millis, June 14, 1934, Millis to Milner, June 20, 1934, Millis to Roger N. Baldwin, July 12, 1934, all *ibid*.
37. Mary Raoul Millis to Roger N. Baldwin, July 24, 1934, *ibid*.
38. Atlanta *Daily World*, June 5, 1934; *Daily Worker*, June 4 and 5, 1934; New York *Times*, June 2, 1934, p. 9.

Nation also attacked Georgia officials. Walter Wilson, whose efforts in 1930 had embarrassed Atlanta authorities in their prosecution of the Atlanta Six, decried Georgia justice in the *Nation*. "If the conviction sticks and if the Atlanta Six are sent to prison," he warned, "the forces of reaction and fascism in Georgia will have temporarily triumphed." [39]

Because of Hudson's renewed offensive against communism, sympathizers remained uneasy over Herndon's safety. But, to their amazement, in mid-June the state unexpectedly agreed to bail for Herndon, perhaps in order to offset the growing criticism. Judge Lee B. Wyatt fixed the amount at fifteen thousand dollars. When ILD members recovered from their surprise, they quickly realized that the sizable bond was an almost prohibitive sum. Requests for a reduction of the amount, supported in a petition signed by over one hundred prominent black Atlantans including the president of Morris Brown College, W. A. Fountain, Jr., and Jesse O. Thomas of the Urban League, went unheeded. Consequently the ILD braced itself for a frantic effort to raise the money within a month's time. [40]

Still shunned by bonding agencies, the ILD was forced to conduct a public campaign to raise the bail. Though difficult, such a campaign did have the advantage from the ILD's perspective of involving thousands of individuals in a common struggle. Exhorting the party faithful and sympathizers to greater efforts, the *Daily Worker* claimed that the granting of bond was victory for mass protest. It warned, though, that the triumph could "be turned into a defeat for the working class unless the money is raised within the next two weeks." The Central Committee of the Communist party of the United States issued a formal statement cautioning against relying on the benevolence of the U.S. Supreme Court. It asserted that only a strong mass movement could force the "supreme legal agent of the white rulers" to hand down a favorable decision. [41]

To help publicize the Herndon and Scottsboro cases, the ILD sent

39. Henry Hart, "Help for Herndon," *New Republic*, July 18, 1934, p. 266; *Nation*, June 6, 1934, p. 633; Walter Wilson, "Georgia Suppresses Insurrection," *Nation*, August 1, 1934, pp. 127–28.
40. Atlanta *Daily World*, June 17, 21, and August 1, 1934; *Daily Worker*, June 29, 1934.
41. *Daily Worker*, June 30, July 4 and 11, 1934. See also Quincy Howe, "Help Herndon," *Nation*, August 15, 1934, p. 185. Most black newspapers cooperated with the ILD appeals.

Ada Wright, a "Scottsboro mother," and Herbert Newton, one of the Atlanta Six, to speak at the annual convention of the NAACP in Oklahoma City. The two were reluctantly permitted to talk briefly. Newton called for vigorous efforts to save Herndon from the chain gang, and, although the convention passed a mild resolution supporting Herndon, no further action was taken. As the month progressed, the *Daily Worker* increased its coverage of the bail-raising drive. Daily articles explained the significance of the case, and special forms for contributions were provided. Prominent Communist leaders appealed for contributions. On July 30, with just three days left in the campaign, only $8,627.40 had been raised, almost entirely through small donations. Frantic last-minute appeals by the *Daily Worker* and the ILD were heeded, as nearly $5,000 poured in during the final two days. In fact, the fund drive was eventually oversubscribed by about $3,000. All in all, it was an impressive fund-raising feat, but a final victory for Herndon remained far away.[42]

Immediately following the transfer of the money into government bonds, ILD attorney Joseph Brodsky flew to Atlanta, arriving on Friday night, August 3. The next morning Brodsky and John Geer presented the bond at the Fulton County Courthouse. But there they discovered one last obstacle—the need for a formal order signed by Judge Wyatt releasing Herndon. Although Wyatt had been originally scheduled to arrive in the city that day, he had postponed his appearance and still was at home in La Grange, seventy-five miles southwest of the city. The two lawyers quickly departed on a wild, dusty, four-hour drive, returning with the desired signature.[43]

Shortly after 5 P.M., in the company of Brodsky, Geer, and two detectives of the Seaboard Railroad, Angelo Herndon walked through the heavy iron doors of Fulton Tower, breathing fresh air for the first time in over eighteen months. Blinking in the unaccustomed sunlight, the joyful Herndon turned to Brodsky and remarked quietly, "Not to have my head confined in a small place seems strange and wonderful.

---

42. *Daily Worker*, July 3, July 13–August 4, 1934; Pittsburgh *Courier*, July 14 and August 4, 1934.

43. Atlanta *Daily World*, August 5, 1934; *Daily Worker*, August 6, 1934; Atlanta *Constitution*, August 5, 1934; Joseph Brodsky to *Daily Worker*, August 5, 1934, in ILD Papers.

Gee, air smells good." Following a brief stop at Geer's law office, Herndon, accompanied by Brodsky, the Reverend J. A. Martin, and the two detectives, left for the train station, where they boarded a train for New York City. Before leaving, an excited Brodsky telegraphed the *Daily Worker* that Herndon appeared to have suffered physically but that his spirit remained unbroken. The exhilaration of the day's activities still lingering, Brodsky confided that he was "so sleepy tired hot still teeny weeny scared but damn happy." [44]

Yet, ILD leaders in New York feared that Herndon might not be allowed to leave the state peacefully. On August 3 the National Committee for the Defense of Political Prisoners had received a call from Atlanta warning that the Ku Klux Klan planned to seize Herndon before he left Georgia. As a result, numerous demands for protection were lodged with the U.S. attorney general's office and with Governor Talmadge. When writer Theodore Dreiser personally called Talmadge for assurance that there would be no trouble, the governor reassured him that such rumors were greatly exaggerated. "I get letters and telegrams every day from people worried about the matter," he told the skeptical Dreiser, "but the people down here don't molest a nigger for any crime except raping a white woman." He added that Herndon would be safe even if he remained in Atlanta. Although the ILD was not fully convinced by Talmadge's statement, there seemed indeed no public outcry over Herndon's release. The Atlanta *Constitution*, denying that any danger existed, noted that he left jail just like any other prisoner. "Two negro boys unloading tin liquor cans in front of the jail did not even look up as the party left the tower," the newspaper reported. The Seaboard Railroad acted more cautiously, assigning two detectives to meet Herndon at the jail and accompany him on the train until he left the South. [45]

While the train carrying Herndon raced northward, bands of sympathizers prepared to welcome him. Small delegations greeted the train

---

44. *Ibid*. Herndon had, of course, left Fulton Tower briefly in May to go to Grady Hospital for an X-ray examination.

45. ILD news release, August 9, 1934, in ILD Papers; ACLU to Eugene Talmadge, August 3, 1934, and transcript of telephone conversation from Theodore Dreiser to Talmadge, August 3, 1934, both in ACLU Archives; Atlanta *Constitution*, August 5, 1934. Lest Dreiser's fears seem unduly exaggerated, it should be recalled that Georgia led the nation in lynchings in 1930, 1932, and 1933. See Frank Shay, *Judge Lynch: His First Hundred Years* (New York: Ives Washburn, 1938), 107.

in Washington, Baltimore, Philadelphia, and Newark, but by far the largest demonstration occurred in New York City. When Herndon's train pulled into Pennsylvania Station on Tuesday evening, August 7, an enthusiastic crowd estimated at six thousand persons awaited him. Leading the well-wishers were numerous Communist leaders, including Earl Browder, Robert Minor, James W. Ford, and Anna Damon. The joyous crowd swarmed around Herndon as his brother Milton and Robert Minor carried him on their shoulders. After brief formal greetings, Herndon was whisked away to a private residence. The crowd then spilled into the street, halting traffic and eventually marching to Union Square. There Minor addressed the gathering at an impromptu Communist rally.[46]

For several days, Herndon remained under doctor's supervision, refraining from most public appearances. He did hold a press conference the day following his arrival, where he told reporters that he was "more determined than ever to carry on the struggle for the oppressed working class and the Negro people." The *Daily Worker* praised Herndon's courageous conduct and discovered in it proof of the growing unity of black and white workers in their struggle against oppression. Anna Damon of the ILD suggested that Herndon had "become a symbol of working class heroism, of the new spirit of the American youth, Negro and white." Both Herndon and the ILD credited the *Daily Worker* with playing the crucial role in the campaign for his freedom. "Without the *Daily Worker*, it would have been impossible to raise the bail for Herndon in the short time we had, and our young leader would still be sitting in Fulton Tower jail," the ILD's executive committee declared. The Richmond *Planet* acknowledged the ILD's key role, praising the organization's "splendid services" and declaring that it deserved the support of black Americans everywhere. Not until August 17 did Herndon make a public appearance, joining Earl Browder and Joseph Brodsky in addressing a large, energetic crowd at Rockland Palace in Harlem. Again numerous spokesmen lauded the young Communist for his courage and leadership. In his speech, Herndon attacked the southern ruling class and such "misleaders" of blacks as W. E. B. Dubois.

46. *Daily Worker*, August 6–9, 1934; Atlanta *Daily World*, August 15, 1934; Norfolk *Journal and Guide*, August 18, 1934, in clippings file, ILD Papers.

Following several appearances in the New York City area, Herndon departed in September on a Communist-sponsored speaking tour of the Midwest along with Ida Norris, mother of one of the Scottsboro boys. [47]

Before Herndon left, however, he became involved in a public exchange with black newspaperman George Schuyler. In his column "Views and Reviews" in the Pittsburgh *Courier*, the iconoclastic Schuyler had bitterly attacked the Communist party. Not only did he charge that the Communists' slogan of self-determination for the Black Belt was race chauvinism at its worst, but he even asserted that the party was a financial "racket." He also commented rather cynically that Herndon was "out on bail and will probably skip it, like all the rest." Herndon responded in a blistering telegram, vigorously defending Communist tactics and accusing Schuyler of attempting to stab him in the back. In typical Communist rhetoric, Herndon further charged that the columnist, like other "misleaders" of black people, such as the NAACP, had tried first to disrupt the Scottsboro defense and now Herndon's defense. The *Daily Worker* echoed these allegations, describing Schuyler as a "pen-prostitute" and a "toady of the white ruling class." [48]

While Herndon lectured in the Midwest, defense attorneys prepared their request for a rehearing with the Georgia Supreme Court. Ben Davis and John Geer belatedly received much-needed legal assistance. Several experienced New York lawyers, coordinated by leftist attorney Carol Weiss King, rewrote the briefs to strengthen the grounds for attacking the constitutionality of the insurrection statute. [49] But, in late September, the court again ruled against Herndon, denying the petition for a rehearing. It dismissed the protest over its interpretation of the statute as a thinly veiled effort to reintroduce the issue of constitutionality. The court explained: "Regardless of the construction placed upon this statute either by the trial court or by this court, the defendant could have

47. *Daily Worker*, August 8, 9, 15, 17, and 24, September 10, October 9 and 12, 1934; Richmond *Planet*, August 15, 1934, and New York *Amsterdam News*, August 18, 1934, both in clippings file, ILD Papers; Atlanta *Daily World*, September 17 and 25, 1934.

48. George S. Schuyler, "Views and Reviews," Pittsburgh *Courier*, August 25, 1934; *Daily Worker*, August 27, 28, September 7 and 8, 1934; Atlanta *Daily World*, August 29, 1934.

49. Davis, *Communist Councilman from Harlem*, 91; Atlanta *Constitution*, September 7, 1934.

presented to the court below the construction which he deemed to be the proper one and in connection therewith could have attacked the statute upon any chosen constitutional ground." The court also retreated from its earlier position concerning the immediacy of danger necessary before restrictions on speech would be permitted. Abandoning the idea of a "single spark," it declared that the phrase "at any time" did not mean literally that, but should be construed to mean "within a reasonable time." The court added that "it would be sufficient if he intended that it should happen at any time within which he might reasonably expect his influence to continue to be directly operative in causing such action by those whom he sought to induce." This modification did not denote an abandonment of the "dangerous tendency" rule by the court, but merely the adoption of a more flexible interpretation of that test.[50]

In a concurring opinion, Associate Justice John Bell attempted to satisfy defense objections and still uphold the law's constitutionality. Bell quoted from Louis Brandeis' dissent in *Whitney* v. *California* to show that even Justices Oliver Wendell Holmes and Brandeis maintained that free speech was not absolute, citing a passage which included the phrase "a clear and imminent danger." Arguing that even if this construction were applied to the Herndon case, Bell stated that the insurrection "statute does not fail for want of sufficient certainty." Thus the evidence and the law could be found to meet even this more rigorous test.[51]

This second rejection of Herndon's appeal cleared the way for a plea to the United States Supreme Court. Anticipating such a setback from the Georgia court, the ILD had already begun to select attorneys for the next round of legal maneuvering. Meanwhile, Herndon remained free on bond, using the time to publicize his case and various Communist causes in the Midwest and along the West Coast. Back in Atlanta, a new wave of activity by local officials resulted in even more arrests under the embattled insurrection statute.

50. *Herndon* v. *State*, 176 S.E. 620–24 (1934).
51. *Ibid.*

CHAPTER SEVEN

Red Scare, 1934

DURING the fall of 1934, Georgia officials continued their crusade to combat communism and suppress radical activity within the state. In September, while attorneys for Angelo Herndon worked on his appeal to the U.S. Supreme Court, Atlanta authorities paused briefly, then resumed and expanded their anti-Communist activities. So vigorously did John H. Hudson and his zealous associates pursue the alleged Bolshevik "menace" that they actually created a Red scare in the city during October and November.

The great textile strike of 1934 served as both prologue and catalyst to the outbreak of hysteria. On September 4, 1934, thousands of American textile workers began leaving their jobs. Eventually some 400,000 workers, half of them in the South, joined this "largest single strike in American history to that time." In Georgia about 40,000 of the state's 60,000 textile workers eventually walked off the job. Predictably, outbreaks of violence flared across the country. At Honea Path, South Carolina, 6 strikers were killed and 15 injured in the bloodiest encounter of the walkout. Georgia's worst incident came at Trion in north Georgia, where a deputy sheriff and a strike sympathizer were killed during a pitched battle. Although Atlanta experienced no serious clashes, jittery police used tear gas at the Exposition Cotton Mill to clear strikers away from a switch engine removing a loaded boxcar.[1]

1. Atlanta *Constitution*, September 2–11, 1934; Macon *Telegraph*, August 31 and September 1, 1934; George B. Tindall, *The Emergence of the New South, 1913–1945* (Baton Rouge: Louisiana State University Press, 1967), 509–11, Vol. X of Wendell Holmes Stephenson and E. Merton Coulter (eds.), *A History of the South* (10 vols; Baton Rouge: Louisiana State University Press, 1949–).

On Wednesday, September 12, in the middle of the strike's second week, Georgia's Governor Eugene Talmadge won renomination in a smashing victory in the state Democratic primary. Talmadge, who had previously refused to take any measures which might alienate the labor vote, now undertook efforts to quiet the growing fear of widespread violence. On September 14, Talmadge ordered two companies of national guardsmen to Cartersville to maintain peace and help keep textile plants open. When many of the state's factories announced that they would reopen in defiance of the strike, the governor authorized complete mobilization of the guard to head off trouble. The state's press not only supported Talmadge's forceful actions but "took the view that the strikes were fomented by outsiders who were radicals and perhaps communists." [2] When many Georgia mills reopened on Monday, the governor took even stronger action by declaring martial law in those areas where national guardsmen were on duty. Later that day at Newnan, forty miles west of Atlanta, guardsmen surprised and arrested a flying squadron of 128 strikers. The prisoners were transported to a hastily erected internment camp, ringed with barbed wire, at Fort McPherson on the outskirts of Atlanta. By Wednesday, September 19, just one week after the Democratic primary, a troubled peace had descended upon the textile areas of the state. Talmadge's intervention had clearly broken the back of the strike. By the end of the week, strike leaders formally capitulated and urged workers to return to the mills. Subsequently, the workers interned at Fort McPherson were released. [3]

It was at the strike's end that Georgia officials, repeating the pattern of so many southern labor disputes, belatedly raised the issue of Communist influence. As frustrated strikers sullenly trickled back to the mills, state officials raided a mill village in Shannon, arresting fifteen workers they labeled hard-core "radicals." Authorities reported that members of this group had been responsible for several violent incidents including the bloody clash at Trion. Adjutant General Lindley Camp

2. Atlanta *Constitution*, September 5, 6, 14, 15, and 16, 1934; Macon *Telegraph*, September 15, 1934; Sarah M. Lemmon, "The Public Career of Eugene Talmadge, 1926–1936" (Ph.D. dissertation, University of North Carolina, 1952), 179–81.

3. Atlanta *Constitution*, September 18–23, 1934; Macon *Telegraph*, September 18 and 23, 1934. The national guard was also called out in the Carolinas, Maine, Connecticut, and Rhode Island. See *Time*, September 24, 1934, p. 22.

described the suspects as "the biggest trouble-makers" the national guard had encountered, remarking that several of them could not even speak English. He also announced that Communist literature had been seized during the raid. No further details were revealed, except that the fifteen were being held incommunicado at a secret prison under martial law. Five more radicals were arrested the following day.[4]

The discovery of these alleged radicals upset many Georgians. The Atlanta *Constitution* concluded that troublemakers were once again trying to gain a foothold in the state. After blaming these "agitators" for causing much of the violence during the strike, the newspaper proclaimed: "There is only one way to deal with communism, and that is to crush its ugly head whenever it shows above the surface. It is the enemy of good government, serves no good purpose, and prospers only through the creation of discontent and the violation of law and order."[5] Although the *Constitution*'s position was not unexpected, the most surprising reaction came from W. T. Anderson, the normally liberal editor of the Macon *Telegraph*. He had tried to remain open-minded toward labor but had been disturbed by the strike. The editor's concern for the sacredness of private property, his abhorrence of violence, and his devotion to the right-to-work principle all combined to frighten him into an uncharacteristic position. In an editorial entitled "Reds at Our Gates," Anderson stated that the arrest of the fifteen agitators proved that Communists were a major factor in the growing national unrest. Blaming these radicals for instigating violent clashes from previously content workers, he declared that, as soon as their undesirable influence had been removed, workers in the Shannon area had flocked back to their jobs. To Anderson, this confirmed the accusation that Communists tried to manipulate strikes for their own advantage.[6]

Press accounts failed to reveal much about the twenty radicals held incommunicado. George L. Googe, southern representative of the American Federation of Labor, asked the United States district attorney to investigate, explaining that he had found no evidence of Communist

4. Atlanta *Constitution*, September 27 and 28, 1934; Macon *Telegraph*, September 27 and 28, 1934.
5. Atlanta *Constitution*, September 28, 1934.
6. Macon *Telegraph*, September 28, 1934. In both 1930 and 1933 Anderson had publicly defended the right of free speech, even for Communists.

activities by the prisoners. Finally, on October 3, the national guard released the strikers but still failed to provide any information. Who the prisoners were, what they did, and why they were arrested remained a puzzle.[7]

Once the mysterious radicals had been released, public attention shifted to Atlanta, where the only self-professed Communists arrested during the strike were jailed. On September 5, the second day of the walkout, police had arrested on "suspicion" Nannie Leah Young, thirty-four, and her sister Annie Mae Leathers, twenty-eight, at the Exposition Cotton Mill. The two had been distributing Communist literature, including the *Daily Worker*, to the pickets. Because authorities continued to hold the women without formal charges, white attorney Louis Tatham and John Geer initiated habeas corpus proceedings. As a result, local officials formally charged the two women with circulating insurrectionary literature. After the grand jury speedily returned indictments, Recorder John L. Cone set bond for the sisters at five thousand dollars each.[8]

The women's selection of Geer as defense counsel shocked local officials. Court observers could not remember a comparable situation in which southern white women had chosen to be represented by a black attorney. Such a move only reinforced the sisters' image as extreme radicals and convinced officials that Geer was acting improperly.[9] When the two impoverished textile workers failed to post bond, Geer and Tatham filed a motion requesting a reduction. Judge G. H. Howard took up the request at a hearing on Tuesday, October 2. In an unusual procedure, he allowed Young to take the stand in support of the plea and to talk as long as she desired.

Undoubtedly, Howard had not anticipated her loquaciousness. The outspoken mill worker delivered a rambling, poignant monologue lasting nearly three hours. Even the Atlanta *Journal* conceded that she

---

7. Atlanta *Constitution*, September 29, October 3 and 5, 1934. When the strikers returned to Shannon, a vigilante committee of mill hands chased them out of town.

8. *Ibid.*, September 6 and 8, 1934. Arresting officers stated that the two sang the "International" while being taken to police headquarters.

9. *Ibid.*, September 9, 1934; Atlanta *Daily World*, September 30, 1934; Washington, D.C., *Tribune*, November 31, 1934. Ben Davis had once spoken on behalf of a white female ILD worker in a confrontation with Hudson, but never appeared in court for her.

"graphically described the hardships of the average textile worker."
Young, who had begun working in cotton mills at the age of eight,
explained the difficulties she had encountered during her work in
numerous mills. In Atlanta she had tried to obtain relief to feed her four
hungry children, since her husband was ill and unable to provide for the
family. But what little support she received was inadequate and the
welfare workers were indifferent. In short, there was virtually no one to
whom a needy textile worker could look for deliverance. Young also
spoke of the need for black and white workers to unite and to overcome
racial antipathy. A "harangue," declared the *Constitution*. "A moving
account," retorted the *Daily Worker*. Unmoved, Judge Howard refused
to lower the bond and the two women remained in jail.[10]

Eleven days later, police in Atlanta and in suburban Decatur (in
De Kalb County) swooped down late at night on two area residences and
arrested twelve suspected Communists. Decatur Police Chief W. O.
Parker led a raiding party to the home of Mrs. R. W. Alling, where they
interrupted what he described as a "Communist meeting." Arrested
were five whites—Alling; her daughter Kay; Sarah Lee, a friend of
Kay's; Nathan Yagol, an Emory University graduate student; and Alexander Racholin, a New York City attorney—and one black man, Clarence Weaver, head of a Negro painters' and plasterers' union in Atlanta.
Yagol, Racholin, and Weaver were all held in the De Kalb County Jail
without bond and charged with attempting to incite insurrection. Police
stated that Racholin was an organizer for the Communist party and that
they had enough evidence to send him "up for life." The three women,
released temporarily, were ordered to report the next day to post bond.[11]
About the same hour in Atlanta, police raided a house at 446 Lindsay
Street, arresting five black residents and seizing a large quantity of
Communist literature. The five, who were booked on "suspicion," were
identified as Joseph and William Moreland, Fannie Hunter, Lucille

10. Statement of Nannie Leah Young at bail hearing, undated, in International Labor Defense
Papers, Schomburg Collection, New York Public Library, hereinafter cited as ILD Papers; author's
interview with Nannie Leah Young Washburn, Atlanta, Ga., September 21, 1970; *Atlanta
Constitution*, October 3, 1934; Atlanta *Journal*, October 3, 1934; *Daily Worker*, October 5 and 6,
1934; Atlanta *Georgian*, October 4, 1934.
11. Atlanta *Constitution*, October 16, 1934; Atlanta *Journal*, October 15, 1934; Altanta
Daily World, October 16, 1934; Atlanta *Georgian*, October 15, 1934; Macon *Telegraph*, October
16, 1934.

Lawrence, and Zelman Ware. Officials said additional Communist literature was found by police at Weaver's home, where they also arrested his wife.[12]

Following the arrests, the Atlanta *Constitution* congratulated the police for keeping a close watch on "outside agitators who may seek to spread their radical doctrines in the community." The newspaper suggested that, if the charges were proved, the courts should deal with the accused "in the same firm and vigorous manner in which radicals who have in the past attempted to stir up discontent in Atlanta have been handled." Stating that the Founding Fathers had not intended the First Amendment to sanction unlimited attacks on the American political system by disgruntled agitators, the *Constitution* urged that "the destructive activities of communists and other types of radicals . . . be sternly suppressed."[13]

On Wednesday, October 17, Justices of the Peace David Ansley and Neal Sheppard conducted a hearing into the De Kalb County arrests. John H. Hudson, assistant solicitor general of Fulton County and chief mastermind of the Red hunt, directed the prosecution in place of Solicitor General Claude Smith of the Stone Mountain Circuit, who was out of town. Police Chief Parker testified that all six defendants were present when officers entered the Alling home. As evidence Hudson introduced a large body of allegedly Communist literature seized in the raid. This material included copies of the *New Masses*, the *Daily Worker*, the *New Republic*, the *Nation*, *Liberty* magazine, and the *Labor Defender*. Books and pamphlets included Bishop William Montgomery Brown's *Communism and Christianism,* Pearl Buck's *The Good Earth, The Communist Way Out, Are Petting Parties Dangerous?, What Every Girl Should Know*, and *What a Woman of Forty Should Know*. Following this move, the prosecution then introduced what it said were copies of Communist party membership books dis-

---

12. Atlanta *Constitution*, October 16, 1934; Atlanta *Journal*, October 15, 1934; Atlanta *Daily World*, October 16, 1934.

13. Atlanta *Constitution*, October 17, 1934. Emory President Harvey Cox hastily denied reports that Yagol was a faculty member, explaining that in return for a tuition scholarship Yagol performed occasional duties for the chemistry department.

covered at Weaver's residence and several documents found on Racholin and Yagol.[14]

The defendants all denied being Communists. The purpose of the
meeting, they explained, had been to discuss current events, especially
the prevention of war. Alling stated that most of the confiscated material
had belonged to her late husband and that she was unfamiliar with many
of the items. Yagol testified that the papers found on him were nothing
more than a class schedule, a problem in calculus, and notes containing
quotations from General Douglas MacArthur and other authorities on
war. Clarence Weaver told the court that he had been invited to the
gathering by Yagol, whose family he had known for many years. The
two had accidentally met earlier in the day, and, when Yagol learned
that Weaver had just returned from an antiwar conference in Chicago, he
urged him to attend the discussion. Racholin, the only authentic Communist in the group, did not take the stand and tried to remain as
unobtrusive as possible throughout the proceedings. At the end of the
day's session, the justices of the peace dismissed charges against Kay
Alling and Sarah Lee but postponed a decision on the other four until the
following day.[15]

During Thursday's session, police detained an additional suspect
outside the hearing room. Authorities arrested Ralph Spooner of Atlanta
when he was discovered handing out what they said was Communist
literature inside the courthouse. Down the hall, Justice of the Peace
Ansley, after hearing additional evidence, ordered the four defendants
held over for the grand jury. He set bonds of five thousand dollars each

14. Several Emory students had to be threatened with contempt of court when they broke into
laughter at the introduction of *Are Petting Parties Dangerous?* as evidence. Atlanta *Constitution*,
October 18, 1934; "Trigonometry Problem," *Emory Alumnus*, X (November–December, 1934),
7; Atlanta *Journal*, October 17, 1934; Atlanta *Daily World*, October 18, 1934; author's interview
with R. A. Day, Atlanta, Ga., September 22, 1970; author's interview with William H. Jones,
Atlanta, Ga., September 22, 1970; Glenn Hutchinson, mimeographed pamphlet, undated, in
Nathan Yagol File, Emory University Archives.

15. Yagol's calculus problem had been at first mistaken for a secret Communist message.
Author's interview with Jones; Atlanta *Constitution*, October 18, 1934; Atlanta *Daily World*,
October 16, 1934; Atlanta *Journal*, October 18, 1934; Atlanta *Georgian*, October 18, 1934; *New
Masses*, November 6, 1934, p. 5; Mrs. R. W. Alling to the Reverend Harry F. Ward, undated, in
American Civil Liberties Union Archives, Princeton University Library, hereinafter cited as ACLU
Archives.

for Racholin and Weaver, a one-thousand-dollar bond for Alling, and a three-hundred-dollar bond for Yagol. But, at a special bail hearing the next day, the acting solicitor Roy C. Leathers asked that the four defendants be held without bond, arguing that a conviction under the insurrection law carried with it a possible death penalty. After listening to debate, Judge Davis remanded the four to jail without bond. Subsequent efforts to obtain bonds for the defendants likewise failed. Spooner too remained behind bars.[16]

While the four De Kalb defendants were confined to jail, Fulton County officials continued their own investigation of Communist activities in Atlanta. Following careful study of materials seized at the Lindsay Street residence, Solicitor General John A. Boykin made the startling announcement that his office had uncovered a secret Communist operation. Boykin declared that the arrested blacks had been operating an insurance company known as the International Workers' Order (IWO), which was a front for the Communist party. According to Boykin, several words used in the group's materials, such as *amiketos*, *eureka*, and *ki-cu-wa*, were secret Communist passwords.[17]

Boykin's chief assistant John H. Hudson and other Atlanta officials spent a busy week hunting Communists both real and imagined. De Kalb officials had discovered on Clarence Weaver an advertisement for a Negro Workers' Council meeting at the Urban League headquarters. Suspecting that the assembly might be a cleverly disguised Communist gathering, police invaded league offices on October 15. After searching the building for forty-five minutes, they left without finding any evidence of Communist activity. An irate Jesse O. Thomas, southern field secretary of the league, denounced the raid and rebuked city officials for creating an unwarranted "insurrection hysteria." Emphasizing that police officers had no respect for black Atlantans, he declared that this hostile attitude would continue so long as blacks could not vote and were not regarded as normal citizens.[18]

16. Atlanta *Constitution*, October 19 and 20, 1934; Atlanta *Journal*, October 19 and 20, 1934; Atlanta *Georgian*, October 20, 1934; Atlanta *Daily World*, October 19, 1934. While in jail Yagol kept his mind alert by playing chess and studying physical chemistry.

17. Atlanta *Constitution*, October 18 and 20, 1934; Atlanta *Journal*, October 19, 1934; Atlanta *Daily World*, October 19, 1934.

18. Atlanta *Daily World*, October 17 and 18, 1934; *Daily Worker*, October 26, 1934; Mary Raoul Millis to Roger N. Baldwin, October 23, 1934, in ACLU Archives. The Urban League

Later in the week, the Fulton County Grand Jury considered indictments against the six original suspects, as well as against John Grant, a boarder at the Lindsay Street residence, and Clarence Weaver, who remained lodged in the De Kalb jail. John Geer and Louis Tatham represented the suspects on behalf of the ILD. Following several hours of testimony, the grand jury indicted all eight on the charge of circulating insurrectionary literature, which carried a five-to-twenty-year prison sentence upon conviction. Bail was set at five thousand dollars each. When the state refused to lower the bonds, Geer announced that he and Tatham would file a formal demand for trial, forcing the state to try the group before the end of the year.[19]

In the midst of this turmoil, the case of Nannie Leah Young and Annie Mae Leathers came to trial on October 23. Immediately before the proceedings, Geer announced his withdrawal, stating that he did not wish to prejudice the women's chances. White attorneys H. O. Hubert of Decatur and C. B. Powell of Birmingham, Alabama, replaced him. These lawyers, along with Tatham, filed demurrers attacking the constitutionality of the insurrection law, forcing Judge Howard to postpone the trial. Later in the week the judge heard arguments on the demurrers, eventually overruling the defense objections.[20]

Boykin and Hudson remained hard at work throughout the month. Upon their request the grand jury prepared to call as many as one hundred witnesses to investigate local radical activity. Boykin also announced that his office might seek indictments and extradition proceedings against William Weiner and Max Bedacht of New York City, the national directors of the International Workers' Order.[21]

declined to press charges for the raid, fearing that such action might endanger their fund-raising efforts. The police also visited the Butler Street YMCA in search of Alexander Racholin's living quarters.

19. Atlanta *Constitution*, October 20, 1934; Atlanta *Journal*, October 20, 1934; Atlanta *Daily World*, October 21, 1934.

20. Atlanta *Journal*, October 23, 24, and 28, 1934; Atlanta *Constitution*, October 28, 1934; Atlanta *Georgian*, October 23, 1934; Atlanta *Daily World*, October 24, 1934. John Geer later reintered the cases in an unsuccessful effort to have them transferred to the federal district court. Not until 1963 would a federal court, faced with a similar request by civil rights workers in Americus, Georgia, agree to intervene in such cases during state court proceedings.

21. Attorney C. B. Powell wrote the ILD, "This sounds foolish to an Alabama lawyer but after my visit there I would not be surprised at anything." Atlanta *Journal*, October 22 and 23, 1934; Atlanta *Daily World*, October 19, 1934; C. B. Powell to ILD, October 24, 1934, in ILD Papers.

On October 25, Solicitor General Boykin disclosed plans to extend his war on communism across the Southeast. Boykin explained that he had drafted a model "anti-Red" law, copies of which he had mailed to prosecutors in the southeastern states. The virtue of this new measure, he said, would be its provisions to head off Communist-led disorders. According to the proposal, the mere *possession* of insurrectionary literature would become an offense punishable by imprisonment for five to twenty years. "My motive in asking passage of this bill," Boykin stated, "is to prevent the spread of Communism and to punish acts in preparation of the crime." [22] On the same day, a special session of the grand jury quizzed a long line of witnesses in its probe of radical affairs. The Reverend J. A. Martin spent nearly two hours behind closed doors with the investigators, and John Hope, Jr., son of the Atlanta University president, was questioned for thirty minutes. Young Hope had been connected with the National Students' League, an organization which Boykin labeled pro-Communist. [23]

While Hudson and Boykin busied themselves with their anti-Communist labors, opposition to their policies grew. The arrest of Mr. and Mrs. Clarence Weaver, as well as raids on the Urban League headquarters and the Butler Street YMCA, angered Atlanta's black middle class. A. T. Walden, president of the local NAACP, offered unofficially to defend the Weavers. Leaders of the local chapter discussed the situation at a mass meeting, where they disclosed that private conferences with community leaders were in progress. [24]

Both Jesse O. Thomas of the Urban League and the Reverend J. Raymond Henderson of Wheat Street Baptist Church publicly attacked the Communist scare. In an article for the *Daily World*, Thomas complained that during the present confusion the mere possession of unorthodox literature was enough to make one seem an insurrectionist. He ridiculed officials' fears by observing that it was a "sad commentary

22. Atlanta *Constitution*, October 26, 1934; Atlanta *Journal*, October 25, 1934. The *Kourier*, the magazine of the Ku Klux Klan, reported that Boykin's discoveries had "heightened his apprehension of danger to the southern social order and the peace of the territory." See *Kourier*, X (November, 1934), 3.

23. Atlanta *Daily World*, October 26, 1934.

24. Atlanta *Daily World*, October 21 and 24, 1934; Mercer Evans to Lucille Milner, November 5, 1934, in ACLU Archives. The *World* reported that ILD attorney Joseph Brodsky had been mentioned as possible defense counsel for the IWO defendants.

upon our sense of governmental security when our public officials get so disturbed they can't sleep for fear some Negro may take a Communist pamphlet . . . and overthrow a government of three hundred thousand citizens." Thomas, a keen observer of contemporary social trends in Atlanta, pointed out that the real basis "of this whole question is this fear that the Negro workers and white workers will make common cause." He sarcastically added that, if the frenzy continued, it would not be too farfetched to find even prayer meetings closely supervised.[25] Henderson also took exception to the prevailing furor. On October 27, in an open letter to Boykin, Mayor James L. Key, Police Chief T. O. Sturdivant, and the white citizens of the community, the minister warned "that the city of Atlanta is unduly alarmed over Communism" and that it was caught up in an "unwarranted hysteria." Proclaiming that he stood solidly for law and order and opposed communism, Henderson nonetheless cautioned that the rights of innocent citizens could easily be trampled by overzealous officials.[26]

These Red raids also disturbed Atlanta's white liberals. Mary Raoul Millis informed the ACLU of the situation, blaming Solicitor General Boykin for the trouble. "I think he is a fanatic," she commented, "utterly ignorant and entirely uninformed, in that he believes in the existence of a red menace, standing on our doorsteps and especially around the doors of our factories, sent here direct from Moscow."[27] But Professor Mercer Evans of Emory argued that John H. Hudson provided the chief impetus for the persecutions. In a letter to the League for Industrial Democracy, a labor-oriented affiliate of the Socialist party, he stated: "Hudson is willing to damn anybody or any organization as Communist, and is willing to throw them into prison, if they in anyway deviate from the path of the King James version of the Christian Bible, if they in any way countenance discussion of sex or birth control, or if they in any way show interest in any 'radical' criticism of the present economic or political organization of society." After commenting that Hudson strongly resented those whites who showed any respect for

25. Atlanta *Daily World*, October 27, 1934.
26. Atlanta *Constitution*, October 28, 1934; Atlanta *Daily World*, October 28, 1934; Atlanta *Journal*, October 28, 1934.
27. Mary Raoul Millis to Roger N. Baldwin, October 23, 1934, Edgar Watkins to ACLU, November 1, 1934, and ACLU to Thomas Hardwick, October 31, 1934, all in ACLU Archives.

blacks, Evans assured the LID that local liberals were actively discussing the situation with prominent citizens and that public statements in behalf of free speech would be forthcoming.[28]

In the midst of the controversy, Dr. M. Ashby Jones, one of Atlanta's most distinguished white ministers, pleaded for reason and calm discussion. Speaking at a community service in the Central Congregational Church on Sunday, October 28, he warned that a new wave of hysteria threatened to engulf the city. Cautioning that the "promiscuous and irresponsible" use of the communism issue could result in great injustice, he implored Atlantans to refrain from hasty conclusions. A week later, in his regular Sunday column in the *Constitution*, Jones charged that the Red hunt was "a terrible assault upon the spirit of American democracy." The Baptist minister deplored the fact that such efforts attempted to punish a citizen "not for his acts, but for his thoughts," and he concluded that the dearest of American liberties—free assembly, free speech, and free thought—were endangered.[29] On November 2, an interracial committee of Atlanta ministers added yet another plea for calmness and sanity. The group declared that the popular fear of Communist gains among the city's black population was "practically groundless" and that the number of black Communist sympathizers was "negligible." The committee further asserted that Atlanta blacks were loyal, patriotic citizens to whom revolutionary movements had no appeal and suggested that the best way to fight communism in the long run would be to correct "the ills and injustices upon which revolution thrives."[30]

By far the most important development came with the involvement of Emory University in the controversy. Affiliated with the Methodist church, this liberal arts college functioned as a pacemaker for "enlightened opinion" in the area, although some residents considered

28. Mercer Evans to Mary Fox, October 28, 1934, and ACLU to Evans, October 31, 1934, both *ibid*.
29. Atlanta *Constitution*, October 29 and November 4, 1934; Atlanta *Journal*, October 29, 1934. Jones was one of the founders of the Commission on Interracial Cooperation, which was organized in 1919.
30. Atlanta *Journal*, November 4, 1934; Atlanta *Daily World*, November 4, 1934; New York *Times*, November 4, 1934, Sec. 1, p. 17; *Sunday American* [Atlanta *Georgian*], November 4, 1934.

the university too liberal. The testimony of two Emory professors at Herndon's trial had been unpopular, and John H. Hudson had often complained about Dean Edgar A. Johnson's using *The Communist Manifesto* in his economics class. Following Yagol's arrest, the school once again came under attack. Upset by accusations that the university served as a "hot-bed of Communism," sixty-eight Emory faculty members petitioned President Harvey W. Cox to issue a public statement. The faculty resolution declared its opposition to communism and its belief in democracy, tolerance, and free discussion. Cox warmly endorsed the resolution, and, in an eloquent appeal, he reaffirmed his opposition to communism but condemned the curtailment of free speech. "We believe . . . that the most effective way to combat revolutionary doctrines is through full, frank and honest discussion of all questions that affect our welfare as a people," he said. Cox concluded by urging "an intelligent and calm approach to the vexing questions" of the day.[31]

Student newspapers at Emory and nearby Agnes Scott College defended Nathan Yagol. Depicting him as a popular student, a man of high intellect, and "a good old boy," the Emory *Wheel* denied that Yagol was guilty of any wrong. Instead, the newspaper suggested that his sole "crime" had been the social "indiscretion of attending a meeting with a Negro in a section where such association is generally frowned upon." To a man, asserted the *Wheel*, the Emory student body believed in Yagol's innocence. In a similar vein, the Agnes Scott student newspaper deplored his arrest and defended the right of free speech.[32]

President Cox's forthright declaration evoked much favorable comment. Writing in the New York *Times*, southern correspondent Julian Harris, advertising director of the Atlanta *Constitution*, charac-

31. Atlanta *Constitution*, October 28, 1934; Atlanta *Daily World*, October 28, 1934; *Sunday American*, October 28, 1934; Thomas H. English, *Emory University, 1915–1965: A Semicentennial History* (Atlanta: Emory University, 1966), 40–41; "Trigonometry Problem," 7–8. Among the faculty members signing the statement were Professors Cullen B. Gosnell, I. W. Brock, Mercer Evans, Thomas Govan, J. Samuel Guy, William H. Jones, Fletcher Green, and Dean Raymond Paty.

32. Emory University *Wheel*, October 25 and November 1, 1934, and Agnes Scott College *Agonistic*, November 7, 1934, all in Nathan Yagol File. Socialist leader Norman Thomas announced that the League for Industrial Democracy was prepared to do everything possible in Yagol's behalf. Atlanta *Constitution*, October 29, 1934; Atlanta *Journal*, October 29, 1934.

terized the statement as "fully worthy of the head of one of the South's greatest and most liberal universities." Harris blasted the attitudes of local officials, satirically suggesting than even Thomas Jefferson would have to be cautious with his public comments in present-day Atlanta. The official voice of Atlanta's labor movement, the *Journal of Labor*, praised the "dignified protest" of President Cox and warned that misguided prosecutions of radicals would only strengthen communism. Stressing a favorite theme, the magazine proclaimed, "A strong labor union is worth more than a whole riot squad of arresting officials." [33]

Although the stand of Emory students, faculty, and administration apparently turned the tide against Boykin and Hudson, the two prosecutors still retained sizable community support. On October 30, two days after it had printed President Cox's declaration, the Atlanta *Constitution* urged patriotic citizens to support Boykin's proposed anti-Red law. "There is no need, and should be no place, for radical activities in the United States," it asserted. The *Constitution* demanded that potential troublemakers "not be permitted to continue their nefarious activities under pleas of constitutional rights." The Greater Atlanta Post No. 390, Veterans of Foreign Wars, joined the newspaper in commending the actions of Boykin and Hudson and attacking what it termed "villainous, despicable and dastardly" efforts to undermine local tranquillity. [34]

The *Commonwealth*, an anti-Talmadge weekly political newspaper, also supported the two officials. On October 4, it began a ten-part series, "The Hand of Moscow in Georgia," which presented an amazing potpourri of half-truths, exaggerations, and falsehoods. Written by editor Reavis O'Neal, Jr., the articles charged that the "Red Serpent" had been coiling in the heart of Dixie for ten years, biding its time to strike. Party efforts had been aimed primarily at recruiting gullible blacks by advocating social equality and racial amalgamation. Moreover, because Communists had cleverly captured control of the major educational foundations (except for the Julius Rosenwald Fund), these

33. New York *Times*, November 4, 1934, Sec. 4, p. 1; *Journal of Labor*, November 9, 1934; Harvey W. Cox to Mrs. Julian L. Harris, November 1 and 14, 1934, both in Julian L. Harris Papers, Emory University Archives; Hunt Clement, Jr., "Capitol-izing Georgia News," Gainesville *Eagle*, November 8, 1934, in Nathan Yagol File.

34. Atlanta *Constitution*, October 29, November 2 and 3, 1934.

foundations served as excellent fronts for Communist efforts at southern black colleges.[35] In typical rhetoric, the *Commonwealth* warned that Communists planned "to overthrow organized government, make of wives and mothers common sexual chattels, destroy homes, break up families, and vest the very title of the family hearth in the name of a Communist government which takes orders from Soviet Russia." To the newspaper, Hudson's recent raids had graphically demonstrated the extent of this threat to Georgia. The involvement of two teachers, Yagol and Alling, was particularly disturbing. "The exposure of the tender minds of Atlanta school children to the insidious propaganda of a Communist school teacher should arouse" officials to further action, declared the *Commonwealth*.[36]

Following its investigation into Communist activity, the Fulton County Grand Jury issued its recommendations in early November. It declared that undesirable literature calling for social equality between the races had been circulating in the city. Because such propaganda "inflames racial prejudices, stirs up strife and a general breakdown of our law," the grand jury therefore strongly urged that careful surveillance of radical activities be maintained and requested that the legislature adopt those laws which would "better safeguard our institutions in this respect."[37]

In this confused atmosphere of conflicting charges, the De Kalb defendants gained another chance to tell their story. The De Kalb County Grand Jury considered charges against them in an all-day session on November 2. The defendants again denied that they had been holding a Communist meeting when arrested. Clarence Weaver repeated his earlier statement that he had attended the gathering only at Yagol's special invitation. Defense attorneys stressed the harmlessness of the seized literature. To the surprise of most observers, the grand jury listened sympathetically to these explanations, then voted not to indict any of the defendants.[38] This unexpected decision came as a major

35. *Commonwealth*, October 18, 1934.
36. *Ibid.*, October 25 and November 1, 1934.
37. Atlanta *Constitution*, November 3, 1934; Atlanta *Daily World*, November 3, 1934.
38. Atlanta *Constitution*, November 3, 1934; Atlanta *Daily World*, November 3, 1934; Atlanta *Journal*, November 3, 1934; Atlanta *Georgian*, November 3, 1934; *Daily Worker*, November 6, 1934. Edgar Watkins wrote the preceding day that he had learned that the grand jury

setback for Boykin and Hudson's crusade against communism. Sensing the shift in public opinion, the prosecutors began to soften their attacks. On Thursday, one day before the grand jury action, the solicitor's office had permitted John Grant, one of the Atlanta defendants, to be released on his own recognizance. On Saturday, following a conference with John Geer, Hudson agreed to reduce the bonds of four Atlanta defendants, which they subsequently met. Their trial was postponed indefinitely.[39]

The Emory *Wheel* applauded the grand jury action, terming it a "sharp rebuke" to local authorities. The newspaper added that a great injustice had been done to Emory's reputation. When cornered by friends, a shaken Yagol declared, "I guess the only thing a student can do is to drop all interest in anything that isn't just so. . . . I used to think this was a free country, but I know better now." Hunt Clement, Jr., an Emory graduate and political columnist for the Gainesville *Eagle*, also praised the decision. "The refusal of the county grand jury to indict is a sufficient answer to the particular ravings of Solicitor Boykin," he stated, remarking that Boykin and his staff had simply gone crazy on the subject of communism.[40]

Although the grand jury decision delighted Alling, it did not end her problems. Upon her arrest, she had been fired from her substitute teaching post, but her vindication in court did nothing to remedy this

might refuse to return indictments. See Edgar Watkins to ACLU, November 1, 1934, in ACLU Archives. Racholin, the only authentic Communist arrested on the raids, later inherited a prosperous real estate business in New York City and left the party.

39. Atlanta *Daily World*, November 4, 6, and 7, 1934; Atlanta *Journal*, November 7, 1934; Atlanta *Constitution*, November 2 and 7, 1934. John Grant was merely a boarder at the Lindsay Street residence and had no dealings with the IWO. Because of his injudicious choice of residence, Grant spent ten days in jail. Zelman Ware also had no connection with the IWO; neither did William Moreland, Joseph Moreland's son. The entire proof of Lucille Lawrence's radical activities consisted of an application for IWO membership found in her room. See C. B. Powell to the ILD, October 24, 1934, in ILD Papers.

40. Emory University *Wheel*, November 7, 1934, and Hunt Clement, Jr., "Capitol-izing Georgia News," Gainesville *Eagle*, November 8, 1934, both in Nathan Yagol File. Yagol and Emory University experienced one more brief furor over communism in February, 1935, when Yagol tried to speak to a group of Oglethorpe University students. When he arrived on the campus, nearly one hundred athletes blocked his path and forced him to leave without giving his speech. Oglethorpe President Thornwell Jacobs termed the affair "a refreshing exhibition of good, old-fashioned American patriotism." The Gainesville *Eagle* saw a different moral, sarcastically commenting that "Oglethorpe football players ought to be ready at all times to protect their Alma Mater from anybody who has learned to think." See Emory *Wheel*, February 7, 1935, and Gainesville *Eagle*, February 14, 1935, both in Nathan Yagol File.

situation. Despite pleas from ministers Witherspoon Dodge and Claud Nelson and labor leader A. Steve Nance, school officials refused to place her name back on the list of approved substitute teachers. Moreover, De Kalb officials refused to return her late husband's papers. Inquiries by a procession of liberals and even the ACLU over the next two years failed to modify these authorities' intransigence. [41]

Unable to obtain employment and shadowed by police, Alling returned to Emory to work on a master's degree. In May, 1935, though, President Cox informed her that she would not be permitted to register for the fall semester, citing numerous complaints against her alleged propagandizing at the school. Apparently Cox feared that the university would be seriously harmed by new rumors that the school continued to harbor Communists. These developments disillusioned her. "This whole affair seems more like a nightmare than like reality," she wrote Roger Baldwin. "I can sympathize now with Communists," she said in a despondent letter. "If I am treated like an outcast and criminal when I have done the little I have, think how cruel they would be to a regular Communist." Eventually Emory relented and permitted her to enroll again, but as of December, 1936, she had not been able to regain her teaching position. [42]

The halting of Boykin's prosecutions delighted area liberals. Optimistically, the Reverend M. Ashby Jones told the ACLU that the next step would be to press for repeal of the insurrection law itself. But Mercer Evans cautioned against this move, doubting that liberals could even prevent enactment of Boykin's proposed anti-Communist law. Although he reported that there was a possibility "that Talmadge would veto it at the instigation of his close political supporter, W. T. Anderson," Evans was skeptical concerning the long-term influence of Atlanta liberals. [43]

41. Mrs. R. W. Alling to Lucille Milner, November 6 and 15, 1934, July 11, and September 23, 1935, Milner to Alling, November 9, 1934, Witherspoon Dodge to Roger N. Baldwin, October 8, 1935, and A. Steve Nance to Milner, November 27, 1936, all in ACLU Archives.
42. Mrs. R. W. Alling to Roger N. Baldwin, October 15 and 21, 1935, Alling to ACLU, January 9, December 11 and 16, 1936, Alling to Lucille Milner, June 10, July 6 and 13, 1936, all *ibid*. Actually there was little political activity at Emory during those years by either faculty or students. Mercer Evans was one of the few activists on campus. Author's interview with Day.
43. M. Ashby Jones to Lucille Milner, November 12, 1934, and Mercer Evans to Milner, November 5, 1934, both in ACLU Archives.

Though forced to modify his strategy, John H. Hudson did not undergo any change of heart. On November 22 he told the Junior Chamber of Commerce, "There's nothing the Communists can do to stop me from exposing them short of putting me under the sod." Hudson asserted that Communists were working to undermine the home, marriage, and the American economic system. Apparently a few chamber members remained skeptical, because Hudson invited the group to the courthouse to study his collection of confiscated Communist literature. The Atlanta *Constitution* also remained unmoved by liberal protests. Later in the month it attributed the lack of Communist success in Georgia to the firm action of local courts and law enforcement officials. "There is no difference in law violation, whether committed by known criminals or by radical malcontents operating under the disguise of political crusaders," it declared.[44]

Evidence came in mid-November that the Communist scare had not completely subsided in Georgia. Officials at Brenau College, a women's college in Gainesville, informally proposed that a former congresswoman, Jeannette Rankin, be invited to fill a "chair of peace" at the school. Upon learning of the idea, Kenneth Murrell, commander of the American Legion Atlanta Post No. 1, quickly condemned the suggestion as "un-American" and tending to promote Communistic ideas. He also declared that Rankin was unfit to hold such a position. Although the establishment of a peace chair was not a likely possibility, given Brenau's shaky finances, it was more than enough to frighten nervous Legionnaires. During the next month they issued numerous protests in a running battle with Brenau President Dr. Haywood Pierce, Sr., but the legion's crude efforts won little popular following. Even the Atlanta *Journal* observed, "It is hard to see anything 'un-American' in such a proposal."[45]

The failure of the peace chair controversy to spark widespread indignation demonstrated public surfeit with the Communist issue. It did

44. Atlanta *Journal*, November 23, 1934; Atlanta *Constitution*, November 18 and 26, 1934.
45. Atlanta *Journal*, November 15, 22, and 30, 1934; Atlanta *Constitution*, October 27, November 15 and 16, 1934; New York *Times*, December 16, 1934, Sec. 4, p. 6; Emory University *Wheel*, November 22, 1934; *Sunday American*, December 23, 1934; Hannah Josephson, *Jeannette Rankin* (Indianapolis: Bobbs-Merrill, 1974), 135–37. Rankin later won a libel suit over these charges.

not mean, however, that the general public had been converted to the causes of free speech and free inquiry. Although the antics of Boykin and Hudson had been momentarily checked, both men still retained considerable power and influence within the area. Hence there was no assurance that similar incidents would not occur in the future. Hunt Clement, Jr., writing in the weekly Gainesville *Eagle*, summed up the significance of the De Kalb prosecutions in words that applied equally well to the entire Red scare: "The case of the State versus Nathan Yagol is the opening gun in a battle that will be fought throughout the South whenever the old order tests lances with the new. The new order demands, in the prophetic words of Dr. Cox, 'tolerance and free discussion.' The old order, as exemplified by the John A. Boykins, demands suppression and terrorism." [46] Yet, despite this setback, the "old order" was far from defeated, as the following years would clearly show.

46. Hunt Clement, Jr., "Capitol-izing Georgia News," Gainesville *Eagle*, November 8, 1934, in Nathan Yagol File.

CHAPTER EIGHT
The Supreme Court Evades a Ruling

WHILE the Red scare raged in Atlanta, the ILD began preparing for its appeal of the Angelo Herndon case to the United States Supreme Court. On behalf of the ILD, which was particularly interested in obtaining distinguished legal counsel for the appeal, lawyer Carol Weiss King, an independent-minded leftist, sounded out several experienced attorneys about the possibility of arguing the case. She first approached Jerome Michael, professor of law at Columbia University and a native Georgian. Although sympathetic to the idea of challenging the constitutionality of the Georgia insurrection statute, previous commitments forced him to decline the offer. Then she contacted Walter Gellhorn, a twenty-eight-year-old Columbia law professor, who agreed to serve and promptly departed for Atlanta in August, 1934. There he and local attorney W. A. Sutherland prepared papers requesting a rehearing from the Georgia Supreme Court, setting in motion a new round of legal efforts in the Herndon case.[1]

Upon returning to New York, Gellhorn discussed the proceedings with Whitney North Seymour, under whom he had briefly served in the solicitor general's office in Washington, D.C. Seymour, a dedicated civil libertarian, accepted a subsequent invitation to head the appeal. He then asked Gellhorn and Herbert Wechsler, another young Columbia law professor, to help with preparing the briefs. However, Seymour

---

1. Reminiscences of Roger N. Baldwin, 139–40, in Oral History Collection, Nicholas M. Butler Library, Columbia University; Walter Gellhorn to the author, May 6, 1970; author's interview with Walter Gellhorn, New York, N.Y., September 10, 1970; author's interview with Howard N. Meyer, New York, N.Y., September 4, 1970.

made it clear to the ILD that he alone would be responsible for the final decisions on legal strategy. As plans for the appeal to the U.S. Supreme Court went ahead, Seymour asked Sutherland if he and his partner Elbert P. Tuttle would be willing to assist, thus bolstering the defense by the presence of Atlanta attorneys. Sutherland readily accepted, completing the staff arrangements for the next two years.[2]

In Seymour, who later served as president of the American Bar Association, the ILD obtained the services of a brilliant legal strategist. Graduating from the University of Wisconsin at age nineteen and the Columbia Law School at twenty-two, he joined in 1923 the prestigious New York City law firm of Simpson, Thacher, and Bartlett. Eight years later, Thomas Thacher, then U.S. solicitor general under President Herbert Hoover, brought Seymour to Washington as his top assistant. A Republican and an Episcopalian, Seymour might have seemed an unlikely candidate to defend a black Communist from Georgia. But his dedication to the preservation of civil liberties and his strong belief that lawyers should defend unpopular causes and clients motivated his involvement. Moreover, Seymour became convinced not only of Herndon's innocence but also of the physical dangers in a chain gang sentence. Because of his concern, he volunteered to work without fee. The ILD agreed to bear the court costs and miscellaneous expenses. In their preparations, Seymour and his associates concentrated on attacking the constitutionality of the Georgia insurrection statute, declining to pursue the earlier challenge to the jury system. The ILD concurred in this decision and neither interfered with Seymour's handling of the proceedings nor attempted to manipulate the defense attorneys. Seymour further insisted that the case be handled as a legal matter without any attempted pressure on the courts. The ILD readily agreed and directed its mass pressure campaign mainly at Georgia political officials, especially Governor Eugene Talmadge.[3]

Walter Gellhorn and Herbert Wechsler, who assisted Seymour on

2. Author's interview with Whitney North Seymour, New York, N.Y., September 8, 1970; author's interview with Gellhorn; "Whitney North Seymour," *Current Biography, 1961* (New York: H. W. Wilson, 1961), 417–18; ILD press release, August 31, 1934, in International Labor Defense Papers, Schomburg Collection, New York Public Library, hereinafter cited as ILD Papers.

3. Author's interview with Seymour; *News-Week*, April 20, 1935, p. 25; "Whitney North Seymour," 417–19.

the various briefs during the next two years, brought to the defense team keen legal minds. After an outstanding record at Columbia Law School, Gellhorn had worked in the U.S. solicitor general's office for two years before joining the Columbia faculty in 1933 at age twenty-seven. A native of New York City, Wechsler received his law degree from Columbia in 1931, where he edited the *Columbia Law Review*. After a stint as legal clerk to Justice Harlan Fiske Stone, he joined the Columbia faculty in 1933 at the age of twenty-four. Gellhorn and Wechsler likewise served without fee.[4]

W. A. Sutherland and Elbert P. Tuttle provided Herndon with two talented lawyers from a prominent Atlanta firm. More important, their high community standing added locally a degree of respectability to Herndon's case which it had not previously possessed. A native of Georgia, Sutherland graduated from Harvard Law School in 1917. He worked for two years as legal secretary to Justice Louis Brandeis before opening his practice in Atlanta. Will W. Alexander of the Commission on Interracial Cooperation and President Buell G. Gallagher of Talladega College in Alabama both were impressed by Sutherland's devotion to civil liberties. Gallagher wrote Walter White of the NAACP that Sutherland appeared possessed "by a kind of fanatical passion for free speech." If any man in Atlanta could gain the confidence of the Georgia courts while successfully fighting the insurrection statute, Gallagher declared, it would be Sutherland. Tuttle, a graduate of Cornell Law School, was equally talented. He had assisted black attorney A. T. Walden and other liberal lawyers in obtaining a new trial for controversial black defendant John Downer in 1931 and was quite concerned with the problems of Negro defendants in southern courts. Both he and Sutherland felt that Herndon's race had been largely responsible for his conviction.[5]

While Herndon and his attorneys waited for the U.S. Supreme Court to reconvene, Georgia legislators early in 1935 took up the matter of

4. Author's interview with Gellhorn. Both men earned numerous honors during their careers at Columbia.
5. Reminiscences of Will W. Alexander, 207a–208a, in Oral History Collection; Buell G. Gallagher to Walter White, December 3, 1935, in National Association for the Advancement of Colored People Papers, Library of Congress, hereinafter cited as NAACP Papers; author's interview with Elbert P. Tuttle, Atlanta, Ga., September 22, 1970.

Solicitor General John A. Boykin's model anti-Red law. In the House, Representatives William B. Hartsfield and Bond Almand from Atlanta introduced the sedition bill eagerly desired by Boykin. Not regarded as a major piece of legislation, the bill slowly made its way through legislative channels. When John Geer sought permission to speak before the House in opposition to the proposed act, he was told he couldn't unless he paid a $250 fee. Meanwhile, both the House and Senate considered additional bills aimed at prohibiting the Communist party from obtaining a place on the Georgia ballot.[6]

Finally in March, the legislature acted on both proposals. On March 14, the House adopted the Hartsfield-Almand sedition bill by a unanimous vote of 104 to 0. It subsequently passed the Senate with equal ease. Designed to supplement the infamous insurrection law, the bill warned that "many and diversified attempts are being made to spread seditious doctrines among the people of this state." After defining sedition as writings, publications, or other efforts at eventually encouraging individuals to use force against the government, the legislature fixed punishment at five to twenty years in prison. Another section of the bill struck at the circulation of dangerous publications. The measure declared it unlawful for a person to possess, *with intent to circulate*, any seditious literature. The possession of five or more copies of such material, stated the act, would constitute prima facie evidence of intent to circulate. Violation of this section carried a penalty of one to ten years.[7]

Initially, the Senate and House approved different versions of the separate anti-Communist party act. On March 15, the Senate passed by a vote of 28 to 0 its draft of the bill. The House eventually relented and accepted this version on March 21. In final form, the proposal sought "to discourage, regulate and control communistic activities in Georgia by prohibiting the recognition of political parties advocating communism or similar theories." It declared that no political party that

6. *Journals of the Ten Days Special Session and the Regular Session of the House of Representatives of the State of Georgia, 1935* (Atlanta: Stein Printing Co., 1935), 578, 683, 685, 910, hereinafter cited as *House Journals*; John Geer to Anna Damon, January 21, 1935, in ILD Papers; *Daily Worker*, January 9, 20, and February 4, 1935. Hartsfield served as mayor of Atlanta from 1937 to 1962. Elected as a conservative, in time he became a liberal.

7. *House Journals*, 2407–10; Atlanta *Constitution*, March 15 and 29, 1935.

advocated the overthrow of the government by force or violence or that carried on a program of sedition or treason against the state would be allotted a place on the ballot.[8]

Following the session's conclusion on March 23, Governor Talmadge began signing into law those bills of which he approved. But he also vetoed several measures, including, to the surprise of many, both the sedition bill and the anti-Communist party act. On each he wrote, "The purpose of the bill is good but it could be easily misconstrued and could infringe on the right of free speech." Despite requests for clarification of his decision, Talmadge remained silent, and he never issued a formal veto message. Several months later the governor did tell a visiting delegation that he had acted to protect freedom of the press and free speech, but that was the extent of his explanation.[9] Talmadge's move puzzled local liberals. Doubtful of any sincere commitment to civil liberties by the governor, O. E. Petry, secretary-treasurer of the Georgia Federation of Labor, speculated to the ACLU that the governor's real motive had been to strike at the bill's chief advocate, John A. Boykin, a bitter political rival. Petry warned that Talmadge was noted "for his consistency in one area, that is, he consistently double-crosses everyone he has contact with." The Reverend Claud Nelson, southern secretary of the Fellowship of Reconciliation, likewise reported that the governor's veto indicated no conversion to liberalism. He agreed with Petry that Talmadge's main aim had been to rob Boykin of credit for sponsoring the bills.[10]

As the date for Herndon's hearing before the United States Supreme Court approached, there was some evidence that his plea might receive a favorable hearing. On February 15, 1935, the court had listened to arguments concerning the famous Scottsboro case, which featured an

8. *Journals of the Ten-Days Special Session and the Regular Session of the Senate of the State of Georgia, 1935* (Atlanta: Stein Printing Co., 1935), 1108–1109, 1158, 1397, 1447; *House Journals*, 2513, 2696, 2874.

9. Atlanta *Constitution*, March 29 and August 3, 1935; Roger N. Baldwin to Eugene Talmadge, April 9, 1935, in American Civil Liberties Union Archives, Princeton University Library, hereinafter cited as ACLU Archives.

10. O. E. Petry to Samuel Paul Puner, April 12, 1935, and Claud Nelson to Roger N. Baldwin, April 24, 1935, both in ACLU Archives.

attack on the Alabama jury system by controversial New York City attorney Samuel Leibowitz. Subsequently, on April 1, Chief Justice Charles Evans Hughes delivered the court's judgment. This landmark decision invalidated the conviction of Clarence Norris on grounds that the systematic exclusion of blacks from jury service deprived a black defendant of equal protection of law under the Fourteenth Amendment.[11] Contemporaries viewed the decision not only as a significant advance for blacks but also as a great triumph for the ILD and a brilliant personal victory for Leibowitz. Anna Damon of the ILD optimistically predicted, "Our victory in the Scottsboro case points the road for victory in the Herndon case." Her rhetoric, though exaggerated, was not without basis in fact. Even though Herndon's attorneys had not followed through with the original attacks on the Fulton County jury system, feeling that they had a stronger case against the constitutionality of the insurrection law, the Scottsboro decision offered them hope that perhaps the court was becoming more sympathetic to the problems of black defendants in southern courts.[12]

The *New Republic*, which had taken only slight notice of the Herndon case heretofore, now saw the matter as one of utmost concern. In an April 10 editorial, the magazine proclaimed, "Few cases in American jurisprudence have been of greater importance than the appeal of Angelo Herndon." Since the affair was really a test case for the numerous nationwide attempts to legislate against any form of radicalism, the appeal assumed added significance for the *New Republic*. Should the Supreme Court uphold the verdict, the magazine asserted, "a heavy blow will have been struck at civil liberties." But a decision in

11. Loren Miller, *The Petitioners: The Story of the Supreme Court of the United States and the Negro* (New York: Pantheon, 1966), 265–66; Dan T. Carter, *Scottsboro: A Tragedy of the American South* (Baton Rouge: Louisiana State University Press, 1969), 319–24. Although its significance was not fully recognized immediately, this ruling greatly advanced the legal status of blacks in the long run, not only for the precedent involved but also because it represented a vital shift by the court to a more sympathetic attitude toward civil rights.

12. Author's interview with Seymour; author's interview with Gellhorn; *Daily Worker*, April 6, 1935. Seymour preferred to strike at the insurrection law itself, rather than the jury system, since a successful appeal would virtually end all future prosecutions under that law. The favorable Scottsboro decision, which most legal observers had not anticipated, merely granted the defendants a new trial, rather than fully freeing them. The distinction was crucial, since Alabama officials were determined to convict the youths at any cost. Moreover, the jury issue was less clear-cut in the Herndon case than in the Scottsboro case.

Herndon's favor would be "an equally devastating blow . . . struck at the forces of reaction." [13]

On Friday, April 12, 1935, the Supreme Court assembled to hear arguments on *Herndon* v. *Georgia*. At exactly 2:30 P.M., the nine black-robed justices filed into the chamber and seated themselves in their large black-leather chairs. In the middle of the first row of seats normally reserved for spectators sat Angelo Herndon, intently following the proceedings. After sympathizers and sightseers quickly filled the remaining seats in the small courtroom, Whitney North Seymour calmly rose to present Herndon's case. The lanky attorney stressed that the Georgia insurrection law, as construed by the Georgia Supreme Court, violated the due process clause of the Fourteenth Amendment. He explained that the statute unreasonably restricted constitutional protection of free speech through its failure to conform to the "clear and present danger" test formulated by Justice Oliver Wendell Holmes in his famous *Schenck* v. *United States* opinion. [14] As the justices listened, Seymour asserted that the constitutional objections had indeed been properly raised in earlier proceedings through the petition for a rehearing to the state supreme court. All in all, he presented an eloquent plea for the protection of free speech and other civil liberties. [15]

J. Walter LeCraw, assistant solicitor of Fulton County, represented the state of Georgia. In contrast to Seymour's smooth approach, the slightly built, middle-aged prosecutor delivered an emotional oration, dramatizing his points with sweeping gestures which seemed to irritate the justices slightly. LeCraw declared that the Communists sought to create a "Negro Nation" out of the Black Belt of the South. He maintained that the insurrection statute did not violate the constitution and was entirely consistent with the "dangerous tendency" test laid down by the U.S. Supreme Court in *Gitlow* v. *New York*. His most convincing point was the charge that the court was without jurisdiction because the constitutional issues had not been raised at the appropriate

13. "The Herndon Case," *New Republic*, April 10, 1935, pp. 230–31.

14. *Schenck* v. *United States*, 249 U.S. 47 (1919). Wrote Holmes, "The question in every case is whether the words used are used in such circumstances and are of such a nature as to create a clear and present danger that they will bring about the substantive evils that Congress has a right to prevent."

15. *Daily Worker*, April 13 and 16, 1935; *News-Week*, April 20, 1935, p. 25; letter by Angelo Herndon in *Nation*, May 8, 1935, pp. 540–41.

time. He pointed out that Herndon's lawyers had originally challenged the constitutionality of the statute at a pretrial hearing through a demurrer to the indictment, which the trial judge had dismissed. Subsequently, in the bill of errors presented to the Georgia Supreme Court, the defense had cited the earlier action as reversible error. But the defense had not taken exception to the trial judge's ruling immediately or while the suit was pending, as called for by state criminal procedure. As a result, the state court had properly overruled the complaint. LeCraw asserted that, because of this setback, Herndon's attorneys had indirectly reintroduced the constitutionality issue again by attacking the state court's ruling. Since this was just a subterfuge, LeCraw urged the court to dismiss the appeal for want of jurisdiction.[16]

The printed briefs elaborated on the legal points in contention. Seymour's brief sketched the legal evolution of the insurrection law, noting that it had been originally aimed at slave revolts. Seymour denied the state's accusation that Herndon had advocated the use of violence. He also contended that Herndon possessed only single copies of several of the controversial pamphlets, such as Brown's *Communism and Christianism,* which indicated that the items were for personal study, not mass circulation. The most vital point immediately at stake was whether the issue of the insurrection law's constitutionality had been properly raised. Here Herndon's attorneys were on shaky ground. As Walter Gellhorn later admitted, they had patched the appeal together as best they could following the clumsy introduction of constitutional issues at the original trial. Although the defense attorneys were satisfied that they had established a solid case, their points were not as clear-cut as they would have preferred. Had the constitutional issues been more skillfully handled originally by Geer and Davis, Herndon's chances for a favorable ruling would have been enhanced.[17]

The major substantive point raised by Seymour and his associates

16. *Ibid.*; Brief for the Appellee, *Herndon* v. *Georgia*, U.S. Supreme Court, October term, 1934, No. 665, copy in law office of Sutherland, Asbill, and Brennan, Atlanta, Ga. Angelo Herndon, *Let Me Live* (New York: Arno Press, 1969), 311–12. Communist accounts claimed that LeCraw slipped in his first reference to Negroes and used the word *niggers*. Afterwards he carefully referred to "Negras."

17. Brief for the Appellant, 23–39, 47–59, Brief for the Appellee, *Herndon* v. *Georgia*, copy in law office of Sutherland, Asbill, and Brennan; author's interview with Gellhorn; author's interview with Seymour.

centered on the clear and present danger test for infringements of free speech. As formulated by Justice Holmes in the classic free speech case of *Schenck* v. *United States* (1919), the test required that in order to curtail the First Amendment's guarantee of free speech there must be a "clear and present danger" to the state. Herndon's attorneys argued that the Georgia statute, as construed by the Georgia Supreme Court, violated this test; hence the law should be declared unconstitutional.[18]

The brief for the state of Georgia countered by declaring that the Supreme Court had never adhered to the clear and present danger test as a fixed principle. Instead it had followed the dangerous tendency test defined in the decision of *Gitlow* v. *New York* (1925), which permitted states to restrict and punish utterances that had a "dangerous tendency" which might eventually lead to violence against the state. The state brief cited majority decisions in several other significant cases following the *Schenck* ruling in which the court appeared to adhere to the dangerous tendency test and ignore the clear and present danger principle. In this contention, the state was partially correct. The philosophy of clear and present danger had been primarily the creation of Justice Holmes, supported by Justice Brandeis, not the entire court. Herndon's attorneys were in effect asking the court to reestablish the primacy of this earlier principle. They cleverly argued that, in both the *Gitlow* v. *New York* and *Whitney* v. *California* decisions, a *specifically defined* political doctrine had been prohibited under the more flexible test but that in the long run the principle of clear and present danger had not been "substantially impaired." Defense attorneys noted that the Georgia statute did not outlaw a specific ideology but in fact *any* language which tended to incite to insurrection, thus creating a situation different from those of the *Gitlow* and *Whitney* cases.[19]

18. Brief for the Appellant, *Herndon* v. *Georgia*, copy in law office of Sutherland, Asbill, and Brennan; Alpheus Mason and William M. Beaney, *The Supreme Court in a Free Society* (New York: Norton, 1968), 285–99; Henry Abraham, *Freedom and the Court* (New York: Oxford University Press, (1967), 157–71.

19. Brief for the Appellant and Brief for the Appellee, *Herndon* v. *Georgia*, copy in law office of Sutherland, Asbill, and Brennan. For a discussion of the *Gitlow* and *Whitney* decisions, see Zechariah Chafee, Jr., *Free Speech in the United States* (Cambridge: Harvard University Press, 1941), 318–25, 343–51. Chafee, p. 392, argues that the dangerous tendency test was "fatal to the maintenance of open discussion." Chafee's writings are evaluated in Jonathan Prude, "Portrait of a Civil Libertarian: The Faith and Fear of Zechariah Chafee, Jr.," *Journal of American History*, LX (December, 1973), 633–56.

The decision was announced on May 20, 1935. By a vote of six to three, the Supreme Court dismissed Herndon's appeal, declaring that since he had failed to raise the constitutional question at the earliest opportunity the court lacked jurisdiction. Justice George Sutherland wrote the majority decision, which stated that the original pretrial attack on the law's constitutionality had been too vague and had not been preserved by exceptions according to established practice. Consequently the issue could not be introduced anew upon petition to the state supreme court for a rehearing, unless there were unusual circumstances. Herndon's attorneys had argued that the state court's ruling was unanticipated and hence presented an exception. Justice Sutherland examined the lower court's ruling in *Carr* v. *State*, entered on March 18, 1933, while Geer and Davis' motion for a new trial was still being prepared. He concluded that the implications of the *Carr* ruling were so clear-cut that Herndon's attorneys could have anticipated such a ruling in his case and prepared accordingly: "It follows that his [Herndon's] contention that he raised the federal question at the first opportunity is without substance, and the appeal must be dismissed for want of jurisdiction."[20]

Justice Benjamin N. Cardozo penned a strongly worded dissent in which he was joined by Justices Brandeis and Stone. Cardozo argued that "the protection of the Constitution was seasonably invoked and that the court should proceed to an adjudication of the merits." He maintained that the trial judge had not only refused to invalidate the clear and present danger test but had actually required even more proof of immediate danger to the state. "It is a novel doctrine," protested Cardozo, "that a defendant who has had the benefit of all he asks, and indeed of a good deal more, must place a statement on the record that if some other court at some other time shall read the statute differently, there will be a denial of liberties that at the moment of the protest are unchallenged and intact. Defendants charged with crime are as slow as are men generally to borrow trouble of the future." Moreover, the justice asserted that the decision in *Carr* v. *State* had not indicated an unequivocal rejection of the doctrine of *Schenck* v. *United States*, for the major precedent for the

---

20. *Herndon* v. *Georgia*, 295 U.S. 441–46 (1935); New York *Times*, May 21, 1935, p. 5; Atlanta *Daily World*, May 21, 1935.

state court's ruling—the *Gitlow* v. *New York* decision—applied only to specific doctrines, "carefully defined," not to general restrictions on free speech. Warning against a "web of procedural entanglements" and arguing that the court did have jurisdiction, Cardozo submitted that Herndon amply deserved an answer to the question raised in his appeal.[21]

The Supreme Court rejection was disappointing, particularly because the merits of the case had not been considered. As had been feared, the court had used a technicality to dismiss the appeal, but this evasion was not as unusual as some critics charged. Historically the Supreme Court had frequently avoided ruling on complicated constitutional questions when it could dispose of a case on other grounds. Furthermore, the dissenting trio of Cardozo, Stone, and Brandeis formed an influential minority, one which could be looked to for a sympathetic hearing should defense attorneys eventually succeed in bringing the appeal back on a proper foundation. Plans for such a move were promptly made by Seymour and his associates.[22]

Liberal opinion sharply criticized the ruling. The New York *Post* editorially rebuked the court for sidestepping the issue, dismissing Justice Sutherland's opinion as "a mass of shabby technicalities." The *New Republic* termed the refusal to review the case "discouraging" and added that the court had unwittingly "given tacit support and approval to all the reactionary forces striking at civil liberties in the United States." The *Nation* labeled the affair "a new [Tom] Mooney Case," deploring the possibility that Herndon would be sentenced to the chain gang "on a disputed issue of procedure." It suggested that the court decision "puts a final seal of approval on one of the most indefensible examples of 'class justice' so far recorded in this country."[23] Several major newspapers across the country also criticized the decision. Even one southern daily, the Birmingham *Post*, voiced some sympathy for Herndon.[24]

21. *Herndon* v. *Georgia*, 295 U.S. 446–55 (1935).

22. Author's interview with Seymour.

23. New York *Post*, May 22, 1935; "This Week," *New Republic*, May 29, 1935, p. 58; *Nation*, May 29, 1935, p. 613. See also "Georgia Chain Gang Awaits Peaceful Demonstrator," *Christian Century*, August 21, 1935, pp. 1052–53, and "The Herndon Case," *Survey*, LXXI (October, 1935), 303.

24. San Francisco *News*, May 22, 1935, St. Louis *Star*, July 13, 1935, Denver *Star*, undated, Birmingham *Post*, undated, all in clippings file, ILD Papers. American Socialists also

Several leading law reviews rebuked the Supreme Court, especially for evading a decision on the substantive issues. The *Harvard Law Review* gently chided the court for unreasonably requiring defense counsel to have urged a less favorable construction of the insurrection law than that offered by the trial judge. More outspoken was the *University of Pennsylvania Law Review*, which charged, "The Supreme Court is scarcely to be commended for the assiduousness with which it went about avoiding a decision on the question. The court's ruling should prove distressing to those who love consistency in the law, as well as to those who cherish the rights of free speech and racial minorities."[25]

As expected, the black press universally chastised the ruling as a "miscarriage of justice." The Pittsburgh *Courier* denounced the verdict as a "bow to reaction." Although noting that Herndon's Communist affiliation had not aided his cause, the *Courier* nonetheless charged that "even had he been sponsored by the Baptist Church there is no assurance that the decision of the high court would have been any different." The Richmond *Planet* described the decision as "a judgement which is unsurpassed in hideousness and barbarity" and depicted the evasion as "revolting" and a "mockery" of justice.[26] Communist publications offered similar views. "By its decision in the Herndon case," contended the *Daily Worker*, "the United States Supreme Court stands self-exposed as the champion of lynching, the chain-gang, and the whole drive against the Negro people." After observing that the "myth of impartiality" had been torn from the court, the *Worker* warned that only mass protest could force a rehearing.[27]

---

denounced the ruling. The *Socialist Call* charged that Herndon's real "crime" had been to organize black and white workers together to demand higher wages, and Norman Thomas characterized the action as a "monstrous miscarriage of justice." See *Socialist Call*, May 25, 1935; statement by Norman Thomas, May 28, 1935, in ILD Papers.

25. *Harvard Law Review*, XLIX (November, 1935), 150–51; *University of Pennsylvania Law Review*, LXXXIV (December, 1935), 256–57. Also critical were *Columbia Law Review*, XXXV (November, 1935), 1145–47, and *Minnesota Law Review*, XX (January, 1936), 216–17. Carol Weiss King criticized the ruling, warning that the court sought to eliminate the clear and present danger test. See International Juridical Association *Monthly Bulletin*, IV (June, 1935), 6.

26. Richmond *Planet*, June 1, 1935, Pittsburgh *Courier*, June 1, 1935, Cleveland *Call and Post*, undated, Cleveland *Eagle*, undated, and San Francisco *Spokesman*, July 19, 1935, all in clippings file, ILD Papers; *Crisis*, XLII (July, 1935), 209.

27. *Daily Worker*, May 21 and 22, 1935.

The outcry which greeted the court's ruling indicated that by the summer of 1935 there existed a sizable body of sympathy across the country for Angelo Herndon. Yet, as long as the ILD and other Communist organizations saw themselves as the only progressive forces honestly fighting injustice, cooperation with liberal groups was extremely difficult. But, during the spring and summer of 1935, the philosophies of the Communist party and the ILD underwent a significant reinterpretation. Frightened by the "towering menace of fascism," especially Nazi Germany, the Communist International revised its strategy. Socialists, liberals, trade unionists, and others previously denounced as "parasites" and "social fascists" now were given a clean bill of health and urged to join the so-called united front against fascism. In this new alignment the Communist party promised to share collective leadership, rather than to dictate decisions. The Seventh World Congress of the Communist International formally adopted this policy in Moscow in August, 1935, but the change had been evident for several months.[28]

This shift in strategy had profound consequences for Communist activities in the United States. The Communist party opened its arms to virtually anyone who was antifascist, ranging from Norman Thomas to Father Divine. To the ILD, this new concept meant that it should greatly expand its cooperation with other groups in legal defense work. Therefore, in September, 1935, the ILD approached the NAACP about a broad coalition to assume control of the Scottsboro boys' defense. After lengthy negotiations, representatives of the ILD, NAACP, ACLU, and other groups established the Scottsboro Defense Committee on December 19, 1935.[29]

Events in the Herndon case had foreshadowed this change. On May 24, 1935, shortly after the Supreme Court's ruling, Herndon asked several liberal organizations, including the NAACP, to support his petition for a rehearing. He specifically requested permission to appear before the association's executive committee "to discuss with you the

28. Earl Browder, "Recent Political Developments and Some Problems of the United Front," *Communist*, XIV (July, 1935), 625–40; James W. Ford, "The United Front in the Field of Negro Work," *Communist*, XIV (February, 1935), 158–74; Carter, *Scottsboro*, 331–33; Earl Latham, *The Communist Controversy in Washington: From the New Deal to McCarthy* (Cambridge: Harvard University Press, 1966), 46–53.
29. Carter, *Scottsboro*, 332–35.

basis for united action, involving your entire organization, in the struggle against this barbarous decision." In a second letter on May 31, he begged the NAACP to make a public statement on the matter and to telegraph the Supreme Court, which was preparing to recess for the summer, urging it to reconsider the appeal. After consulting with the association's special counsel Charles H. Houston, the executive secretary Walter White informed both Herndon and Whitney North Seymour that the association had agreed to file an *amicus curiae* ("friend of the court") brief in support of Herndon if it could obtain the approval of the Supreme Court and Georgia authorities.[30]

White then hastily wrote attorney A. T. Walden in Atlanta, asking him to seek permission from J. Walter LeCraw for the association's proposed action. Then the NAACP issued a press release announcing that it intended to assist Herndon's petition for a rehearing, since it feared that he would be " 'railroaded' to a living death because of his radical activities in behalf of the underprivileged." But these hopes were quickly dashed when Walden reported the next day that LeCraw and John A. Boykin had refused to consent to the legal move. This rejection undercut the association's plans and made its future efforts uncertain.[31] At the board of directors meeting on June 10, White brought up Herndon's request for a telegram to the Supreme Court, and after much discussion the board decided to take this unusual step. Subsequently, White telegraphed Chief Justice Charles Evans Hughes, informing him that the NAACP desired to file an *amicus curiae* brief in Herndon's behalf. He declared, "The grave issues involved have vitally stirred our association and its members throughout the country and the Negroes of America now beseech the court to pass upon the law which so gravely threatens their security." Even though the clerk of the court replied ambiguously, the immediate urgency of the plea was considerably

30. Angelo Herndon to NAACP, May 24, 1935, Herndon to Walter White, May 31, 1935, White to Herndon, May 27 and June 4, 1935, White to Arthur B. Spingarn, May 27 and June 3, 1935, Charles H. Houston to White, May 25, 1935, White to Houston, May 27, 1935, and memorandum by White, June 4, 1935, all in NAACP Papers. White told Spingarn, "Both Roy Wilkins and I both feel that despite the fact that the case apparently was badly handled by counsel in the court below, the NAACP cannot remain silent." Houston shared this opinion, blaming Geer and Davis for bringing Herndon "uncomfortably close to eighteen years on the chain gang."

31. Walter White to A. T. Walden, June 5, 1935, memorandum by White, June 5, 1935, Whitney North Seymour to White, June 6, 1935, NAACP press release, June 7, 1935, and Walden to White, June 8, 1935, all *ibid.*

diminished when Justice Owen J. Roberts granted a stay of execution of the sentence until the court reconvened in October.[32]

While the NAACP pondered its strategy, Angelo Herndon and the ILD expanded their publicity efforts. The previous year the young Communist had toured the West Coast, creating discussion and controversy among blacks. Because of the favorable response, the ILD scheduled a similar tour for the summer of 1935. En route to California, Herndon stopped at Oklahoma City to address the NAACP's annual convention, which adopted a resolution supporting his appeal. In addition to Herndon's personal appearances, the ILD constructed a replica of the standard cage sometimes used to house prisoners assigned to a Georgia chain gang. The cage also toured the West, making a vivid impression on those who viewed it.[33] Another ILD tactic designed to drum up support for Herndon was a massive petition campaign, which opened in June but did not gain momentum until the fall. The ILD hoped to acquire two million signatures demanding unconditional freedom for Herndon, and such diverse groups as the Socialist party, the Southern Tenant Farmers' Union, and the National Association of Colored Women circulated the forms. What the petition campaign accomplished is not clear. Although it had no influence on the legal proceedings, this effort generated considerable publicity and acquainted thousands with Herndon's cause and the program of the ILD. Probably the campaign's most beneficial result was the new attitude of Georgia prison officials, who greatly improved their treatment of Herndon when he was eventually returned to Atlanta in October, 1935. At that time Herndon reported jail conditions to be much better than during his previous stay.[34]

32. Board of directors minutes, June 10, 1935, Walter White to Charles Evans Hughes, June 11, 1935, and Charles Elmore Cropley to White, June 12, 1935, all *ibid.*; *Daily Worker*, June 13, 1935.

33. *Daily Worker*, November 12, 14, 16, December 13, 1934, and June 28, 1935; *Labor Defender*, August 1, 1935, p. 3; Donald Burke, "It's Hard to Believe," *Labor Defender*, October 1, 1935, pp. 7–8; Herndon, *Let Me Live*, 318. For a brief dramatization of Herndon's plight, see *Daily Worker*, August 16, 1935.

34. Petition to Governor Talmadge, copy in NAACP Papers; *Labor Defender*, October 1, 1935, p. 9; *Share Croppers Voice*, I (August, 1935), 4, in ILD Papers; *Socialist Call*, July 20, 1935; *Daily Worker*, September 14, 28, October 16, 22, 27, November 6, 7, 16, and 25, 1935; Atlanta *Daily World*, December 8, 1935. Among those signing the petitions were Governor Floyd B. Olson of Minnesota, Congressman Vito Marcantonio, William Allen White, A. Philip Randolph, Roy Wilkins, Upton Sinclair, and the flamboyant black minister Father Divine. Petitions were also received from France, Australia, and apparently South Africa.

The Herndon case received additional publicity when a delegation of writers, sponsored by the leftist National Committee for the Defense of Political Prisoners, interviewed Governor Eugene Talmadge in August. Bruce Crawford of Norton, Virginia, Emmet Gowland of La Vergne, Tennessee, Shirley Hopkins of Truro, Massachusetts, and Alfred Hirsch of New York City, secretary of the national organization, composed the group. To their surprise, they found several other "visitors" awaiting them with Talmadge, including Kenneth Murrell and A. L. Henson of the local American Legion. During the conversation the governor agreed with Crawford that the Herndon case "looks like" a political conviction, adding later that he was "not so hot on political convictions" but that "commands" to free Herndon would bring no results. The group asked Talmadge to pardon Herndon and work for repeal of the insurrection law. The governor indicated that he would consider a formal application for clemency but declined comment on the insurrection law.[35]

During the meeting, Hirsch and Murrell became embroiled in a heated argument. Murrell asserted that the group had been touring the country raising funds for the Communist party and making irresponsible statements, and he told Talmadge, "Governor, these people are in the most gigantic racket in the United States." Hirsch challenged Murrell to prove his charges, threatening legal action. Following the interview, the pair continued their dispute outside and exchanged harsh words. Despite this incident, members of the group praised Talmadge when they left Atlanta. "The warm reception given us by Governor Talmadge is certainly a contrast with the attitude of Governor Bibb Graves of Alabama," they declared.[36]

In September the ILD decided to bolster Herndon's organizational support by creating a general defense committee representing various protest groups. This move had been contemplated for several months. In early July, William L. Patterson, head of the ILD, wrote Walter White

35. Atlanta *Constitution*, July 31 and August 3, 1935; *Daily Worker*, August 5 and 15, 1935; Atlanta *Daily World*, July 23 and August 3, 1935; Alfred Hirsch, "On Behalf of Angelo Herndon," *New Masses*, August 20, 1935, pp. 13–14.

36. *Ibid*. When members of the delegation claimed they had been shot at near Clanton, Alabama, while en route to Montgomery, Governor Bibb Graves had denounced their charge as a cheap publicity stunt.

that the NAACP's telegram to Chief Justice Hughes had indicated a "wish for a united front of struggle for the liberation of Angelo Herndon" but that much more than just the mere filing of a legal memorandum would be needed to effect this coalition. The NAACP remained skeptical of Patterson's overtures. Noting his suggestions of additional measures, Charles H. Houston recommended that the association "stay clear of too many entanglements," a view in which White fully concurred. Later in the year, the association would join a similar united front committee for the Scottsboro boys, but as of July it was not yet ready for such action.[37]

Undaunted, the ILD channeled its energy into the creation of the united front. Finally, on September 3, 1935, six radical groups—the ILD, the General Defense Committee of the Industrial Workers of the World, the League for Industrial Democracy, the League of Struggle for Negro Rights, the National Committee for the Defense of Political Prisoners, and the Non-Partisan Labor Defense—agreed to establish the Joint Committee to Aid the Herndon Defense. Mary Fox of the LID was named secretary-treasurer of the group, whose chief task was to create favorable publicity. In October, along with the ACLU, the joint committee issued a pamphlet explaining the details of the Herndon case. It also sponsored fund-raising rallies. In addition, the committee conferred with Claud Nelson of Atlanta, southern secretary of the Fellowship of Reconciliation, who agreed to urge southern liberals to petition Governor Talmadge for clemency for Herndon. Despite these "united front" efforts, the joint committee had no control over the legal handling of the case. But members did not complain, for they were quite satisfied with Whitney North Seymour as chief defense counsel.[38]

After opening its October session, the Supreme Court considered Seymour's petition for a rehearing. This request concentrated solely upon whether the court had ruled correctly that it was without jurisdic-

37. William L. Patterson to Walter White, undated, and memorandum by Charles H. Houston, July 17, 1935, both in NAACP Papers; Carter, *Scottsboro*, 332–35.

38. Mary Fox to friends, September 30, 1935, in NAACP Papers; *Wisdom, Justice, and Moderation* (New York: Joint Committee to Aid the Herndon Defense, 1935); "Call for a United Herndon Action Conference," mimeographed circular in Socialist Party Papers, Duke University Library; memorandum on committee on Herndon, undated, and minutes of Herndon committee, October 2, 1935, both in ILD Papers. Walter Wilson of the ACLU wrote the pamphlet.

tion because Herndon's initial attorneys had not raised the federal issue at the proper time. Seymour produced a lengthy list of Georgia decisions which he said demonstrated that there was no "appropriate action" for Herndon to have taken in the trial court to attack an expected construction of the insurrection law by the Georgia Supreme Court, even if such a construction could actually have been anticipated. The New York attorney examined the various legal steps theoretically available to the defense under Georgia procedure and showed that each was unsuited to this situation. Therefore, Herndon's appeal had been properly raised, and the court erred in ruling otherwise. Seymour's arguments were supported by the *amici curiae* brief jointly filed by the NAACP, the ACLU, the black National Bar Association, the Methodist Federation for Social Service, the Reverend Allan Knight Chalmers, the Reverend Harry Emerson Fosdick, and Rabbi Stephen S. Wise. The NAACP, which had been unsure if it would be able to file the brief, had seized upon an ambiguous reply from the Georgia attorney general and declared that the state had given its required consent.[39]

This brief, prepared by Charles Houston, chief counsel for the NAACP, concurred with Seymour's claim that the Supreme Court had misinterpreted Georgia procedure. It contended that every Georgia precedent uncovered by the *amici curiae* sustained the defense contention that a new interpretation of the insurrection law by the state supreme court could not have been anticipated. The document's arguments were concise; it did not attempt to duplicate Seymour's detailed analysis. As Houston had earlier explained, the brief would "not be of very great help on the law," since Seymour had already prepared a most thorough case. "But these briefs are important," he declared, "from the standpoint of impressing the court as to the widespread interest felt by all classes of persons and organizations in this case and with the fundamental nature of the issues in the case as related to agitation for social reform."

---

39. Petition of Appellant for Rehearing, *Herndon* v. *Georgia*, copy in law office of Sutherland, Asbill, and Brennan; Charles H. Houston to M. J. Yeomans, September 16, 1935, Yeomans to Houston, September 18, 1935, Houston to Thurgood Marshall, September 16, 1935, Houston to Carol Weiss King, September 29, 1935, Walter White to Whitney North Seymour, August 2, 1935, and Lucille Milner to White, September 27, 1935, all in NAACP Papers. Other *amici curiae* included the Church League for Industrial Democracy, the Justice Commission of the Central Conference of American Rabbis, the Reverend W. Russell Bowie, and the Reverend Hubert C. Herring.

Although the petition apparently had little immediate impact on the court, it did generate favorable publicity. The motion to file the brief was made and granted during the opening session in the new Supreme Court Building. When the names of the *amici curiae* were read aloud in the courtroom, which was jammed with high government officials and prominent attorneys, they "created quite an impression." [40]

But, on October 14, the Supreme Court denied Herndon's request for a rehearing and ordered the case returned to Georgia. Immediately Seymour began to plan new attacks on the insurrection law in the state courts. Disturbed by this second rejection, Herndon's champions redoubled their efforts while the controversial defendant prepared to surrender to Atlanta officials. [41]

Fearful that the court rejection doomed Herndon to a Georgia chain gang, the ACLU, the NAACP, and several southern liberals began quiet, behind-the-scene investigations of the best way to approach Governor Talmadge about a pardon. Walter Wilson, who in 1930 had been extremely successful in developing public support for the Atlanta Six, strongly urged that prominent southern liberals be recruited to sign a public statement affirming Herndon's innocence, thus making his cause more respectable. [42] Claud Nelson, who undertook the project, asked several well-known persons, including President Frank P. Graham of the University of North Carolina, Emory President Harvey W. Cox, Will W. Alexander of the Commission on Interracial Cooperation, and Julian Harris, the new editor of the Chattanooga *Times*, to sponsor the statement. Nelson hoped to obtain the signatures of several hundred

40. Motion for Leave to File Brief as *Amici Curiae* in Support of Motion for Rehearing and Brief in Support Thereof, *Herndon* v. *Georgia*, copy in law office of Sutherland, Asbill, and Brennan; Charles H. Houston to Mary Fox, September 19, 1935, Rober N. Baldwin to Houston, October 15, 1935, and memorandum by Houston, October 11, 1935, all in NAACP Papers. Thurgood Marshall, later appointed to the United States Supreme Court by President Lyndon B. Johnson, was also listed as of counsel.

41. At Columbia University over four hundred students attended a campus meeting protesting the court's move, and the November issue of the *Columbia Law Review* termed the denial "a flagrant and inexcusable miscarriage of justice." The journal added that the hopes raised by the court's sympathetic ruling in the Scottsboro case (*Norris* v. *Alabama*) had been dashed by the recent action. See New York *Times*, October 17, 1935, p. 11; *Columbia Law Review*, XXXV (November, 1935), 1145–47. Other protests came from the *Socialist Call*, October 19, 1935, and *New Republic*, October 23, 1935, p. 283.

42. "Call for a United Herndon Action Conference," in Socialist Party Papers; minutes of joint committee, September 27 and October 2, 1935, in ILD Papers.

southerners. Graham, an outspoken liberal who, according to one historian, "signed enough liberal manifestoes to put the South in the reformer's paradise," readily agreed. But he encouraged Nelson to concentrate on recruiting Georgia residents, suggesting that their presence on the petition would have greater impact on Talmadge. In Atlanta, R. B. Eleazer, educational director of the Commission on Interracial Cooperation, suggested that the commission also consider appealing to Talmadge for clemency. Although Eleazer doubted that such a plea would succeed, he explained to Will Alexander "that it is almost imperative that the Commission make some such statement to put itself in the clear in regard to this case." [43]

Roger Baldwin of the ACLU attained the most success in locating someone who could influence Talmadge when he approached former senator and governor Thomas Hardwick and editor W. T. Anderson of the Macon *Telegraph* about the pardon. To Baldwin's delight, Anderson, a well-known Talmadge supporter, revealed in a confidential letter that he had spoken with the governor in mid-1934, "and he indicated to me that he was favorably inclined towards giving Herndon a pardon." However, Talmadge also stated that his adjutant general Lindley Camp had visited Herndon in jail and had reported that the prisoner was defiant and insolent. Fortunately, "this did not seem to prejudice the case in so far as the governor's comment was concerned," Anderson explained. He concluded that Talmadge probably wanted to dispose of the affair but would not act until all legal avenues had been exhausted. This news cheered Baldwin, but other information proved less sanguine. Reports indicated that the governor put much faith in the opinions of local superpatriots A. L. Henson and Kenneth Murrell, both of whom were quite hostile to Herndon. Although Whitney North Seymour discounted their power, Baldwin reluctantly tempered his confidence in Anderson's influence. [44]

43. Claud Nelson to Frank P. Graham and others, October 5, 1935, Graham to Nelson, October 14, 1935, "An Appeal by Southern Citizens on Behalf of Angelo Herndon," mimeographed circular, undated, all in Frank P. Graham Papers, Southern Historical Collection, University of North Carolina Library; Francis B. Simkins, *A History of the South* (New York: Alfred A. Knopf, 1965), 607; R. B. Eleazer to Will W. Alexander, October 23, 1935, in Commission on Interracial Cooperation Papers, Trevor Arnett Library, Atlanta University.

44. Roger N. Baldwin to Thomas W. Hardwick, July 31, 1935, W. T. Anderson to Baldwin, August 7, 1935, ACLU to Edgar Watkins, October 15, 1935, A. L. Henson to Olive Blake,

Shortly before Herndon left for Atlanta, Charles Houston of the NAACP suggested to Carol Weiss King another way to protect Herndon while attacking the insurrection law. Houston recommended that one of the other Georgia insurrection defendants press for trial. At the resulting hearings, proper groundwork could be laid for a challenge to the insurrection law, as well as to the exclusion of blacks from juries. Houston also confided that the association was willing to use its southern contacts to seek a pardon for Herndon. But King requested that the NAACP defer such efforts pending further legal maneuvers in Atlanta by Seymour.[45]

On the eve of Herndon's departure from New York City, the Joint Committee to Aid the Herndon Defense held an enthusiastic rally at the Manhattan Opera House. There over 2,500 sympathizers dramatically pledged not to rest until they had united the workers of America in a successful struggle to free him. The controversial defendant gained a brief reprieve because of delay in forwarding legal papers to Atlanta, but eventually he departed southward on October 25, accompanied by correspondent Joseph North of the *New Masses*.[46] Somewhat carried away by the experience, North described the trip in flowing prose for the November 5 issue of his magazine, depicting Herndon as a great working-class hero. "This lad stands up with John Brown and Nat Turner," he exclaimed, "with the wisdom of George Dimitrov." Upon arriving in Atlanta, the two spent the night at the home of Viola Montgomery, mother of one of the Scottsboro boys, talking and listening to blues records. Finally, on Monday morning, October 28, in the

---

November 1, 1935, Baldwin to Whitney North Seymour, November 8, 1935, and Seymour to Baldwin, November 15, 1935, all in ACLU Archives. Baldwin became worried when a letter to Talmadge from a seventh-grade schoolteacher in Trenton, New Jersey, Olive Blake, asking for details on the Herndon case, was referred to A. L. Henson for a reply. The Reverend Witherspoon Dodge described both Murrell and Henson as "shyster" lawyers and Henson as a "sycophant at the feet of the Honorable Eugene Talmadge." The ACLU threatened a libel suit against Murrell in July, 1935, over remarks he made concerning the ACLU and Jeannette Rankin, but later abandoned the project. See Roger N. Baldwin to Witherspoon Dodge, July 19, 1935, Dodge to Baldwin, July 23 and 25, 1935, Arthur Garfield Hays to Baldwin, June 14, 1935, Hays to Kenneth Murrell, July 2, 1935, and Murrell to Hays, July 17, 1935, all in ACLU Archives.

45. Charles H. Houston to Carol Weiss King, October 18, 1935, memorandum by Houston, November 4, 1935, and report of the secretary, November 11, 1935, all in NAACP Papers.

46. New York *Times*, October 22, 1935, p. 15, and October 24, 1935, p. 4; *Daily Worker*, October 23 and 24, 1935; Atlanta *Daily World*, October 24, 25, and 27, 1935; *Nation*, October 30, 1935, p. 494.

company of North and attorney Elbert P. Tuttle, Herndon surrendered to Sheriff James L. Lowry, who escorted him through the heavy doors of Fulton Tower Prison.[47]

While in the city, Joseph North took the opportunity to interview the governor. Talmadge told the reporter that, despite personal reservations about the wisdom of the insurrection law, he was sworn to uphold the state constitution and penal code. Initially he declined to comment specifically on the Herndon case. But then, as North later recalled, Talmadge dramatically reversed himself.

The Governor rose and paced the room, turning to stare out the great bay window that opened on the broad plaza outside. He pivoted on me suddenly, a lean finger pointing outside. "See those streets, suh? They'd be piled with corpses like haystacks, the gutters would run blood, if I let Nigras like Herndon run loose. If that Nigra is what they say he is and is stirring up general hell, preachin' equality, he will stay in jail until his black hide rots." If there were others like him, preaching revolution, the Governor would give every Caucasian a shotgun and tell him to use it as conscience dictates.

Although North omitted this inflammatory passage from the article at Talmadge's request, Herndon supporters drew little comfort from his otherwise harsh portrayal of the governor.[48]

With Herndon again behind bars, Tuttle began the groundwork for the next challenge to the insurrection statute by promptly filing a petition for a writ of habeas corpus with Judge Hugh M. Dorsey of Fulton County Superior Court. Dorsey signed the writ, setting the date for a formal hearing in November, when the defense planned to renew its attack on the insurrection law's constitutionality. Apparently it was

---

47. Joseph North, "Herndon Is Back in Atlanta," *New Masses*, November 5, 1935, pp. 15–16; Herndon, *Let Me Live*, 322–25; Atlanta *Daily World*, October 27 and 29, 1935; Joseph North, *No Men Are Strangers* (New York: International Publishers, 1958), 80–83. Herndon's return heightened national concern over Georgia's notorious chain gang system, already under attack from various groups including the American Prison Association. Governor Talmadge defended the chain gang as a "humane way" to deal with prisoners because it removed them from drab prisons and gave them healthy exercise and fresh air. See Atlanta *Constitution*, November 1, 1935; Joseph North, "Chain Gang Governor," *New Masses*, November 12, 1935, pp. 9–12; Myra Page, "Men in Chains," *Nation*, November 13, 1935, pp. 561–63.

48. North, "Chain Gang Governor," 9–12; North, *No Men Are Strangers*, 83–86. North failed to mention this outburst at the time, later explaining in his autobiography that when Talmadge regained his composure he requested that his more outspoken comments be deleted. North subsequently helped write a mass chant for the New Theater about Herndon.

Tuttle who decided to make the plea to Dorsey rather than to another superior court judge. The young Atlanta attorney had recently served as solicitor general pro tem under Dorsey while investigating charges against the regular prosecutor, John A. Boykin, who was exonerated. At first this maneuver shocked Seymour, who uncomfortably recalled Dorsey's notorious role as the prosecuting attorney in the infamous Leo Frank case (1913–1915). To Dorsey's credit, though, he had acquired a liberal reputation during a later term as governor (1917–1921), even sponsoring in 1921 a public conference on the Negro's condition in Georgia. [49] Through his brief association with Dorsey, Tuttle evidently came to feel that the former governor would not only be fair and impartial but might even be sympathetic to the defense case, precisely because of his background. R. B. Eleazer indicated privately that he too felt Dorsey might strike down the law, since Dorsey was "quite fair-minded in his interracial attitudes." [50]

The habeas corpus hearing opened on November 12 in the Fulton County Courthouse under Judge Dorsey. At Seymour's request Herndon appeared in court and sat with his attorneys. Nattily attired in a gray suit, white shirt, and red tie, the young Communist resembled a college student. His concern was evident, though, when he placed a large volume on the table in front of him. In lettering plainly visible to the judge and attorneys could be read the title—*The Letters of Sacco and Vanzetti*. [51]

49. Hugh M. Dorsey, *A Statement from Governor Hugh M. Dorsey as to the Negro in Georgia* (Atlanta: N.p., 1921); Atlanta *Constitution*, November 6, 8, and 9, 1935. For Dorsey's role in the prosecution of Leo Frank, see Leonard Dinnerstein, *The Leo Frank Case* (New York: Columbia University Press, 1968).

50. R. B. Eleazer to A. C. French, November 20, 1935, in Commission on Interracial Cooperation Papers; author's interview with Joseph Brennan, Atlanta, Ga., February 6, 1970; author's interview with Seymour. In 1963 John H. Hudson told an interviewer that he and Solicitor General Boykin, political opponents of Dorsey's, decided to allow him to consider the petition, feeling that a liberal ruling in favor of Herndon could be used against the judge in the following year's election. However, Hudson's memory was at fault in this case, as it was the defense that had the option of making the habeas corpus plea to any judge it chose. Hudson probably had in mind a similar effort in 1936, which will be described in the following chapter. See David Entin, "Angelo Herndon" (M.A. thesis, University of North Carolina, 1963), 56. This error also appears in two otherwise useful accounts—John C. Edwards and Joseph H. Kitchens, Jr., "Georgia's Anti-Insurrection Law: Slave Justice for Twentieth-Century Negro Radicals," *Washington State Research Studies*, XXXVIII (June, 1970), 130, and John Hammond Moore, "The Angelo Herndon Case 1932–1937," *Phylon*, XXXII (Spring, 1971), 68.

51. Atlanta *Daily World*, November 13, 1935; author's interview with Seymour. The suit was

Both Seymour and W. A. Sutherland, Tuttle's law partner, spoke on Herndon's behalf. Sutherland told the packed courtroom that the statute "and this conviction places the state of Georgia in a ridiculous position before the people of this country and the world." Depicting the state's case against Herndon as "flimsy," if not "almost unbelievable," he charged that the insurrection law had been clearly designed for political prosecutions. "The ruling on this case," he predicted, "no matter from whom it may come, will be a landmark in constitutional law." [52] Seymour and assistant prosecutor J. Walter LeCraw repeated their views on the constitutionality of the insurrection law. Seymour argued that the statute not only violated the clear and present danger test for free speech, but it also was too vague and indefinite to set a standard of guilt. LeCraw defended the law, reminding the court that free speech was not absolute. As in previous encounters, the short, fiery prosecutor maintained that Herndon had plotted to overthrow the government and create a Negro republic in the South. At the close of arguments, Judge Dorsey deferred his decision, indicating that it might be several days before he would reach a conclusion. In the meantime, county officials returned Herndon to his cell in Fulton Tower. [53]

While Dorsey pondered his ruling, the Atlanta *Constitution* broke its editorial silence on the case in a hard-hitting attack on the tiny local branch of the Young Communist League, which had circulated handbills defending Herndon. The *Constitution* labeled these circulars "a challenge to the police authorities of Atlanta" and urged that "every effort should be made to round up this group of radicals who would spread their poisonous doctrines among the ignorant classes of the city." Citing A. L. Henson of the American Legion as its chief authority, the newspaper explained that what really happened in the Herndon affair was that Communists had "overstepped the liberal bounds that exist in the United States and planned insurrection and overthrow of the federal

---

technically filed against James L. Lowry, a former railroad conductor who had served as sheriff for nineteen years.

52. Atlanta *Daily World*, November 13, 1935. John Geer had left Atlanta by this time. In September, following his marriage, he had moved to Louisville, Kentucky, hoping to escape public hostility and to find better economic opportunities.

53. *Ibid.*, November 14, 1935; Atlanta *Constitution*, November 13 and 14, 1935; *Daily Worker*, November 14, 1935.

government." The *Constitution* urged that members of the Young Communist League be arrested and punished to demonstrate local resistance to such efforts at stirring up discontent. "Other sections of the country may remain insensible to activities of the reds," stated the editorial, "but Atlanta can be expected to crush this type of over-radicalism whenever it shows its ugly head above the slime in which it breeds." [54]

Three weeks after the habeas corpus hearing, Dorsey announced his decision. To the delight of Herndon and his attorneys, the judge ruled that the insurrection law was unconstitutional because it was "too vague and indefinite to provide a sufficiently ascertainable standard of guilt." He ordered Herndon released on a reduced bond of eight thousand dollars and gave the state twenty days to file notice of appeal. Perhaps hoping to offset any local white discontent over his ruling, Dorsey issued a separate statement pointing out that it should be a simple matter for the state to enact a law protecting its citizens from insurrection as well as meeting all constitutional requirements. "Many of our states have laws that have been upheld by the Supreme Court of the United States which give ample protection against doctrines such as Herndon was advocating," he said. [55]

Shortly before one o'clock that afternoon, Elbert Tuttle and Atlanta *Daily World* reporter Cliff Mackay met Herndon in the office of Sheriff James Lowry at the Fulton County Courthouse. Herndon chatted with Mackay while waiting for the necessary paperwork to be completed, noting that the jail food had greatly improved since his former stay. After Tuttle handed over eight thousand dollars in U.S. Treasury bonds, Herndon signed the release form and walked through the swinging doors into the street. Following a brief conference with Tuttle, Herndon and Mackay spent the rest of the afternoon watching a Tarzan movie and eating a hefty meal. Later that evening, Herndon departed via train for New York. As a precaution, Edward Kane, a young lawyer from Sutherland and Tuttle's firm, accompanied Herndon as far as Washing-

54. Atlanta *Constitution*, November 24, 1935. A local Communist spokesman denounced the editorial as "scurrilous" and the newspaper's publisher Clark Howell, Jr., as "a reactionary of the Hearst type." See *Daily Worker*, December 3, 1935.

55. Atlanta *Daily World*, December 8, 1935; Atlanta *Constitution*, December 8, 1935; Atlanta *Georgian*, December 7, 1935; New York *Times*, December 8, 1935; p. 1.

ton, D.C., where Louis Colman of the ILD replaced him. About three thousand exuberant supporters—including a veritable *Who's Who* of radical leaders—greeted Herndon when his train pulled into New York's Pennsylvania Station. The enthusiastic crowd followed Herndon outside and continued to cheer as he left for a reception in Harlem. Anna Damon of the ILD told reporters that Herndon would rest for a week before beginning a speaking tour.[56]

Herndon's unexpected freedom pleased many blacks, liberals, and radicals. Liberal and black periodicals generally praised Judge Dorsey for his integrity, depicting him as a "big man" who had rendered a "courageous" decision. The New York *Post* saluted Dorsey's ruling as "the first ray of light out of the miasma of Georgia 'justice' in several years." Pointing out that a similarly liberal judgment by Alabama Judge James E. Horton, Sr., in the Scottsboro case had subsequently brought him political defeat, one black newspaper thus found even greater cause to applaud Dorsey's conduct. Angelo Herndon likewise received considerable praise. In its New Year's Day issue, the *Nation* named him to its honor roll of distinguished Americans for 1935, along with such notables as Cordell Hull, Maury Maverick, Hugo Black, and Charles Beard.[57] Communists generally deemphasized Dorsey's role and exalted the influence of the united front and mass protest. The *Daily Worker* exuberantly exclaimed, "If the United Front is so powerful a force on behalf of Herndon, what can it not accomplish in the Scottsboro Case? . . . The United Front freed Herndon! Onward with the United Front!"[58]

Communist involvement in the Herndon case continued to spark debate among black publications. Several black newspapers lauded the

---

56. Atlanta *Daily World*, December 8, 1935; *Daily Worker*, December 9, 16, and 18, 1935.

57. New York *Post*, December 9, 1935; *New Jersey Herald-Guardian* (Newark), December 14 and 21, 1935, in clippings file, ILD Papers; *Nation*, December 18, 1935, p. 699, and January 1, 1936, p. 9. Among those periodicals praising Judge Dorsey were the *Christian Century*, December 18, 1935, pp. 1613–14, *New Republic*, December 18, 1935, p. 157, *Socialist Call*, December 21, 1935, Richmond *Planet*, December 14, 1935, Philadelphia *Tribune*, December 12, 1935, Atlanta *Daily World*, December 19, 1935, and *East Tennessee News* (Knoxville), December 19, 1935, all in clippings file, ILD Papers.

58. *Daily Worker*, December 9, 10, and 18, 1935; Joseph North, "United Front Opens Herndon's Jail," *New Masses*, December 17, 1935, pp. 15–16; *Western Worker*, December 16, 1935, in clippings file, ILD Papers.

ILD for its vigorous defense campaign. The Washington, D.C., *Tribune* observed that the ILD "must be commended for its conscientious adherence to its purpose to seek justice for men under the law," a sentiment fully shared by the Richmond *Planet* and the St. Louis *Argus*. But the Pittsburgh *Courier* and the NAACP's monthly magazine, the *Crisis*, doubted the benefits of Communist involvement. The *Courier* asserted that the Dorsey ruling was not, "as the Communists will doubtless maintain, a triumph of mass pressure, but rather a justification of the legal methods used by organizations such as the National Association for the Advancement of Colored People." In a famous December editorial, the *Crisis* attempted to distinguish between the Herndon case and the Scottsboro case. The magazine explained that, though a politically conscious Herndon knew what to expect from Atlanta authorities, the politically naïve Scottsboro boys had not sought martyrdom to any ideology or cause. The crux of the matter, declared the *Crisis*, was this: "Did the Communists have the right to use the lives of nine youths, who, unlike Angelo Herndon, did not know what it was all about, to make a propaganda battle in behalf of the Negro race or the theories of Communism? The *Crisis* does not believe they had that right." [59]

To courthouse followers in Atlanta, Dorsey's decision came as a "distinct surprise." Most local attorneys had felt that Herndon would never be freed except by a ruling from outside the state, a view shared by northern observers. Dorsey's ruling undoubtedly cost him some popularity, but nothing occurred in Georgia resembling the public outcry in Alabama following Judge Horton's decision for the Scottsboro boys. Although the American Legion and the Men of Justice, a right-wing group that supported Solicitor General John A. Boykin, did attack the ruling, public opinion did not become unduly alarmed, perhaps because it was clear that Herndon planned to leave the state. Yet Boykin,

---

59. Pittsburgh *Courier*, December 14, 1935; *Crisis*, XLII (December, 1935), 369; *East Tennessee News* (Knoxville), December 19, 1935, in clippings file, ILD Papers. The January, 1936, issue of the *Crisis* carried Herndon's picture on the cover, and NAACP officials were less critical in their private communications. See Charles H. Houston to Angelo Herndon, December 17, 1935, in NAACP Papers. Some black newspapers expressed satisfaction with the ILD's efforts, yet refrained from endorsing actions of the Communist party. See St. Louis *Argus*, December 13, 1935, Richmond *Planet*, December 14, 1935, and Washington, D.C., *Tribune*, December 17, 1935, all in clippings file, ILD Papers.

Hudson, and LeCraw remained as determined as ever to press the state's case. On December 11, LeCraw filed a bill of exceptions to Dorsey's decision, thereby keeping the case alive and guaranteeing another hearing before the Georgia Supreme Court. The controversy over Angelo Herndon and the insurrection law remained far from finished.[60]

60. Atlanta *Daily World*, December 8, 1935; Atlanta *Constitution*, December 12 and 19, 1935.

CHAPTER NINE
A Narrow
Victory

DESPITE the setback received from Judge Hugh Dorsey's ruling against the insurrection law, prosecutors John A. Boykin and John H. Hudson continued their antiradical efforts. Confident of a more favorable reception from the Georgia Supreme Court, Boykin and his staff raced to finish their briefs to be able to gain a hearing as quickly as possible. Meanwhile the solicitor general's office continued its surveillance of local radical activity. In January, 1936, Hudson warned members of a local right-wing organization, the Order of 21, that potentially dangerous radical efforts continued in the city. The Atlanta *Georgian*, a Hearst newspaper, photographed Hudson, John Echols, head of the order, and Kenneth Murrell of the American Legion burning stacks of Red literature. Echols told reporters that, although more than 100,000 pieces of Communist material had been seized during the previous year, local authorities had "been able only to scratch the surface." [1]

On January 25, 1936, the Georgia Supreme Court heard oral arguments on the appeal from Dorsey's ruling in Fulton County Superior Court. Solicitor General Boykin, who had not previously involved himself in the legal proceedings concerning Herndon, personally appeared to plead the state's case, thereby demonstrating its importance to local authorities. In his general arguments Boykin charged that "the doctrine of violence is inculcated in the mind of every Communist." According to him, Herndon had been convicted for advocating the armed overthrow of the state of Georgia and the creation of a Negro

1. Cited in *Daily Worker*, January 23, 1936.

republic from the South's Black Belt. Boykin added that the American Communist party "preaches overthrow of the government by force and violence." Defense attorney W. A. Sutherland countered by warning that limitations on free speech only encouraged violence. "When a man like Herndon is made a martyr," he said, "there is real danger to democracy." Whitney North Seymour and J. Walter LeCraw also spoke at the hearing, recapitulating their technical points over the constitutionality of the insurrection statute.[2]

While the state court reviewed the written arguments, local officials pursued an active course. On the night of May 28, 1936, five policemen raided a meeting at 948 Violet Street in southeastern Atlanta. When the Red squad burst into the residence, they found about thirty people packed into the front room. A "wild stampede" ensued when the occupants fled in all directions, scattering furniture and creating general havoc. Officers managed to detain eighteen suspects—ten whites and eight blacks—and arrested them on "suspicion." The next day, charges of disorderly conduct were filed. Still confident that the state supreme court would uphold the insurrection statute, officials also charged the eighteen with attempting to incite insurrection. Among those arrested were Nannie Leah Young, previously indicted under the law in 1934, and Max Singer, a local Communist leader.[3]

In addition to Communist spokesmen across the United States who predictably denounced the arrests, black Atlantans were also disturbed, fearing that these antiradical efforts were poisoning community attitudes and encouraging antiblack and antiliberal movements. On June 9, an unusually large and enthusiastic crowd at the monthly meeting of the NAACP discussed both the recent arrests and the insurrection law. Journalist H. S. Murphy told the group that any organization holding a routine meeting risked prosecution as Communistic under the law, especially if the gathering were interracial. He remarked that police used the "red flag to brand any liberal thinker as a Communist or liberal meetings as Communistic." Forrester B. Washington, branch president, observed that race relations in the state seemed to be deteriorating

2. Atlanta *Constitution*, January 25, 1936.
3. Atlanta *Daily World*, May 30 and 31, 1936; *Daily Worker*, June 1 and 2, 1936; Atlanta *Constitution*, May 29, 30, and June 13, 1936; Atlanta *Georgian*, May 29 and 30, 1936.

as a result of the insurrection statute. Urging the law's repeal, the Reverend Martin Luther King, Sr., president of the Baptist Ministers' Union, pledged his moral and financial support to such an effort.[4]

Several days later, Recorder A. W. Calloway held a preliminary hearing for sixteen of the accused radicals. Police officers described the raid and exhibited examples of the literature seized. Attorney H. A. Allen argued "eloquently" on behalf of the defendants. Following the well-attended hearing, reporters quizzed him about the origin of his retainer. Although Allen reluctantly admitted that he had been hired by an out-of-town group, he countered good-naturedly, "The money is being spent in Georgia, isn't it?" After examining the periodicals carefully, Calloway concluded that, though they were "admittedly Communistic, they did not advocate overthrow of the government." Consequently, he dismissed insurrection charges by observing that there was no evidence to demonstrate "intent to conspire to overthrow the government." But he did find thirteen of the defendants guilty of disorderly conduct and fined them one hundred dollars each. Calloway justified this action by pointing out "that mixed races were assembling in a house in which shades were closely drawn and doors locked." Three black defendants were completely exonerated when it was established that they had no knowledge of the meeting's purpose. Cases against the remaining two defendants were postponed.[5]

The following day, June 13, the Georgia Supreme Court announced its decision in *Herndon* v. *Lowry*, reversing Judge Dorsey's ruling that the statute was unconstitutional and upholding Herndon's conviction. The court concluded that Dorsey had erred in ruling the law "too vague and indefinite to provide a sufficiently ascertainable standard of guilt." The court also brushed aside Seymour's contentions concerning the clear and present danger test by declaring, "It is immaterial whether the

4. *Daily Worker*, June 2, 3, 5, 7, 9, and 18, 1936; Atlanta *Daily World*, June 10, 1936. Also criticized at the NAACP meeting was discrimination against black workers on WPA projects in the city.

5. Atlanta *Constitution*, June 13, 1936; Atlanta *Journal*, June 13, 1936; Atlanta *Daily World*, June 14, 1936. Convicted and fined were Ellie Hawks, Max Singer, Nannie Leah Young, Edith Washburn, Nina Hawks, Ruth Godwin, Henry Wilson, Jack Parker, A. A. Griggs, L. B. Browning, Martha Harris, Carrie Jackson, and Lula Jackson. A reporter for the *Constitution* asked Ellie Hawks if she took her "alleged radicalism seriously." "I most assuredly do," she responded. What about money for the fines and appearance bonds, she was asked. "The party will take care of us," she replied. "They never let their members down."

authority of the state was in danger of being subverted or that an insurrection actually occurred or was impending." [6]

Previously heartened by Dorsey's ruling, liberals, radicals, labor spokesmen, and black leaders now denounced the state court's reversal and looked to the United States Supreme Court to rectify the mistake. "The Herndon decision will come as a shock to all those who were stirred by Judge Dorsey's courageous action," commented the ACLU's Roger Baldwin, adding that an appeal would be made to the U.S. Supreme Court "at once." The St. Louis *Post-Dispatch* asserted that the opinion was "bad law" and symbolized "Georgia justice at its worst." At least one southern newspaper, the liberal Richmond *Times-Dispatch*, edited by Virginius Dabney, added its voice to the protests. The newspaper termed the verdict "one of the darkest blots on Georgia justice" and urged the high court to cleanse the stain. [7] To the Cleveland *Call and Post*, a black weekly, the court decision confirmed the view that it was "difficult for southerners, regardless of their training, to think clearly on any subject pertaining to Negroes." The newspaper prophesied that the only way progress would come to Dixie would be "through decisions by the highest court of the land." Although the Pittsburgh *Courier* agreed, it cautioned that the U.S. Supreme Court's record warranted "considerable skepticism from Negroes." [8]

The controversy over the insurrection statute and Communist advances in Atlanta spread into politics during the spring and summer. Two years earlier, Superior Court Judge G. H. Howard, a veteran of eleven years on the bench, had announced that he would not seek reelection in 1936. Assistant prosecutor John H. Hudson had declared then that he would consider running for the position. However, former county commissioner Paul S. Etheridge, who had been legal counsel for the Ku Klux Klan and was a proved vote getter, and prominent local attorney Edgar Watkins, Sr., both announced for the post. Hesitant to

6. *Herndon* v. *Lowry*, 186 S.E. 429–30 (1936).

7. *Daily Worker*, June 15, 20, 21, and 25, 1936; *Socialist Call*, June 20, 1936; Atlanta *Constitution*, June 14, 1936; New York *Times*, June 14, 1936, p. 1; St. Louis *Post-Dispatch*, June 14, 1936; Richmond *Times-Dispatch*, June 16, 1936, in clippings file, International Labor Defense Papers, Schomburg Collection, New York Public Library, hereinafter cited as ILD Papers; *New Republic*, June 24, 1936, p. 188.

8. Pittsburgh *Courier*, June 20, 1936; Cleveland *Call and Post*, June 18, 1936, Washington, D.C., *Tribune*, June 16, 1936, and Richmond *Planet*, June 13, 1936, all in ILD Papers.

take on two such formidable opponents, the ambitious Hudson soon conceived another plan. Believing that the public had lost faith in Judge Dorsey because of his ruling against the insurrection statute and his generally liberal decisions, Hudson decided to challenge Dorsey by stressing his own anti-Communist credentials.[9]

In the spring of 1936, Hudson resigned as assistant prosecutor, ostensibly to enter private law practice. His real purpose became obvious in early May when he formally declared that he would oppose Judge Dorsey in the September 9 Democratic primary. Following the arrest of the eighteen accused radicals in late May, a shadowy but clever plan began to unfold. Hudson and Boykin worked to have the trials of the eighteen assigned to Dorsey's court, apparently hoping that another liberal ruling would guarantee the judge's political downfall. Claud Nelson reported these developments to the ACLU on June 3, speculating that Hudson might even volunteer to assist in the group's prosecution. "Only one thing more could be thought of to help the scheme along," commented Nelson. "If half-a-dozen liberals would just raise their heads, and let the rabble-rousers connect their names with this example of Communist penetration."[10]

Although Recorder A. W. Calloway's dismissal of insurrection charges against the eighteen on June 12 disrupted Hudson's carefully laid plan, the former prosecutor prepared to wage a vigorous campaign. Local political observers predicted an "interesting" race. Unfortunately for Hudson, the actual campaigning produced unexpected difficulties. A poll of Fulton County attorneys favored his opponent by almost five to one, and several state races captured public attention and completely overshadowed the Hudson-Dorsey clash. In the bitterly fought contest for the United States Senate, Governor Eugene Talmadge challenged incumbent Richard B. Russell, and Talmadge's annointed heir, Charles D. Redwine, locked horns with E. D. Rivers in the governor's race.

9. Atlanta *Constitution*, November 6 and 9, 1934; Atlanta *Journal*, November 5, 9, 1934, and June 23, 1936; David Entin, "Angelo Herndon" (M.A. thesis, University of North Carolina, 1963), 56.

10. *Sunday American* [Atlanta *Georgian*], May 3, 1936; Entin, "Angelo Herndon," 56; Claud Nelson to Roger N. Baldwin, June 3, 1936, in American Civil Liberties Union Archives, Princeton University Library, hereinafter cited as ACLU Archives. As noted before, Hudson told David Entin in 1963 that they had maneuvered Herndon's habeas corpus hearing before Judge Dorsey in November, 1935. The plan, however, clearly applies to the mass arrests in May, 1936.

Locally, Representative William B. Hartsfield presented a serious challenge to Atlanta Mayor James L. Key. Solicitor John A. Boykin defended his post against long-time foe William G. McRae in another heated contest.[11] These statewide clashes, by overshadowing local races, resulted in public apathy and poorly attended rallies. The Atlanta *Constitution* noted just ten days before election time that "little enthusiasm could be found locally." Despite these obstacles and confident predictions from Dorsey's headquarters, Hudson continued to campaign. As early results trickled in on the evening of September 9, he even forged into a narrow lead. But, when additional precincts reported, Dorsey took the lead, holding it tenaciously. Final returns gave Dorsey 18,142 votes to Hudson's 16,385.[12]

By contrast, Paul Etheridge captured the other judgeship at stake by a margin of nearly five thousand votes, and Boykin won reelection by almost a seven-thousand-vote margin. Despite claims by Herndon and northern radicals that the Dorsey success represented a smashing victory over the forces of repression, the results were ambiguous. Given the odds against unseating an incumbent who was a former governor, Hudson had indeed made a strong showing. Furthermore, the overwhelming reelection of Boykin guaranteed that Hudson's partner in working against Communist, radical, and interracial efforts would remain in a position to carry on Hudson's work. Nonetheless, the departure of Hudson from the solicitor general's office removed the single most active antiradical figure in Atlanta from a position of power. Blacks, liberals, and radicals shed no tears when he left.[13]

During the summer and fall of 1936, several national organizations publicly reaffirmed their support of Herndon and their opposition to the insurrection law. The National Bar Association, comprising black lawyers and judges, adopted resolutions on the Scottsboro and Herndon cases at its August convention. The group urged the state of Alabama to

11. Atlanta *Constitution*, May 31, July 25, and September 2–4, 1936.

12. *Ibid.*, August 20, September 6–11, 1936. In Alabama, Attorney General Thomas G. Knight, who twice won convictions against the Scottsboro boys, used his record as part of a successful bid for the lieutenant governor's post in May, 1934. See Dan T. Carter, *Scottsboro: A Tragedy of the American South* (Baton Rouge: Louisiana State University Press, 1969), 273.

13. Atlanta *Constitution*, September 11, 1936; New York *Post*, November 14, 1936; Mary Mack, "We Have Them on the Run," *Labor Defender*, January 1, 1937, p. 13.

free the Scottsboro boys and commended the ILD for its "unselfish and unstinted support of Angelo Herndon." Meeting in Tampa, Florida, the site of numerous violent labor-management clashes during the 1930s, the American Federation of Labor adopted a statement on the Herndon case offered by A. Phillip Randolph of the Brotherhood of Sleeping Car Porters. The resolution condemned the insurrection law, advocated its repeal, and called for Herndon's release. The previous year the AFL had approved a similar resolution supporting Herndon.[14]

The NAACP moved closer toward joining the Herndon defense movement. The decision of American Communists to halt their attacks on such "bourgeois" groups as the association made cooperation with the ILD less distasteful. Having terminated by mutual agreement its warfare with the ILD over the Scottsboro case, the NAACP found itself in a more flexible position. Moreover, it became worried that the Georgia insurrection law would increasingly be used against blacks. In mid-July, the association's chief counsel, Charles H. Houston, recommended to the board of directors that the NAACP join the Joint Committee to Aid the Herndon Defense. Houston noted that many association members, "especially the younger group," wished to see the organization more closely affiliated with the legal defense. More important, he viewed the Georgia court's recent decision as "a crisis in the development of civil rights" in Dixie. "I feel sure that the Herndon Case is just as important as the Scottsboro Case in the long run," he said, "and that there is no more danger of the Association being compromised in the Herndon Case than in the Scottsboro Case." Acting on Houston's recommendation, the board of directors voted on September 14, 1936, to join the committee, "with the understanding that its participation will be similar to that in the Scottsboro Case."[15]

During the latter half of the year, Angelo Herndon busied himself with a variety of activities designed to promote public awareness of his case and of Communist activities. In July he visited the leftist American Youth Congress in Cleveland. Amid confusion resulting from angry

14. *Daily Worker*, August 19, 1936; *American Federationist*, undated, clipping in Angelo Herndon File, Schomburg Collection, New York Public Library.

15. Memorandum by Charles H. Houston, July 20, 1936, and board of directors minutes, September 14, 1936, both in National Association for the Advancement of Colored People Papers, Library of Congress, hereinafter cited as NAACP Papers.

cries of Communist domination and urgent pleas for unity, the congress went on record in favor of freedom for the young Communist. During the fall, Herndon conducted a token campaign for a seat in the New York Assembly from Harlem. Although he polled only 327 votes, New York residents were again reminded of his case. In December Herndon embarked on another speaking tour of the West Coast. Highlighting his trip was a visit to Tom Mooney, perhaps the nation's best-known political prisoner, in a San Francisco jail. Radicals lauded as historic the meeting of the two *causes célèbres*. Commented the *Daily Worker*, "Mooney and Herndon symbolize vividly the fight against oppression with which the American people are confronted in 1937." The Joint Committee to Aid the Herndon Defense likewise remained active, sponsoring various demonstrations and rallies, including a nationwide Herndon Day protest on November 30.[16]

In early 1937, Herndon personally carried his cause to the White House. On February 20, President Franklin D. Roosevelt granted a brief conference to seven leaders from the American Youth Congress. During the chat, Roosevelt asked each delegate his opinion of the recent proposals to reorganize the Supreme Court. When the question was put to the one black member of the group, the visitor responded, "Well, Mr. President, that all depends on how the Supreme Court decides my case." Puzzled, Roosevelt asked what he meant. "I am Angelo Herndon," he explained.[17]

When the United States Supreme Court reconvened in October, 1936, Whitney North Seymour formally requested that the justices review Herndon's appeal. On October 23, the court agreed but set no immediate date for arguments, thus postponing until the next year a resolution of the affair. Nonetheless, the action guaranteed that the defendant would have yet another appearance before the highest court in the land.[18]

16. New York *Times*, July 4, 1936, p. 13, and July 6, 1936, p. 15; *Daily Worker*, February 10, July 7, August 11, 14, September 5, October 5, 14, 21, 27, 30, November 3, 5, 12, 30, December 4, 8, 22, and 23, 1936. Earlier in the year, Herndon spoke at the formation of the National Negro Congress.

17. New York *Times*, February 23, 1937, p. 1, and February 28, 1937, Sec. 4, p. 2; New York *Herald-Tribune*, April 27, 1937, in Angelo Herndon File.

18. New York *Times*, November 24, 1936, p. 19; *Daily Worker*, November 24, 1936.

Concerned about the Supreme Court's current attitudes toward free speech legislation, Herndon sympathizers took special note when a ruling was given in January, 1937, on a case involving an Oregon Communist whose prosecution had been compared to Herndon's. Dirk de Jonge had been convicted under a criminal syndicalism act for his role in a public meeting called to protest police raids and shootings in Portland, Oregon, during July, 1934. Like the relief demonstration led by Herndon, the Portland rally had been orderly; none of the speakers had even advocated the violent overthrow of the government. Nevertheless, an Oregon jury convicted de Jonge, sentencing him to seven years in prison. "His sole offense as charged," noted Chief Justice Charles Evans Hughes of the Supreme Court, "was that he assisted in the conduct of a public meeting, albeit otherwise lawful, which was held under the auspices of the Communist Party." The state's logic was brutally simple. The Communist party advocated violence and sabotage; de Jonge was a Communist and obeyed the party's dictates; therefore he too must advocate violence and sabotage. The state never bothered to provide further evidence of de Jonge's guilt, apparently feeling that this "guilt by association" was quite sufficient. [19]

On January 4, 1937, the Supreme Court overturned de Jonge's conviction in "one of the most striking decisions of recent years." Speaking for a unanimous court, Chief Justice Hughes declared that "peaceful assembly for lawful discussion cannot be made a crime." But the court did not challenge the constitutionality of the law; in fact, Hughes observed in passing that the statute appeared to meet constitutional tests. The court deliberately chose to decide the matter on extremely narrow grounds—that the syndicalism act had been erroneously applied to de Jonge—and avoided formulation of a general rule or test for evaluating sedition and syndicalism laws. Whether Communist party doctrines were inherently seditious and whether party membership could be prohibited were not decided. [20]

19. Zechariah Chafee, Jr., *Free Speech in the United States* (Cambridge: Harvard University Press, 1941), 384–87; New York *Times*, January 5, 1937, p. 1; *De Jonge* v. *Oregon*, 299 U.S. 353–66 (1936); Henry Abraham, *Freedom and the Court* (New York: Oxford University Press, 1967), 53–54. For an account of the original trial, see *Daily Worker*, November 29, 1934.

20. Chafee, *Free Speech in the United States*, 384–87; New York *Times*, January 5, 1937, p. 1; *Columbia Law Review*, XXXVII (May, 1937), 857; *De Jonge* v. *Oregon*, 299 U.S. 353–66 (1936).

"There is something timely as well as impressive about this splendid vindication of a fundamental American right," proclaimed the New York *Times*. The newspaper went on to note that this progressive decision had been rendered by the so-called "narrow-minded reactionaries" on the Supreme Court, thus demonstrating that these justices were indeed concerned with liberty and freedom. But the *Daily Worker* attributed less noble motives to the court, cynically suggesting that the verdict represented nothing more than a grudging concession forced by the previous November's election returns. Nonetheless, Herndon sympathizers took heart, hoping that the ruling indicated a liberal drift in court policy. Certainly Georgia officials found the legal implications disturbing. The logic used by Oregon to convict de Jonge was precisely the logic used by Georgia authorities against Herndon. Both prosecutions lacked evidence that could be construed as an overt attempt at direct action or even inciting immediate action. Nonetheless, a detached observer might have urged caution, for in 1935 a liberal ruling in the Scottsboro case, purported to inaugurate a new court trend, had failed to do so immediately. Although signs for guarded optimism did exist, it remained to be seen if they would bear fruit.[21]

During the first week of February, 1937, both sides submitted written briefs to the Supreme Court. These arguments were similar to those found in previous presentations. The chief innovation was the inclusion of the *De Jonge* v. *Oregon* ruling in both briefs. Predictably, the state contended that the decision did not apply to the Herndon case, and Whitney North Seymour and his associates maintained just the reverse.[22] At precisely 12:27 P.M., on Monday, February 8, a "hushed silence" fell over the courtroom as nine justices filed in and the case of *Herndon* v. *Lowry* was called. Spectators filled every seat in the room

21. New York *Times*, January 6, 1937, p. 22; *Daily Worker*, January 6 and 26, 1937; Mack, "We Have Them on the Run," 13; Anna Damon, "The Struggle Against Criminal Syndicalist Laws," *Communist*, XVI (March, 1937), 279–86; Chafee, *Free Speech in the United States*, 387; American Civil Liberties Union, *Let Freedom Ring!: The Story of Civil Liberty, 1936–1937* (New York: American Civil Liberties Union, 1937), 16–18. The Oregon legislature soon repealed the syndicalism law. Noted constitutional attorney Osmond K. Fraenkel handled de Jonge's appeal for the ILD.

22. Brief for the Appellant and Brief for the Appellee, *Herndon* v. *Lowry*, U.S. Supreme Court, October term, 1936, Nos. 474 and 475, copy in law office of Sutherland, Asbill, and Brennan; New York *Times*, February 4, 1937, p. 14.

and eagerly strained for a glimpse of Herndon, who was seated in the front row. Among those present were ILD head Anna Damon, Joseph Gelders, Carol Weiss King, W. A. Sutherland, Ben Davis, and several representatives of Random House, which planned to release Herndon's autobiography, *Let Me Live*, the following month. The oral arguments by Seymour and LeCraw differed little from earlier clashes. Seymour told the justices that Herndon had been engaged in lawful political activity which represented no danger to the state. LeCraw stressed that Herndon wanted to take land away from white property owners in the Black Belt and give it to blacks. Waving photostatic copies of the *Daily Worker*, the Georgia prosecutor declared that as a Communist "Herndon took his orders from the Communist International, not from any American Communist party, and the Communist International advocates violence to gain its end." Despite indications of some slight amusement at LeCraw's style of delivery, the nine judges gave no hint of how they might rule.[23]

While the Supreme Court pondered Herndon's fate, the Georgia legislature considered a proposed sedition bill designed to supplement the embattled insurrection statute. Acting at the request of John A. Boykin, Senator G. Everett Millican introduced the proposal in late January, 1937. As constructed, the bill outlawed not only the crime of sedition, but even the possession of seditious literature with *intent* to circulate. The proposed statute set the penalty for a conviction under the sedition section at five to twenty years in prison, and punishment for possessing seditious literature with intent to circulate was fixed at one to ten years. Passed in the Georgia Senate by a vote of thirty-two to zero on February 10, the bill then went to the House of Representatives, where it stalled.[24]

The sedition bill's early success disheartened liberals, labor officials, and the ACLU. Former senator and governor Thomas Hardwick warned the ACLU at midmonth that no serious opposition to the proposal had yet emerged. Witherspoon Dodge, a local minister whose

23. *Daily Worker*, February 4 and 9, 1937; New York *Times*, February 9, 1937, p. 5; Atlanta *Journal*, February 8, 1937.

24. *Journals of the Ten-Days Special Session and the Regular Session of the Senate of the State of Georgia, 1937* (Atlanta: Stein Printing Co., 1937), 680, 836, 838, 932; Atlanta *Constitution*, February 11, 1937.

liberal radio program had been discontinued for what he felt were political reasons, informed Roger Baldwin on February 20 that the outlook was extremely discouraging. "The forces of darkness are in absolute control at the present time in Georgia," he wrote. Dodge depicted the public expression of unorthodox views as "suicidal," adding that he might even be forced to go underground. Later, in a more optimistic mood, he spoke with A. Steve Nance and O. E. Petry of the Georgia Federation of Labor. The two labor leaders agreed to work diligently behind the scenes to kill the sedition bill. In turn, Dodge agreed to keep local liberals out of the affair to avoid undesirable publicity.[25] As March approached, it became apparent that this strategy had succeeded. Nance and Petry convinced sympathetic legislators to keep the sedition proposal bottled up in the judiciary committee, from which it never emerged. This victory not only pleased liberals and labor leaders, but it underscored the growing involvement of the labor movement, both locally and nationally, with the crusade against the insurrection law and similar statutes. This concern no doubt resulted from labor's growing militancy and fears that such laws would be used against union activity.[26]

Nance and Petry took great pains to protect themselves against charges of Communist leanings while fighting the sedition bill. In April, Petry defended the Georgia labor movement against "implied charges" of Communist infiltration by AFL organizer Holt Ross. Petry indignantly replied that he knew of no individual in the state labor organization who could be classified as a Communist and that "there is no room for Communism in the Democratic Georgia Federation [of Labor]." The conservative Atlanta *Constitution* praised Petry's statement, commending labor for its steadfast opposition to radicalism. Observed the newspaper, "There is ground for comfort in knowledge that there is no

25. Thomas W. Hardwick to ACLU, February 16, 1937, Claud Nelson to Roger N. Baldwin, February 19, 1937, and Witherspoon Dodge to Baldwin, February 20, 1937, all in ACLU Archives. Dodge later served as a regional director of the Fair Employment Practices Commission during World War II.

26. Witherspoon Dodge to Roger N. Baldwin, March 5, 1937, *ibid.*; American Civil Liberties Union, *Let Freedom Ring!*, 18–19; *Journals of the Ten-Days Special Session and the Regular Session of the House of Representatives of the State of Georgia, 1937* (Atlanta: Stein Printing Co., 1937), 1393.

encouragement in this state for those who would preach the doctrines of Communism, Socialism, Sovietism, Naziism, Fascism or any of the other strange and strangling isms that have run rampant in other portions of the world." [27]

The Atlanta chapter of the NAACP did not participate in the maneuvering against the sedition act. But, in attempting to carry out its regular activities in early 1937, the branch found itself once again accused of being Communist influenced. At an evening meeting on April 23 in the First Congregational Church, the speaker J. L. LeFlore had just begun when about thirty white men, representing the American Legion, marched into the auditorium, taking seats at the front. Following LeFlore's address, the group's leader, later identified as W. L. Van Dyke, stood up and began questioning the speaker about the NAACP's alleged Communist ties. During this interrogation, a young man in the audience angrily rose and "fearlessly" defended the association. Clarence Mitchell, then a student at the Atlanta University School of Social Work, explained the purposes of the organization and suggested that the white group talk to the national office if they wished to pursue the matter. Taken aback by Mitchell's defense, Van Dyke sat down without asking any more questions. As the group departed, its members said that they had come because they understood that the association was a "bunch of reds." Van Dyke also explained that advertisements for the session used the word *force*, which he said was a favorite of Communists. [28]

The Legionnaires' withdrawal did not terminate local doubts about the association. Two days later, the closing gathering of a regional NAACP conference came under suspicion. Branch President Forrester B. Washington and featured speaker Charles H. Houston received a tip that the meeting would be raided by police. Unable to reach anyone by telephone, the two went to police headquarters, where they met with Chief Guy Hornsby. Although he denied that a raid was planned, Hornsby conceded that he had heard rumors that the association was Red, adding that Communist rallies were not permitted in the city. Not

27. Atlanta *Constitution*, April 14 and 15, 1937.

28. Pittsburgh *Courier*, May 8, 1937; Atlanta *Daily World*, April 24, 1937; *Louisiana Weekly* (New Orleans), May 8, 1937; *Crisis*, XLIV (January, 1937), 7; Eugene M. Martin to Walter White, April 24, 1937, in NAACP Papers; Clarence Mitchell to the author, August 5, 1974. Mitchell later served as director of the NAACP's Washington, D.C., bureau for over twenty years.

fully reassured by the NAACP leaders, the suspicious chief and several plainclothesmen attended the rally, where they heard Houston eloquently attack unequal educational opportunities for blacks in the South, as well as lynching and disfranchisement. Even though the officers eventually left quietly without taking any action, black Atlantans regarded their mere presence as yet another effort to intimidate blacks.[29]

While the Supreme Court justices weighed Herndon's case, they found themselves the center of a profound national controversy. President Roosevelt and his supporters had long been angered by the court's stubborn refusal to uphold as constitutional important New Deal measures, such as the National Recovery Administration and the Agricultural Adjustment Act. In the spring of 1936, the court went even further by striking down several liberal state laws as well as additional federal programs, causing many New Dealers to despair of ever gaining the court's approval. To these liberals and to Roosevelt the central problem was not the Constitution but the Supreme Court. Accordingly, the president and his advisers studied plans to remedy this situation. On February 5, 1937, Roosevelt stunned the nation by sending to Congress his controversial court reorganization plan, better known as the "court-packing" scheme. According to the proposal, the president would be empowered to appoint an additional justice to the Supreme Court (up to six) for each justice over seventy years of age who declined to retire. The plan also applied to all federal judges. Roosevelt's unexpected action unleashed a wave of indignant protest, confusing his supporters and delighting his enemies. For 168 days the furor raged. Then in late July the weary president, reluctantly accepting defeat, withdrew his proposal.[30]

The president's attempt at court reform found vigorous support among leftists and Communists. The *Daily Worker* warmly applauded Roosevelt's labors to curb the power of the "autocratic" and "dicta-

29. Pittsburgh *Courier*, May 8, 1937; *Louisiana Weekly* (New Orleans), May 8, 1937.
30. William E. Leuchtenburg, *Franklin D. Roosevelt and the New Deal* (New York: Harper and Row, 1963), 231–38; Joseph Alsop and Turner Catledge, *The 168 Days* (Garden City, N.Y.: Doubleday, Doran, 1938), 1–21; James MacGregor Burns, *Roosevelt: The Lion and the Fox* (New York: Harcourt, Brace, and World, 1956), 229–34, 291–315.

torial" court. But some liberals were less sure of the long-range benefits of the proposed legislation, especially to blacks. "If I were a Negro I would be raging and tearing my hair over this proposal," wrote Oswald Garrison Villard to Congressman Maury Maverick. "Woodrow Wilson introduced segregation in the departments in Washington . . . a future Woodrow Wilson could pack the Supreme Court so that no Negro could get within a thousand miles of justice." Amused Communist writers quickly belittled such fears. Benjamin Davis, Jr., charged that the court was already packed *against* black defendants. Favorable judgments by the court he attributed not to the justices' concern for civil rights but to pressure from "enraged public opinion." In testimony before the Senate Judiciary Committee, John P. Davis, executive secretary of the National Negro Congress, likewise attacked the court's reputation for protecting the constitutional rights of blacks. [31] He told the committee that rights guaranteed to black citizens by the Thirteenth, Fourteenth, and Fifteenth amendments had been consistently "defeated by biased decisions of the Supreme Court." [32]

Amid this national debate, the Supreme Court announced its decision on Monday, April 26. By a vote of five to four the court threw out Herndon's conviction, declaring that the Georgia insurrection statute, as construed and applied, violated the Fourteenth Amendment because it unduly interfered with freedom of speech and assembly and furnished no reasonable standard of guilt. Justices Owen J. Roberts, Louis Brandeis, Benjamin Cardozo, Harlan Fiske Stone, and Chief Justice Charles Evans Hughes all supported the ruling. The conservative bloc, compris-

31. *Daily Worker*, February 9, 10, 15, 20, March 19, 27, and April 17, 1937. Villard's quote is from Leuchtenburg, *Franklin D. Roosevelt and the New Deal*, 235.

32. Capitalizing on the notoriety surrounding Herndon's hearing before the Supreme Court, Random House released Herndon's autobiography in March, 1937. In plain, straightforward prose the young Communist told of his childhood, his conversion to the Communist party, his activities in Atlanta, and his arrest, trial, and imprisonment. *Let Me Live* closed on a dramatic note by asking whether the high court would ultimately free Herndon or send him to a Georgia chain gang. Although reviewers generally found the book lacking in literary grace, they agreed that it was a compelling and even unsettling story. Its greatest value they depicted as its revelations concerning the injustices suffered by black Americans. See the reviews in *Opportunity*, XV (May, 1937), 152–53, New York *Herald-Tribune*, March 14, 1937, *Atlantic Monthly*, CLIX (June, 1937), 748, *Saturday Review of Literature*, April 3, 1937, pp. 10–11, *Crisis*, XLIV (July, 1937), 219, *Nation*, April 10, 1937, pp. 414–16, and *New Republic*, March 31, 1937, p. 245. In 1969 the Arno Press and the New York *Times* issued a reprint of the book with a new preface by attorney and civil rights historian Howard N. Meyer.

ing Justices George Sutherland, Willis Van Devanter, James C. McReynolds, and Pierce Butler, dissented.[33]

Justice Roberts, a recent convert to the liberal bloc, wrote the majority decision. Dismissing most of the literature introduced by the state as evidence, he observed that there was no proof that Herndon had actually circulated the documents or that he had ever advocated forcible subversion of government. The real basis of the state's case, the justice explained, was its contention that Herndon's recruitment of members for the Communist party and his possession of Communist literature constituted an attempt at inciting others to join in combined resistance to the lawful authority of the state. Roberts noted that the Georgia legislature had not prohibited membership in the Communist party, yet this application of the insurrection statute left to the discretion of a jury the power to make recruitment of members a capital offense. To the justice this constituted an "unwarranted invasion of the right of freedom of speech."[34]

Justice Roberts also dismissed the state's arguments concerning the dangerous tendency test derived from the court's earlier decision in *Gitlow* v. *New York*. He stated that the New York law upheld in the *Gitlow* decision carefully defined the prohibited utterances, but the wording of the Georgia statute was unduly vague. Hence the clear and present danger test was the appropriate yardstick, not the dangerous tendency test. "The power of a state to abridge freedom of speech and of assembly is the exception rather than the rule," noted Roberts, adding that such limitations "must have appropriate relation to the safety of the state." To Roberts the statute's application seemed particularly dangerous, because under it any person who advocated a change in government could conceivably be punished by death if a jury felt that his actions might in twenty or thirty years contribute to forcible resistance to the government. He concluded that the insurrection law, "as construed and applied, amounts merely to a dragnet which may enmesh anyone who agitates for a change of government if a jury can be persuaded that he ought to have foreseen his words would have some effect in the future conduct of others."[35]

33. *Herndon* v. *Lowry*, 301 U.S. 242–78 (1937).
34. *Ibid.*, 242–61.
35. *Ibid.*, 255–64.

As one of his last actions on the bench, Justice Van Devanter wrote the dissenting opinion. On May 18, only twenty-two days after the *Herndon* decision, the elderly conservative would announce his long-awaited retirement. Van Devanter stressed that Herndon was a Negro endeavoring to recruit other Negroes for the Communist party and that Communist literature was aimed at "a people [southern blacks] whose past and present circumstances would lead them to give unusual credence to its inflaming and inciting features." After examining the seized Communist documents, the justice concluded that the party's aims were so fantastic that they could never be achieved short of violence. Moreover, the usage of such words as *revolution* and *national rebellion* convinced Van Devanter that the use of force must have been contemplated. Since forcible resistance to the state's authority was anticipated and since the Georgia law was not unnecessarily vague, Van Devanter concluded that the judgment of the state supreme court upholding the statute should be affirmed.[36]

The Supreme Court's decision evoked great pleasure from those sympathetic to Herndon and civil liberties. The ILD, the NAACP, and the ACLU all greeted the news with elation. The *Daily Worker* reported the event with a banner headline and editorially proclaimed that an aroused public had forced the favorable decision from the court, which was bending before widespread demand for judicial reform. Praising the heroic courage of Herndon, the *Worker* also credited the success to hard work by the labor movement, Socialists, Communists, and other sympathizers. In a formal statement released through the ILD, Herndon summed up the court action as a "decisive victory for all the progressive forces in the country" and a major blow "at the Jim Crow oppression of the Negro people." Anna Damon, acting national secretary of the ILD, hailed the decision as a defeat for the forces of reaction and a "victory in the fight for the civil and democratic rights of the Negro people." She found the judgment especially gratifying since it would apparently free seventeen others indicted under the same law in Atlanta.[37]

The liberal press warmly applauded Herndon's success and occa-

---

36. *Ibid.*, 264–78.
37. *Daily Worker*, April 27, 1937; *Southern Worker*, May 1, 1937; ILD press release, April 26, 1937, in ILD Papers; New York *Times*, April 27, 1937, p. 10.

sionally sniped at the court. Three major New York dailies—the *Post*, the *World-Telegram*, and the *Daily News*—endorsed the decision. The *Post*, which sarcastically asserted that the action represented the first time in 150 years that the court had declared unconstitutional a law restricting civil liberties, editorialized, "In the past the Supreme Court's decisions on civil liberties have been noteworthy chiefly for the agility with which the Court has been able to ignore the Bill of Rights." The *Christian Century* lauded the court for rendering a "national service of the highest importance." The *New Republic*, the *Nation*, and the St. Louis *Post-Dispatch* voiced similar opinions. Even two southern newspapers, the New Orleans *Item* and the Richmond *Times-Dispatch*, welcomed the ruling. The *Times-Dispatch* judged Herndon's offense "trivial" at worst and hoped that the affair would teach the city of Atlanta that repression of all unorthodox ideas could not be allowed.[38]

To black leaders and the black press, Herndon's long-awaited vindication warranted considerable celebration. "One does not need to espouse Communism in order to rejoice with Herndon over his freedom," commented the New York *Amsterdam News*. The Richmond *Planet* stressed that the decision meant "as much to oppressed white Americans as it does to the oppressed blacks," a theme echoed in the St. Louis *Argus* and the *Louisiana Weekly* (New Orleans). The *Carolina Times* (Durham, N.C.) commended the ILD for its steadfast defense of the young Communist, suggesting that, had it not been for the organization, "Herndon would have been wearing a number instead of a respectable citizen's clothes." The Pittsburgh *Courier*, one of the most consistently anti-Communist black newspapers of the day, was less generous with its praise. Although happy with Herndon's freedom, the *Courier* cautioned against drawing erroneous conclusions and stated, "The Herndon decision is purely a legal victory that brings the frontiers of freedom a little closer in the South." Not mass pressure but intelligent use of the courts had procured the favorable verdict, the newspaper asserted, and it

38. New York *Post*, April 27, 1937; New York *World-Telegram*, April 27, 1937, and New York *Daily News*, April 27, 1937, both in clippings file, ILD Papers; *Christian Century*, May 5, 1937, pp. 572–73; *New Republic*, May 5, 1937, p. 370; *Nation*, May 1, 1937, p. 494; St. Louis *Post-Dispatch*, April 27, 1937; New Orleans *Item*, April 26, 1937; Richmond *Times-Dispatch*, April 28, 1937. See also *Socialist Call*, May 1, 1937; Manchester *Guardian*, April 30, 1937, in Angelo Herndon File.

correctly warned that future Communist organizers would not be meekly received in Dixie regardless of the ruling.[39]

The Atlanta *Daily World* exhibited a curious reaction. Although the newspaper had sympathetically covered the original trial when Herndon was merely an obscure Communist organizer, it had recently become more circumspect about calling attention to abuses of constitutional rights. The *World* lauded this victory for free speech, but regretted "that some will abuse this right by advocating radical philosophies which might be detrimental to the order of society." Moreover, the *World* feared that the affair had given Georgia a bad image. Urging blacks to steer clear of all "isms" except Americanism, it voiced hope "that the Herndon decision will be accepted purely as a protector of the right of free speech and not as encouragement to radicalism." But Jesse O. Thomas, southern field director of the Urban League, took a more sympathetic position in an article for the *World*. Even though some people might disagree with Herndon's politics, Thomas said, "all are appreciative of the death blow struck at that obsolete and antiquated sedition law on the statute books of our state."[40]

The reaction of the Atlanta *Constitution* demonstrated the decision's limited effect on conservative Georgia opinion. A firm upholder of the state's case, the newspaper took the position that "Communists of all shades, whether deep-dyed reds or mere dilettante pinks, may take warning from this case that they are not wanted in Georgia." It emphasized that the state could not permit "attacks upon the sanctity of constitutional government." Surprisingly, the *Constitution*'s view received support from the Macon *Telegraph*, once the state's most liberal daily. In 1930 editor W. T. Anderson had vigorously denounced the prosecution of the Atlanta Six, and in January, 1933, he had again blasted Atlanta officials for their prosecution of Herndon. In the intervening years, though, bitter textile strikes had apparently driven Anderson into a more conservative outlook. In an editorial entitled "Herndon Beats the Rap," the *Telegraph* indirectly attacked Herndon by charging that freedom was never intended for those seeking to tear down the

39. New York *Amsterdam News*, May 1, 1937, Richmond *Planet*, May 8, 1937, *Carolina Times* (Durham, N.C.), May 8, 1937, and St. Louis *Argus*, April 30, 1937, all in clippings file, ILD Papers; *Louisiana Weekly* (New Orleans), May 1, 1937; Pittsburgh *Courier*, May 8, 1937.
40. Atlanta *Daily World*, April 29 and 30, 1937.

government by force. Noting the involvement of Communist leaders in Congress of Industrial Organizations (CIO) unionizing efforts, the newspaper warned that "clear and drastic measures may well be taken to protect the state and federal government from these radical assaults." [41]

Black newspapers, regardless of their degree of support for the ILD's role in gaining Herndon's freedom, displayed little reverence for the Supreme Court's reputation. The court's initial evasion of a ruling in the case now seemed irresponsible, and the conservative bloc and Justice Van Devanter were described with disgust. The Norfolk *Journal and Guide* expressed dismay "that four of its members are yet unshackled from the shibboleths of a degenerate racial philosophy that discolors their legalistic thinking." [42] Liberal supporters of President Roosevelt's court reform plan agreed, arguing that the slender margin of one vote which gave Herndon his freedom was too fragile to protect constitutional liberties. Only the appointment of additional liberal justices could insure dominance by the liberal bloc and guarantee that the court would vigorously guard civil liberties. Columnist Heywood Broun of the New York *World-Telegram*, who espoused this view, stated that, though five-to-four decisions upholding civil liberties were preferable to five-to-four defeats, "they are not good enough to stand as fundamental settlements of pressing problems, since it is not beyond the bounds of experience for a Justice of the Supreme Court to change his mind." The New York *Daily News*, along with the New York *Post* one of the few solidly liberal newspapers backing Roosevelt's proposals, went even farther by suggesting, "We need not only the President's stopgap reforms; we need also an amendment limiting the federal courts' powers to veto acts of Congress." [43]

Several black spokesmen concurred that court reform was still necessary. Columnist Kelly Miller asserted that judges were as vulnerable to human bias and prejudice as other people. Since the justices' political and economic views influenced their decisions, he asked,

41. Atlanta *Constitution*, April 28, 1937; Macon *Telegraph*, April 28, 1937.
42. Norfolk *Journal and Guide*, May 1, 1937, and Oklahoma City *Black Dispatch*, May 1, 1937, both in clippings file, ILD Papers; Pittsburgh *Courier*, May 1, 1937.
43. New York *Herald-Tribune*, April 27, 1937, in Angelo Herndon File; New York *World-Telegram*, April 28, 1937, and New York *Daily News*, April 27, 1937, both in clippings file, ILD Papers. Most of the country's newspapers opposed the court plan. See Alsop and Catledge, *The 168 Days*, 145–47.

"Why not have a bench imbued with a basic political and economic philosophy which the nation has approved?" Court reform would also protect the legal rights of blacks under the Constitution, Miller said. The Oklahoma City *Black Dispatch* stressed that, when only one vote stood "between liberty and tyranny, the time has arrived to constitutionally revamp our judiciary." And Adam Clayton Powell, Jr., no doubt spoke for many when he declared that blacks would "not be satisfied until the Supreme Court does something about permanent enforcement of the Thirteenth, Fourteenth, and Fifteenth amendments." In a similar vein, Communist leaders continued to demand court enlargement. The *Daily Worker* decried efforts by "clever reactionary forces" to portray the court as an enlightened body, characterizing the "liberal" court as nothing but a "guardian of backwardness and entrenched privilege which makes concessions only when forced to do so." Benjamin Davis, Jr., who had originally defended Herndon in his Atlanta trial, stated that the five-to-four vote "shows how whimsically uncertain the nine old men are about clear violations of the people's fundamental rights." For Davis the best way to guard against such abuses was by implementing Roosevelt's court reorganization plan. Herndon himself espoused this view in an interview at Communist party headquarters. When asked by a reporter if court reform were still needed, he replied, "Yes, more than ever." [44]

Opponents of the court plan saw a different significance in Herndon's freedom. These critics, including many erstwhile New Deal supporters, argued that the liberal bloc's triumph thus demonstrated that the court could be relied upon now to defend civil liberties. Hence court enlargement was unnecessary. The New York *Times*, which epitomized this attitude, editorially praised the court for remaining "true to the tradition which makes it the guardian of civil rights belonging to even the humblest citizen." Critics of the court had overlooked this aspect, the newspaper stated. Such critics had unjustly accused the court of obstructing social progress, when in reality "injustice, hysteria and tyranny" were the forces "obstructed" by the nine justices. The St.

44. Washington, D.C., *Tribune*, May 15, 1937, Oklahoma City *Black Dispatch*, May 1, 1937, and unidentified clipping, all in clippings file, ILD Papers; *Daily Worker*, April 27 and 28, 1937; *Western Worker*, May 3 and 6, 1937, and unidentified clipping, both in Angelo Herndon File.

Louis *Post-Dispatch* and the Richmond *Times-Dispatch* concurred. The *Post-Dispatch*, which opposed the court plan as unwise and unnecessary, told readers that the "Supreme Court again stands out in bold relief as an indispensable bulwark of human rights against invasion by unwarranted governmental authority." [45]

Despite the efforts of supporters and opponents of Roosevelt's court plan to incorporate the *Herndon* ruling into their arguments, the decision apparently had little impact on public opinion. It was primarily the court's upholding of the Wagner Act and several other pieces of New Deal legislation that enhanced its image and killed the possibility of enlarging the court. "A switch in time saves nine," aptly suggested one observer. But the realignment of the justices in their voting behavior, particularly the addition of Hughes and Roberts to the now dominant liberal bloc, did influence the *Herndon* decision, since the five justices who upheld the Wagner Act were the same five who ruled against the insurrection law. [46]

Although the *Herndon* ruling had little effect on the politics of the court fight, it did represent a significant legal advance in the struggle for free speech and other civil liberties. Heretofore, the Supreme Court had indicated that the dangerous tendency test applied to specific, carefully defined laws restricting free speech, but had avoided formulating a policy concerning general prohibitions. *Herndon* v. *Lowry* applied Justice Holmes's clear and present danger test to these general statutes. In fact, Justice Roberts suggested in his opinion that even specific laws should come close to meeting this stricter standard. The great milestones in free speech would come later, but for the present the *Herndon* decision was a step in the right direction. [47] Furthermore, *Herndon* v. *Lowry* assumed broader significance as an expression of the court's feelings about infringements of civil liberties. Because of the unsettled

45. New York *Times*, April 27, 1937, p. 22; St. Louis *Post-Dispatch*, April 27, 1937; Richmond *Times-Dispatch*, April 28, 1937.

46. Leuchtenburg, *Franklin D. Roosevelt and the New Deal*, 236–37; Alsop and Catledge, *The 168 Days*, 145–47.

47. *Harvard Law Review*, L (June, 1937), 1313; author's interview with Whitney North Seymour, New York, N.Y., September 8, 1970. See also Wallace Mendelson, "Clear and Present Danger—From Schenck to Dennis," *Columbia Law Review*, LII (April, 1952), 313–33. Mendelson referred to the clear and present danger test as "an oblique underpinning for the court's position" in the *Herndon* decision.

social and economic conditions of the 1930s, jittery state legislators and frightened local authorities frequently used repression when faced with unpopular attitudes or radical politics. The stance of the court, demonstrated in the *De Jonge* and *Herndon* decisions, sometimes served to restrain such conduct. Legislatures were warned that the highest judicial body in the land frowned upon restrictions of fundamental constitutional rights. The ACLU reported a freer exercise of civil liberties in 1936 and 1937 and attributed part of this improvement to favorable decisions by the Supreme Court. Although the forces of repression were hardly destroyed, the long-range outlook appeared much brighter.[48]

Unfortunately in Georgia, though, there was little evidence to indicate that state or local authorities had modified their attitudes. Despite the fact that the insurrection law's demise had robbed them of a means of harassing social activists, they remained hostile to civil liberties and civil rights. The repressive nature of "southern justice" had been tempered but not eliminated.

---

48. Chafee, *Free Speech in the United States*, 391–93; American Civil Liberties Union, *Let Freedom Ring!*, 3–4; author's interview with Walter Gellhorn, New York, N.Y., September 10, 1970.

CHAPTER TEN

Conclusion

IN JUNE, 1932, Atlanta police arrested an obscure nineteen-year-old black Communist named Angelo Herndon as he picked up mail from his post office box. By the next day probably less than a dozen people outside the police department knew of his arrest. But five years later, in April, 1937, when the U.S. Supreme Court overturned Herndon's conviction under Georgia's notorious insurrection law, the event received front-page coverage across the United States and even attracted attention in several foreign countries. How had such a drastic change come about? The explanation lies in five years of efforts by the International Labor Defense, the Communist party, black Americans, white liberals, and thousands of ordinary citizens to remedy a serious abuse of justice and free Angelo Herndon. During these years the Herndon case raised several controversial issues. What was the ILD really accomplishing for black defendants? Did blacks care about Herndon's fate? Why were Georgia officials so frightened of a black teenager? How could white liberals best assist his cause? Would "southern justice" render a prejudiced decision or decide the case solely on its legal merits? The answers to these questions were not always easy to provide.

One of the most complex problems in the Herndon case concerns the role of the ILD, which supervised Herndon's legal battle. The ILD's involvement raised such issues as the alleged manipulation of blacks by the ILD and other Communist organizations, Communist disruption of alliances with different political groups, radical criticism of the American legal system, and the substantive accomplishments and failures of the ILD in its campaign to help blacks.

Traditional accounts often depict ILD and Communist labors for black defendants as nothing more than callous attempts to manipulate and exploit them for devious Communist purposes without providing any tangible benefits in return. Hence Communists are frequently portrayed as lacking a sincere commitment to ending injustices against blacks.[1] Whatever truth there may be in such portrayals when applied to the party's higher leadership, they certainly do not tell the full story about most persons involved in the Herndon defense. Virtually all radicals who rallied to Herndon's banner were genuinely committed to his freedom. Moreover, to maintain this commitment in the face of dogged resistance from Georgia officials was no easy task.

Such charges of exploitation were also heard in connection with the Scottsboro rape case. But, unlike the Scottsboro boys, Angelo Herndon was not politically naïve. As a professed Communist who had already been jailed in Birmingham, Herndon knew what to anticipate from Atlanta authorities. When the expected did happen, he contacted the ILD. Herndon's Communist ties and his awareness of what an ILD defense would entail spared the group much of the criticism it received over the Scottsboro case. Thus, the ILD "tricked" no one into signing over control of the Herndon case, thereby escaping one of the bitterest charges raised about its maneuvers in Scottsboro. As a result, the NAACP, after an initial rebuff, left the legal proceedings in the hands of

1. William A. Nolan, *Communism Versus the Negro* (Chicago: Henry Regnery, 1951), vii, 84–85; David Entin, "Angelo Herndon" (M.A. thesis, University of North Carolina, 1963), 74–75, 93; Wilma Dykeman and James Stokely, *Seeds of Southern Change: The Life of Will W. Alexander* (Chicago: University of Chicago Press, 1962), 155–56; E. Merton Coulter, *Georgia: A Short History* (Chapel Hill: University of North Carolina Press, 1947), 446–47; David M. Potter, "C. Vann Woodward," in Marcus Cunliffe and Robin Winks (eds.), *Pastmasters: Some Essays on American Historians* (New York: Harper and Row, 1969), 376–77; Ralph E. McGill, *The South and the Southerner* (Boston: Little, Brown, 1959), 198. More balanced though basically hostile to Communist efforts is Wilson Record, *The Negro and the Communist Party* (Chapel Hill: University of North Carolina Press, 1951), 86–90. For a reply to anti-Communist accounts, see Hugh Murray, *Civil Rights History-Writing and Anti-Communism: A Critique*, Occasional Paper 16 (New York: American Institute for Marxist Studies, 1975). A balanced overview of the problem is Vaughn D. Bornet's "Historical Scholarship, Communism, and the Negro," *Journal of Negro History*, XXXVII (July, 1952), 304–24. Nolan refers to one particular example of Communist cynicism concerning the Herndon case. He writes that Anna Damon of the ILD expressed disappointment when she met Herndon for the first time, complaining that he would have been more useful to the party had his skin been darker. See also Murray Kempton, *Part of Our Time: Some Ruins and Monuments of the Thirties* (New York: Simon and Schuster, 1955), 255. I have been unable to either prove or disprove the authenticity of the story, and Herndon declines to answer any such inquiries today. Certainly Georgia officials never doubted that Herndon was dark enough.

the ILD. Since the ILD ultimately did gain Herndon's freedom, it would be difficult to imagine what more the organization could have done, save win his freedom sooner. Another charge frequently heard was that the ILD and the Communist party raised huge sums of money for helpless defendants, such as the Scottsboro boys, but then diverted these funds to other projects. Recent research on Scottsboro by Dan T. Carter discounts this accusation.[2] For the Herndon affair, the ILD financial reports show that income exceeded expenses in two years but fell slightly below expenses in two others. Overall, the ILD ultimately raised about $3,900 more than it spent on the case, exclusive of 1933, when no itemized figures on general defense expenses (there was a $1,700 deficit) were kept. Thus the Herndon case proved only moderately profitable to the ILD, whose leaders always feared that promised funds would not materialize.[3] Less prominent cases proved a serious drain on the ILD treasury. The cost of maintaining bonds on the Atlanta Six, for example, constantly siphoned money away from the financially plagued ILD.

Another liberal criticism concerns Communist rule-or-ruin tactics within alliances, which grew from the frustrations experienced by liberals who worked with Communists on common concerns. To evaluate this criticism for the 1930s one must distinguish between Communist behavior during the period 1929–1934, when Communists scorned joint ventures with liberals and labor leaders, denouncing them as "social fascists" and stooges for reactionaries, and the more cooperative period of the "united front," 1935–1939. In the former phase Communists persistently alienated their logical allies in the South. Instead of winning recruits, this antagonism toward ideological heretics consistently dis-

2. Dan T. Carter, *Scottsboro: A Tragedy of the American South* (Baton Rouge: Louisiana State University Press, 1969), 170.
3. Financial reports for 1933, 1934, 1935, 1936, and 1937, in International Labor Defense Papers, Schomburg Collection, New York Public Library, hereinafter cited as ILD Papers; *Labor Defender*, April 1, 1935, p. 23, and February 1, 1937, p. 18. The Socialist party contributed a check for $510.62 in December, 1935, and presumably additional amounts thereafter. The ACLU, in addition to contributing several hundred dollars from time to time, also spent nearly $1,000 on legal expenses for the Atlanta Six and perhaps twice that much on their bond premiums. See also *Socialist Call*, December 14, 1935; Oliver Hancock to ACLU, April 22, 1930, W. A. McClellan to Forrest Bailey, September 17, 1930, and Roger N. Baldwin to Carol Weiss King, April 13, 1935, all in American Civil Liberties Union Archives, Princeton University Library, hereinafter cited as ACLU Archives. The total funds raised by the ILD in the Herndon campaign amounted to $29,500, plus $16,000 for his bail.

rupted potential alliances and discouraged prospective sympathizers. If this policy was less common on the local level, where the so-called united front from below (cooperation with members of liberal organizations but not with their leaders or the formal organizations) was tried, it still ultimately reared its divisive head to spread dissension and thereby negate the local united front's initial success. The unnecessary split in the local Herndon defense movement in March, 1934, as well as the smaller schism in May, 1933, was provoked by this national policy of attacking liberal and black groups, which the ILD unwisely applied to Atlanta.[4]

Eventually the ILD and Communists, influenced by developments in the world Communist movement and international politics, changed their attitudes. Despite its foreign inspiration, this more flexible approach proved quite successful in the United States. Organizations such as the NAACP, the Socialist party, the ACLU, and labor groups now could work with Communists against common enemies. But in Atlanta this change came too late to be effective. The earlier sectarianism and dogmatism of the ILD had so thoroughly alienated sympathetic local blacks and liberals that most were unwilling to re-form their alliance. Moreover, an isolated ILD had been virtually destroyed by the continuous opposition of Atlanta authorities. Thus the ILD's sectarianism ultimately proved self-destructive in Atlanta.

Despite its excessive contentiousness, the ILD did capture the respect of a significant number of black Americans for reasons that are clear. Although Communist theory held little appeal for blacks, they were impressed by visible ILD actions in behalf of black grievances. The ILD's determined defense of Angelo Herndon, particularly its attack on the exclusion of blacks from Fulton County juries, deeply influenced Atlanta Negroes, especially when the ILD followed up its initial efforts for one person with a series of protests against common difficulties of the city's blacks. Capitalizing on the Glover Davis affair, it used Davis' death to dramatize police brutality and blacks' concern for their personal safety. The ILD's fearless if not reckless activism contrasted with the

4. See Chapters Five and Six herein for details. William L. Patterson acknowledged that "narrow sectarianism" was handicapping the ILD in July, 1934, but neither he nor the ILD did anything about it until the following year. William L. Patterson, "The I.L.D. Faces the Future," *Communist*, XIII (July, 1934), 727.

"armchair activism" of the NAACP and southern white liberals. Thus the ILD, more than other Communist organizations, received much support from Negroes; ILD deeds, not words, were what impressed blacks.[5]

The fundamental philosophy of the ILD was mass protest. As Dan T. Carter observes, "Mass action—the two words invoked a profound response from American communism in the 1930's." Although the ILD did not create this approach, it certainly could claim credit for popularizing it during the thirties. The ILD regarded mass protest as far superior to the "reformist" legal action associated with the NAACP. To the ILD the NAACP's concentration on the individual legal merits of a case while ignoring the broader social and economic forces involved was a short-sighted if not blind approach to the realities of American life. Mass protest offered far greater opportunity for success. Not only would the appropriate legal points be introduced but, more important, through mass protest large numbers of people could be organized into a movement to challenge the social forces underlying legal prosecutions. In this process sympathizers would be "educated" to sociopolitical realities and thereby motivated to become Communists. In short, the ILD believed that law did not exist in a vacuum; organized citizens in a mass movement could change the political environment and thus the manner in which the legal system functioned.[6]

As a means to achieve publicity, mass protest succeeded. This was particularly important to Herndon, for as a little-known, indigent black defendant he had small hope of acquiring the free services of a prominent attorney. Publicity was and still is vital to such defendants. By making the Herndon case into a *cause célèbre*, the ILD gained support for Herndon from thousands of people, several major national organizations, national periodicals, and a battery of skillful attorneys. All these forces contributed to his ultimate vindication. But the ILD was not alone in advocating such publicity. The ACLU agreed that such tactics were vital in political cases. In the summer of 1930, ACLU field representative Walter Wilson had developed such successful publicity concerning the

5. St. Clair Drake and Horace R. Cayton, *Black Metropolis* (Rev. ed.; New York: Harper and Row, 1962), 736, found this to be true in Chicago during the 1930s.
6. Carter, *Scottsboro*, 138; Record, *The Negro and the Communist Party*, 35–36, 88. For William L. Patterson's explanation of mass protest, see *Daily Worker*, April 7, 1933.

Atlanta Six that the solicitor general's office was forced to suspend its plans to bring the defendants to trial. As Roger Baldwin explained to Wilson, "We always take the position of pushing our propaganda even when trials are pending. As a matter of fact, it's the best time." [7]

But the ILD sought through mass protest much more than just widespread news coverage. In its campaign the group reached many individuals previously uninvolved in Communist activity. Most of these people simply wanted to help remedy a shameful abuse of fundamental American rights. Historian C. Vann Woodward was a typical example. As he later recalled about his brief youthful involvement in the affair, "I came home [from a summer tour of the Soviet Union] and then this Herndon case broke, and I said, 'Now here is another thing that is going to disgrace us abroad . . . like the Scottsboro case, and I ought to get into it." [8] Because the ILD was less contentious in the Herndon case than in Scottsboro, it successfully reached a broader range of individuals. The next step was to "educate" them and win them to the Communist movement. But, prior to the adoption of the united front, the ILD almost inevitably alienated these newly gained sympathizers with its inflexible attitude toward any divergence from the official party line. Hence the ILD defeated its own efforts. Furthermore, another negative result of mass protest was its intensification of local resistance. Bitterly resentful of ILD attacks, Atlanta officials redoubled their determined crusade to crush any radical activity or thought in the area. But, even if the ILD had acted more graciously and less belligerently, it could hardly have won a more sympathetic hearing from Atlanta officials, given their fundamental intransigence concerning social change. Perhaps expediency should have dictated a more cautious policy, but it was precisely this lack of caution upon which rested the ILD's chief appeal.

The quality of the ILD's legal efforts in the Herndon case varied considerably. Black attorneys Ben Davis and John Geer were quite inexperienced and ill prepared to handle a case of such magnitude. But more knowledgeable white lawyers refused to work with them. Moreover, had Davis and Geer withdrawn, the ILD would still have been unable to employ a local white attorney willing to challenge *both* the

7. Roger N. Baldwin to Walter Wilson, August 6, 1930, in ACLU Archives.
8. Author's interview with C. Vann Woodward, Atlanta, Ga., November 8, 1973.

insurrection law's constitutionality and the exclusion of blacks from local juries. Despite their inexperience, Geer and Davis applied themselves diligently and raised the correct issues. Also, by utilizing their services the ILD demonstrated its commitment to accepting blacks as equals. ILD leaders felt that the fact that white attorneys would not serve with a Harvard Law School graduate (Davis) solely because of his skin color should not deter them from their commitment to establishing equality for blacks in the courtroom.[9] Certainly Atlanta blacks were impressed by any organization bold enough to utilize the services of black lawyers.

Davis and Geer's inexperience unfortunately was made evident on the appeal of Herndon's conviction. In 1935 the U.S. Supreme Court used the confusion resulting from their clumsy introduction of the constitutionality question to evade a ruling. Nonetheless, three justices at that time felt that the issue had been adequately raised and urged a full hearing of the fundamental issues in question. From a legal point of view, the ILD should have provided additional assistance at the original trial in laying the technical groundwork for an appeal. But the difficulty of arranging suitable lawyers remained understandably complicated.

The later legal undertakings of the ILD were unquestionably of the highest caliber. In Whitney North Seymour the ILD obtained the services of a brilliant legal mind. Those attorneys who assisted him— Walter Gellhorn, Herbert Wechsler, W. A. Sutherland, and Elbert P. Tuttle—were likewise extremely talented. The ILD could not have assembled a more formidable band had it even abandoned its belief in the merits of mass protest. Furthermore, the ILD agreed to Seymour's stipulations that he alone would decide legal strategy and that there would be no political interference with the proceedings. By keeping its word, the ILD demonstrated a flexibility not often implied by its rhetoric. This flexibility was significant because Seymour chose to emphasize the free speech aspect of the case and drop the jury exclusion issue, which the ILD had considered to be more politically symbolic.[10]

9. White reporter James H. Street was criticized merely for sitting next to Davis while discussing a point of law concerning the case.

10. Seymour's choice was extremely important, however, for the ultimate victory in the Supreme Court ended *all* prosecution of Herndon under the insurrection law. If Seymour had attacked the jury system and won, he would merely have gained a new trial for Herndon.

Of course the greatest test of the ILD's legal efforts was their ultimate success or failure. By virtue of the favorable ruling in *Herndon* v. *Lowry* and the resulting death blow to the Georgia insurrection law, the ILD successfully demonstrated its ability to gain legal justice and to provide tangible results for blacks.

But mass protest did not always succeed. Despite an initial victory in Maryland's Euel Lee case, the ILD eventually proved unable to save Lee from the gallows. In the Scottsboro case the ILD did save the nine black youths from the electric chair, but it could not free all of them, even with later assistance from a broad united front committee. Moreover, the ILD's crusade had not changed the basic social structure or legal system of the South. Yet the ILD and Communists had at least made a valiant effort to challenge the forces of southern repression, one which did not pass unnoticed by blacks and one which contrasted with the frequent "armchair exhortations" of liberals. Although relatively few Negroes were willing to expose themselves to the double stigma of being both black *and* Red, the ILD did make them aware that at least a few people were concerned about their sufferings. Considering the lack of national concern over civil liberties and civil rights, that was something worthwhile.[11]

Along with the ILD, Whitney North Seymour shared the credit for winning Herndon's freedom. In spite of his own establishment background, Seymour remained sensitive to abuses of justice and was not distracted from the larger issues in the case by Herndon's Communist ties. Thus he demonstrated that defenders of justice could come from a variety of backgrounds, despite Communist teaching to the contrary. Though its significance should not be exaggerated, his willingness to serve without fee certainly helped Herndon, for the chronically underfinanced ILD probably could not have afforded his services otherwise. As a true civil libertarian, Seymour believed that attorneys were

---

11. *Lee* v. *Maryland*, 161 Atl. 284 (1932). Mass protest did not die after the 1930s, of course. In the late forties and early fifties the ILD's successor, the Civil Rights Congress, also headed by William L. Patterson, used this approach to dramatize the legal difficulties of several black defendants. The civil rights struggles of the following two decades, as well as the judicial confrontations involving the New Left, antiwar leaders, and black liberation spokesmen, likewise produced similar protests. Perhaps the most similar in spirit to the Herndon case was the political defense of Angela Davis. On the Civil Rights Congress, see Record, *The Negro and the Communist Party*, 253–62.

obligated to defend unpopular figures and that quality legal services should not be available only to the wealthy and the famous. In placing his considerable legal talents to work for Herndon, the New York attorney produced an eloquent defense of free speech and the need for careful limits on restrictions of basic constitutional rights. His forceful advocacy of the clear and present danger test convinced the high court to begin once more to utilize the concept, a considerable step toward greater judicial protection of free speech. Seymour's articulate oral presentation matched his shrewd written arguments. None other than Assistant Solicitor J. Walter LeCraw confirmed this when he observed of the 1937 decision that the Supreme Court ruled "in favor of Herndon, or rather in favor of Whitney North Seymour, who made a fine and powerful address . . . on freedom of speech and its implications." [12] Although Herndon greatly benefited from Seymour's assistance, the American system of justice also profited. By demonstrating that attorneys could transcend their class interest and that superior legal advice could be made available to an obscure defendant, Seymour thus contributed to a more progressive image for the American judicial system.

Many Negroes followed the Herndon case from its inception. Since black newspapers publicized developments in the case, blacks were far better informed than whites until the first hearing before the United States Supreme Court. The vast majority of blacks experienced no difficulty in identifying with the young Communist organizer despite his ideology. To them Herndon was merely a black Everyman entangled in a web of racism and legal injustice. His sufferings they viewed as the almost inevitable fate of assertive blacks who spoke the truth about oppressive conditions in the South. Lacking any sympathy for Herndon's prosecutors, blacks were further drawn to his cause by his youthfulness, his fearless advocacy of equal justice, and the seeming harshness of his lengthy sentence. [13]

Although blacks were open-minded, perhaps even a trifle naïve, about Herndon's Communist ties, they were more uneasy over the ILD's

12. J. Walter LeCraw to the author, May 7, 1970.
13. For an excellent account of a Herndon speech in Cleveland and the favorable audience reaction, see the column by W. D. W. in the Cleveland *Call and Post*, undated, in Commission on Interracial Cooperation Papers, Trevor Arnett Library, Atlanta University.

obvious Communist leanings. In general, sympathetic blacks preferred to ignore the touchy issue of communism and concentrate on what the ILD was actually doing for blacks. By following such a pragmatic policy they avoided, among other things, having to reconcile Communist atheism and jibes at the black church with the deep religious fervor of black America.[14] Consistently black spokesmen stressed that any group, regardless of its formal ideology, which combated discrimination and the Jim Crow system was on the Negro's side. Editor W. P. Dabney of the Cincinnati *Union* captured this feeling in a symposium on communism by asking, "When a man is drowning does he demand reasons for the helping hand?"[15] Some blacks did find the ILD's Communist ties unacceptable. The NAACP and the Pittsburgh *Courier* declined to support the Herndon defense movement until 1935, doubting Communist and ILD sincerity and fearing that their rash actions would only make matters worse for black people. Yet these spokesmen still agreed that Herndon did not deserve his harsh sentence and lamented his prosecution. But their hesitancy in joining the fight for Herndon's freedom struck some blacks as an outmoded conservatism which, they feared, might dilute an already weak progressive alliance. Although the majority of sympathetic blacks never became enthusiastic over communism, the ILD's tireless efforts in Herndon's behalf impressed them and made them quite appreciative of this particular Communist-dominated organization.

Atlanta blacks easily identified with Herndon and detested his white prosecutors. His indictment under the insurrection law they viewed as a precedent for future harassment of anyone who criticized the status quo. Prominent middle-class blacks, such as the Reverend J. Raymond Henderson, Ben Davis, Jr., Jesse O. Thomas, and the Reverend J. A.

14. Despite their attacks on religion, Communists realized the significance of the black church to the black community and held numerous rallies and fund-raising benefits in them for Herndon, Scottsboro, and other causes. See Ralph Lord Roy, *Communism and the Churches* (New York: Harcourt, Brace, 1960), 107.

15. "Negro Editors on Communism: A Symposium of the American Negro Press," *Crisis*, XXXIX (April, 1932), 156. See also comments by E. Washington Rhodes of the Philadelphia *Tribune*, Carl Murphey of the Baltimore *Afro-American*, and William D. Kelley of the New York *Amsterdam News* in the previous month's installment. Even Wilson Record, *The Negro and the Communist Party*, 94, concedes that blacks joined Communist organizations "because Communists were frequently the only ones attempting to do something immediately about jobs, relief, and general welfare."

Martin, willingly cooperated with the Provisional Committee for the Defense of Angelo Herndon and the ILD. Their sympathy even extended to other white and black radicals prosecuted by local white officials. Prominent black druggists L. D. Milton and C. R. Yates posted bond for Herndon in December, 1932, shortly before the young Communist's trial, and Milton and J. R. Wilson also posted bond for Ann Burlack, one of the Atlanta Six, in October, 1933. Several faculty members from the city's black colleges signed petitions and spoke in Herndon's behalf. Attorneys Ben Davis and John Geer provided legal advice to white radicals, and Geer even represented in court Annie Mae Leathers and Nannie Leah Young, southern white radicals. And in October, 1934, a group of black ministers joined their white counterparts in denouncing the public hysteria over communism during Atlanta's Red scare.[16]

Atlanta blacks viewed the Herndon prosecution as an effort to silence anyone who attempted to help blacks improve their "place" in southern society, as well as an attempt to disrupt biracial economic cooperation. Jesse O. Thomas of the Urban League repeatedly stressed white officials' fears of black and white workers making common cause. When blacks formed coalitions with radicals and white liberals, a veritable *ménage à trois*, they faithfully carried out their share of the labor. Except for the more extreme anti-Communist spokesmen, they did not permit differences with these other groups to handicap unduly their work. Their chief complaints were that white liberals failed to act decisively when needed and that Communists introduced extraneous issues into disputes. As long as the ILD maintained a sincere united front, blacks willingly cooperated with the group. But when sectarianism intruded, as in the controversy over John Downer's execution and alleged NAACP complicity, black Atlantans rejected the ILD and the provisional committee and remained loyal to traditional community leaders and institutions. Basically, blacks identified with the ILD because it acted aggressively and because it was going their way. But, when the ILD ventured too far afield or attacked other blacks or allies, then despite their previous approval blacks parted company with the

16. Angelo Herndon, *Let Me Live* (New York: Arno Press, 1969), 220; ILD press release, October 17, 1933, in ILD Papers; Atlanta *Constitution*, October 28, 1934; Atlanta *Daily World*, November 4, 1934.

radicals. Thus black sympathy for the ILD rested heavily on convenience and mutual acceptance and ignored ideology. As Adam Clayton Powell, Jr., later observed, "The Negro neither fears the Communist nor leans over backwards in admiration. The Communist is the same to him as a Holy Roller, Republican or Elk. He is just another human being to be judged individually on one basis—is he fighting for full and complete equality of opportunity for black people?" [17] Black response to the ILD rose and fell on this point. But, even when at odds with the ILD, blacks never lost sight of Angelo Herndon, to them the abiding symbol of Jim Crow justice.

Most white liberals were slow to rally to Herndon's side, frequently because of a lack of information. As the case acquired notoriety, liberal spokesmen increasingly denounced the young Communist's conviction, adding their voices to the public outcry. Southern liberals, especially in Georgia, were reluctant to speak out publicly in the early years of the affair. Editor W. T. Anderson of the Macon *Telegraph* stood virtually alone inside the state when he denounced Herndon's conviction in 1933. The relative weakness of Georgia liberals made them hesitant to act, especially since their protests only inflamed the opposition. Some liberals, like Will W. Alexander of the Commission on Interracial Cooperation, shunned involvement with the Herndon defense because of hostility to any joint action with Communists, whom he labeled "political Holy Rollers." Alexander proved so reluctant to speak out that, on an earlier occasion, the ACLU's Walter Wilson privately accused him of trying to sabotage liberal publicity concerning the Atlanta Six.[18] Although some of the liberal reticence may seem unduly cautious in retrospect, it should be recalled that during the 1930s virtually any form of interracial activity was still considered subversive and dangerous in the South. Moreover, Communist denunciations of liberals as social fascists and tools of the ruling class hardly motivated southern liberals, any more than their national counterparts, to embrace the ILD.

Following the creation of the united front, liberals found it much easier to work with the ILD. Even though Alexander and the interracial

17. Adam Clayton Powell, Jr., *Marching Blacks* (New York: Dial Press, 1945), 70.
18. Will W. Alexander to Roger N. Baldwin, July 30, 1932, in Commission on Interracial Cooperation Papers; Walter Wilson to ACLU, July 13, 1930, in ACLU Archives.

commission remained aloof, other liberals took a more active role. Several prominent figures, including the ministers Allan Knight Chalmers, Harry Emerson Fosdick, and Hubert C. Herring, joined with the ACLU and the NAACP in the 1935 *amici curiae* petition to the U.S. Supreme Court. Chalmers and Fosdick had been active in the Scottsboro case too. State and national labor leaders also nervously noted Herndon's prosecution under the insurrection law. Such spokesmen were hostile to Communist ideology, but, fearing that the statute could be used against AFL organizers too, they worked with the ILD against the Georgia law and efforts to supplement it.[19] Their assistance proved vital. In 1937, while Atlanta liberals and blacks watched helplessly, labor leaders sidetracked and defeated a proposed sedition bill which had earlier seemed certain to pass the Georgia legislature. Subsequently, following the Supreme Court's blow to the insurrection law, Georgia officials found themselves lacking a substitute legal tool for use against political and economic dissenters. Although labor leaders did not stress the Herndon case as a typical example of biased southern justice, they did agree that his prosecution was part of a broader strike against black and white labor unity and, potentially, any union activity. Hence labor leaders had a personal interest in seeing Herndon triumph, as well as a more general commitment to justice.

If one classifies the ACLU as a liberal group, then it can be said that not all liberals were slow to respond to the Herndon case. Because of its entry into the bizarre world of Georgia political prosecutions in 1930 on behalf of the Atlanta Six, the ACLU was already familiar with John A. Boykin, John H. Hudson, and their associates by the time of Herndon's arrest. The ACLU did not merely concern itself with the traditional libertarian aspects of restrictive laws; rather the group fully appreciated the social, political, and economic forces behind the prosecution of Herndon and the other Atlanta defendants. But, though the ACLU was much healthier financially than the ILD or even the NAACP, it was still a far cry from the powerful institution it later became. In fact, it did not even have a Georgia chapter at the time, relying on a brief list of "friends" in the state for assistance. Despite these handicaps, the ACLU

19. Walter Wilson to ACLU, May 31, 1930, in ACLU Archives, quotes Jerome Jones of the Atlanta *Journal of Labor* to that effect.

worked to help Georgia's insurrection defendants and was the single most important force in blocking the trial of the Atlanta Six in the summer of 1930. The ACLU volunteered to help the ILD following Herndon's conviction, offering to supply Arthur Garfield Hays or a southern white attorney to work on an equal or even a subordinate basis with Geer and Davis on the appeal. Although the ILD declined the proposition, the rejection did not discourage the ACLU, which closely monitored the case. It published a pamphlet exposing the affair and raised several hundred dollars to help finance the appeals. Unlike some liberals, the ACLU did not let the ILD's often exaggerated rhetoric deter it from supporting a just cause. As the ACLU's Roger Baldwin explained to Mary Raoul Millis in November, 1933:

> But when issues arise such as the Scottsboro Case, the Herndon Case, and the Tuscaloosa lynchings, violent extremes are thrown into conflict. We are then facing problems of passion with the Klan on one side and the Negroes and their new left wing allies on the other. There is no way of escaping that conflict; no way of dissociating the ILD from these cases. We confront a practical situation in which we are forced to stand for legal defense in any form it is organized, whatever we may think of the wisdom of selection of counsel or of tactics in court.[20]

Thus the ACLU consistently transcended the limitations of liberalism better than any other group in actively supporting the Herndon defense. Yet it too could do little alone. A common front was not only good theory, it made common sense too.

Conservative Georgia officials and their allies did not always distinguish between such groups as the ILD, the NAACP, and the ACLU. To them and to many southern whites each of these organizations was a menace to the region. Satisfied with the status quo, such officials viewed any attempted change or criticism as a threat to the entire fabric of southern society. Communists were bad enough on their own, but, when these radicals came to the assistance of southern blacks, Georgia officials reacted much like their ancestors had to the abolitionist attack nearly a century before. Prosecutors John H. Hudson and especially J. Walter LeCraw vociferously denounced Communist teachings con-

20. Roger N. Baldwin to William L. Patterson, January 24 and 26, 1933, and Baldwin to Mary Raoul Millis, November 21, 1933, both *ibid.*

cerning "self-determination for the Black Belt."[21] To them this slogan raised the ultimate specter of land redistribution, black domination, and, ironically (in light of Georgia's actions in 1861), secession from the United States. Actually, most southern blacks simply ignored the phrase, but not Atlanta officials. The fact that the ILD also had many non-Communist members made no impression on these men. ILD legal efforts for blacks in southern courtrooms, particularly the use of black attorneys, merely confirmed their earlier fears. Communist efforts to organize black and white workers proved equally disturbing, as did the large biracial relief demonstration led by Herndon in June, 1932, which inspired his arrest.[22]

The attitude of the average white Georgian is more difficult to determine. Many whites were slow to learn the details of the case because of the reluctance of local white newspapers to grant undue publicity to potentially sensational racial incidents. Reporter James H. Street noted that the Atlanta dailies preferred not to "play" racial troubles because of the often criticized role of the press in the infamous 1906 race riot and the Leo Frank disorders.[23] But, when the Atlanta *Constitution*, the city's leading newspaper, did take a stand, it firmly endorsed the various insurrection prosecutions, denounced any radical activity (including the mere existence of radicals) as a threat to public order, and defended the status quo against any criticism. The Macon *Telegraph* was the only major Georgia newspaper to decry Herndon's conviction, and by 1937 even it had modified its stance.

One noticeable difference between the Herndon case and the Scottsboro rape case was the greater restraint exercised by conservative white Georgians compared with their Alabama counterparts. Unlike Scottsboro, no angry mob stormed the jail demanding vengeance. One

21. A. L. Henson, head of the American Legion in Atlanta, likewise stressed the dangers of a black republic in the Deep South. Another American Legion leader, Kenneth R. Murrell, who was a friend of Governor Talmadge's and an anti-Communist, denounced the ACLU as "the breeder of all atheists, anti-Americans, Communists, socialists and off-color religious organizations now active in promoting class war, social unrest and revolution in the United States." See *Daily Worker*, November 14, 1935; Kenneth Murrell to Arthur Garfield Hays, July 17, 1935, *ibid*.

22. The Fulton Cotton and Bag Mill was one center of radical activity. Communists sporadically published the *Fulton Bag Worker* for employees there, and it was at the plant entrance that police arrested Annie Mae Leathers and Nannie Leah Young under the insurrection law in October, 1934.

23. James H. Street, *Look Away!: A Dixie Notebook* (New York: Viking Press, 1936), 150.

reason perhaps was the fact that Herndon's crime, essentially that of organizing black and white workers together under the auspices of the Communist party, was basically a "thoughtcrime." His alleged misbehavior was somewhat abstract and hence more difficult for the average person to grasp. Moreover, since this was a victimless crime, there were no victims' relatives to clamor for immediate retribution. Perhaps the two cases demonstrate that, though white southerners feared political revolution and social equality, their supreme phobia was black rape.[24] Nonetheless, large numbers of antagonistic whites packed the courtroom for Herndon's trial and many of the hearings for the other defendants. Ku Klux Klan members kept a wary eye on radical activists and periodically left their unique calling card—a burning cross. Certainly the possibility of extralegal action often lurked in the background. If by deemphasizing the controversy the major Atlanta dailies kept mob violence from emerging, then perhaps their restrictions were well founded.

Also important in preventing the case from arousing massive hysteria on the scale of Scottsboro was Governor Eugene Talmadge's restrained behavior. For some reason the governor chose not to exploit the case politically. The northern delegations that periodically descended upon him, the flood of pro-Herndon propaganda sent to him, and the bitter caricatures of him painted in northern periodicals all offered ample provocation for Talmadge to have defended violently the southern way of life against the outside world. Miraculously, he chose not to do so. Unlike during the 1950s and 1960s, it was the governor of Georgia who worried about the state's image and Atlanta's officials who held the city and state up to national condemnation and ridicule. Considering Talmadge's stormy career, it would seem that he had few moral or ideological compunctions against such behavior. Perhaps his restraint and caution were motivated more by his dislike for Boykin, Hudson, and their associates, who were bitter political rivals, than by his respect for constitutional rights.

24. At Herndon's January, 1933, trial, prosecutor John H. Hudson introduced the interracial sex taboo when he asked Professor T. J. Corley if the Communist platform endorsed racial intermarriage. Although Corley cautiously skirted the issue, Hudson succeeded in conveying to the jury his implication that Communist teachings departed radically from traditional southern mores concerning miscegenation.

It was John H. Hudson who tried unsuccessfully to exploit the case politically. Had Judge Hugh M. Dorsey not proved such a formidable opponent, Hudson probably would have succeeded in unseating the former governor and in expanding his anti-Communist crusade. Prosecutors Hudson, Boykin, and LeCraw all believed that Communists planned to overthrow existing southern society using gullible blacks as their vanguard. Not only were these officials determined to eradicate radical thought from the state, but they strenuously opposed practically all discussions of controversial or unorthodox ideas. Hudson's often expressed desire to prosecute Emory Dean Edgar A. Johnson for using *The Communist Manifesto* in class is just one example of the prosecutor's basic animosity toward independent thinking, if not the intellectual process itself. As Professor Mercer G. Evans remarked of Hudson, in words that apply equally well to Boykin and LeCraw, "Hudson is willing to damn anybody or any organization as Communist, and is willing to throw them into prison, if they in any way deviate from the path of the King James version of the Christian Bible, if they in any way countenance discussion of sex or birth control, or if they in any way show interest in any 'radical' criticism of the present economic or political organization of society." Evans added that this hostility particularly extended to persons who showed "evidence of a decent regard for Negroes." [25]

In these attitudes Atlanta officials were not unrepresentative of many white southerners. Their response, along with that of their supporters, the Atlanta press, and the public, demonstrated the Deep South's opposition to free speech, independent thinking, and "outside" ideas. Any discussion of the race issue was greeted with righteous indignation. Dominant community values were not to be discussed. Public order must be maintained at any cost. Present society was a fair and just society; an attack on any part of it endangered the entire social fabric. Instead of modifying these beliefs, the Herndon case only reinforced them. The basic values of conservative white southerners remained unchanged.

Although most blacks and many liberals viewed the Herndon case as

25. Mercer Evans to Mary Fox, October 28, 1934, in ACLU Archives.

a civil rights case, from the legal perspective it was more properly a civil liberties case, particularly after Whitney North Seymour chose to stress the insurrection law's excessive restrictions on free speech, rather than the exclusion of blacks from juries. Most writers stressed that the case was typical of the legal difficulties suffered by blacks, but the free speech aspect served to broaden its public appeal. Liberals who might otherwise have been unconcerned, as well as persons of moderate or conservative political leanings, could appreciate the basic constitutional principles involved, even though they might have difficulty identifying with the defendant. After all, Seymour was himself a Republican and a conservative who nonetheless supported Herndon's cause because of the threat to civil liberties.

In his attack on the insurrection law, Seymour pleaded eloquently for the revitalization of the clear and present danger test by cleverly arguing that this was the appropriate standard for laws of a general nature restricting free speech. Since the U.S. Supreme Court had not firmly established whether the dangerous tendency test for laws prohibiting specifically defined doctrines also applied to more general statutes, this line of reasoning permitted the court to accept the clear and present danger test in one area while continuing the older test for specific prohibitions, thereby avoiding having to reverse itself. The favorable ruling in the Herndon case thus resurrected the clear and present danger test and advanced the cause of free speech.[26] Although later rulings would further reduce restrictions, *Herndon* v. *Lowry* indicated that the court was becoming more sensitive to such abuses. Ironically, if Ben Davis and John Geer had introduced the constitutionality question so clearly that the court could not have evaded a ruling in 1935, the result might have been unfortunate for Herndon and for civil liberties. The 1937 majority of five justices was the newly emerging liberal bloc on the court, but in 1935 this bloc had not yet been formed. Precisely how Chief Justice Hughes and Justice Roberts might have voted then is unknown, but their reluctance even to hear the case in 1935 suggests that they might have remained with the conservatives. Therefore Herndon

26. Zechariah Chafee, Jr., *Free Speech in the United States* (Cambridge: Harvard University Press, 1941), 318–25, 343–51, 384–87.

and the clear and present danger test both benefited from the two-year delay and President Roosevelt's court fight.

As for Angelo Herndon the individual, he remained to the public more of a symbol than a real person. The various pamphlets published by the ACLU and ILD and the occasional magazine accounts do not succeed in humanizing Herndon the political prisoner. Not until the publication of Herndon's autobiography *Let Me Live* in 1937 did the young Communist's life receive a more in-depth popular treatment. Even then Herndon remained to most people a symbol of Communist militancy, of southern injustice, of black assertiveness, and of the dedicated young social activist of the 1930s.

If the public remained ignorant of Herndon's personal qualities, those persons who came to know him usually found him an engaging young man with an alert, promising mind. Blacks who heard him speak on ILD tours also responded favorably. Here was a young black man upstaging established leaders by fearlessly denouncing discrimination and oppression, something which most blacks had secretly longed to do. Herndon's devotion, courage, and sense of mission deeply impressed them as well as sympathetic whites. But most of his ideas at the time were hardly original; they usually reflected a simplified version of the correct Communist position of the moment. This is not surprising. Since Herndon had been primarily an activist, not a theoretician, he had found little time for study. But, as the young man matured intellectually, he learned to think more independently. During the early forties he and Ralph Ellison edited the *Negro Quarterly: A Review of Negro Life and Culture*, a short-lived journal partially funded by Communist sources. Departing from the official Communist line, editorial comment strongly condemned continued denials of equal rights to blacks and insisted that rectifying such faults should not be subordinated to the cause of winning the war.[27]

Although most observers ultimately regarded Herndon himself as a distinctive individual, they interpreted his case as a typical product of

27. Roger N. Baldwin to the author, March 5, 1970; author's interview with Whitney North Seymour, New York, N.Y., September 8, 1970; *Negro Quarterly: A Review of Negro Life and Culture*, I (1942–43), 3–4, 196, 295–302. Herndon was listed as the sole editor of the first issue. Subsequent issues listed Herndon as editor and Ralph Ellison as managing editor.

the southern legal system. If the Deep South were firmly committed to white supremacy, social control of blacks, and suppression of any challenge to the status quo, as most observers agreed, then it would be naïve at best to believe that such fundamental values would not affect the legal system. In fact, "southern justice" often contributed to the defense of the status quo against any challenge.[28] The behavior of local and state courts in the Herndon case bears out this conclusion. A discussion of the case strictly on its legal merits was rare. The federal courts proved more open-minded, but even Justice George Sutherland apparently let his distaste for Communist teachings about self-determination for the Black Belt influence his legal reasoning. One southern exception to this, and indeed the chief redeeming feature of the Georgia legal system, was Judge Hugh M. Dorsey. Something of a maverick, Dorsey demonstrated that at least a few white southerners were capable of dealing fairly with black and radical activists. But Dorsey's subsequent political difficulties, like those of the Scottsboro judge, James E. Horton, Sr., demonstrated the political risk inherent in departing too far from prevailing social attitudes.

Despite this criticism of southern justice, it must be conceded that the legal system eventually did free Herndon, though the ultimate decision came from Washington, D.C., not Atlanta. The ILD ignored such accomplishments because in its attacks on the legal system the group was in effect trying to have its cake and eat it too. If the courts upheld Herndon's conviction, the ILD could depict this as proof of their biased justice. If the courts freed Herndon, the ILD could still argue that they were biased but that only the ILD and mass protest, not any sense of justice, had forced them to make the correct decision. Nonetheless, the Herndon case earned little credit for the southern legal system. The fact that it took five long years to establish what should have been obvious from the beginning—Herndon's innocence—was hardly a stirring endorsement of the southern and American legal systems. For blacks, radicals, and many liberals, southern justice remained synonymous with the white man's law.

28. This was particularly true during the civil rights controversies of the 1950s and 1960s. One book which examines several facets of this problem is Leon Friedman (ed.), *Southern Justice* (New York: Pantheon, 1965), especially Michael Meltsner, "Southern Appellate Courts: A Dead End," 136–54.

Epilogue

SURPRISINGLY, the favorable decision rendered to Angelo Herndon by the United States Supreme Court in 1937 did not change the status of the seventeen others indicted under the insurrection law in Georgia. Completely ignoring the *Herndon* v. *Lowry* ruling, Solicitor General John A. Boykin refused to drop the charges against these suspects, sticking to his decision for the next two years. Fearful of Boykin's ability to incite unfavorable publicity and skeptical of the objectivity of Georgia juries when the issues of race and radicalism were involved, the International Labor Defense prudently declined to exercise its right to demand a prompt trial. But, while the seventeen remained at liberty on bail, the cost of the annual premium for their bonds, especially those of the Atlanta Six, proved an irritant to the financially plagued ILD. Upon several occasions the ACLU made emergency payments to the bonding company when the ILD proved unable to produce the money on time.[1]

In February, 1939, ACLU director Roger N. Baldwin and ILD leaders warily considered a trial request for the Six but concluded that such a move would be, as Anna Damon phrased it, "most inadvisable" at the time. Several months later, though, as the date for yet another premium payment approached, the ILD became bolder. Overcoming its fears of Georgia juries and of Boykin, the ILD had attorney Elbert P. Tuttle write the solicitor general to inquire formally if his office planned

---

1. The premiums amounted to $260 annually. Report of board of directors meeting, September 12, 1938, in American Civil Liberties Union Archives, Princeton University Library, hereinafter cited as ACLU Archives.

any action and if the charges could now be dropped. To Tuttle's relief, Boykin reluctantly agreed to the *nolle prosequis* of the cases. Finally, on August 30, 1939, the indictments against the Atlanta Six and their fellow suspects were officially dropped.[2]

In the months following his vindication, Angelo Herndon enthusiastically plunged into work for the Communist party. In May, 1937, he was elected national vice-president of the Young Communist League. During the next few years he labored on various Communist projects and contributed occasional articles to the *Daily Worker*. Yet as the years passed Herndon slowly found that he was no longer a celebrity. Instead of the excitement of a grand struggle for justice he encountered the monotony of routine party activities.[3]

But in the early 1940s Herndon discovered a challenging new venture. With Ralph Ellison he edited the short-lived periodical, the *Negro Quarterly: A Review of Negro Life and Culture*. Founded by the Communist-sponsored Negro Publication Society of America, the journal published articles, poems, and reviews by such writers as Ellison, Sterling A. Brown, Langston Hughes, Herbert Aptheker, L. D. Reddick, E. Franklin Frazier, and Jorge Amado. Moreover, after 1941, the *Negro Quarterly* displayed some independence from the official Communist position. Instead of echoing the standard Communist declaration that domestic complaints over civil rights should be subordinated to the higher goal of winning the war, the review demanded that injustices be immediately exposed and corrected and that blacks be given an equal opportunity to participate in the war effort. Criticizing the Western powers for their paternalism and their hesitancy to apply the Four Freedoms at home, the journal declared that black Americans shared with colonial peoples throughout the world the desire for freedom.

2. Roger N. Baldwin to W. A. Sutherland, February 1, 1939, Elbert P. Tuttle to Baldwin, February 20, 1939, Anna Damon to Baldwin, February 20, 1939, Baldwin to Whitney North Seymour, July 25, 1939, Tuttle to John A. Boykin, August 30, 1939, and Boykin to Jerome M. Britchey, September 22, 1939, all *ibid*. Charges were dropped against Joseph Carr, M. H. Powers, Mary Dalton, Ann Burlack, Herbert Newton (Gilmer Brady), Henry Story, Annie Mae Leathers, Nannie Leah Young, Julia Jones, Clarence Weaver, William Moreland, Fannie Aderhold, Joseph Moreland, Edgar King, Zelman Ware, John Grant, and Lucille Lawrence.

3. New York *Times*, May 6, 1937, p. 18. In 1938 Herndon married Joyce M. Chellis of Gadsden, Alabama. See Angelo Herndon File, Schomburg Collection, New York Public Library; John Hammond Moore, "The Angelo Herndon Case, 1932–1937," *Phylon*, XXXII (Spring, 1971), 61.

While working on the quarterly, Herndon encountered some difficulty with Colonel Arthur V. McDermott, a local Selective Service director in New York. McDermott twice tried to revoke Herndon's occupational deferment, which was based on his work with the *Negro Quarterly*. In each instance, though, the local board upheld Herndon's appeal and renewed his 2-A classification. Whether McDermott's actions were prompted by personal or political motives is not clear.[4]

During the early forties Herndon remained a sincere Communist. But in subsequent years his faith wavered. By the war's end, he had apparently abandoned the party, along with several other prominent blacks including Langston Hughes.[5] The precise reasons for this decision are not known. Perhaps like other black Communists he became alienated by the party's deemphasis of domestic black problems during the war. Ellison later recalled that Herndon was searching for his own identity, which seemed to have become confused over the years. In any case, the break was final. Although Herndon continued to follow civil rights events, he withdrew from active public participation. In the middle or late forties he left New York and moved to a midwestern city. There he worked as a salesman and lived quietly, refusing to discuss his earlier life with anyone but trusted friends.[6]

Benjamin J. Davis, Jr., Herndon's original attorney, led a more publicized career. He remained a loyal Communist and rose high in party ranks, eventually receiving a seat on the Central Committee. A dynamic public speaker, Davis eventually entered New York City politics as a Communist candidate. Elected a city councilman in 1944, he successfully retained the position until 1949, when a new system of representation contributed to his downfall. In 1950, along with ten other top Communist leaders, he was indicted and convicted under the Smith

4. William A. Nolan, *Communism Versus the Negro* (Chicago: Henry Regnery, 1951), 157; *Negro Quarterly: A Review of Negro Life and Culture*, I (1942–43), Nos. 1–4; New York *Times*, August 20, 1943, p. 7, and August 31, 1943, p. 19.

5. Jessie Parkhurst Guzman (ed.), *Negro Year Book: A Review of Events Affecting Negro Life, 1941–1946* (Tuskegee, Ala.: Tuskegee Institute Department of Records and Research, 1947), 280; Murray Kempton, *Part of Our Time: Some Ruins and Monuments of the Thirties* (New York: Simon and Schuster, 1955), 255.

6. Moore, "The Angelo Herndon Case," 61; author's interview with Ralph Ellison, Washington, D.C., April 7, 1972. In 1967 Herndon initially agreed to cooperate with Moore's project but refused to reply to subsequent letters. He also declined to respond to my numerous inquiries.

Act for belonging to the Communist party and was sentenced to five years in prison. In 1951 the United States Supreme Court upheld the convictions in *Dennis* v. *United States*, thereby severely restricting the clear and present danger test. While serving his sentence in the federal penitentiary at Terre Haute (in a segregated section), Davis composed his memoirs, but when he was freed in 1955 authorities refused to release the manuscript. Not until 1965, a year after his death, did federal officials surrender the memoir, which was later published as *Communist Councilman from Harlem*. John Geer, Davis' former law partner, subsequently lived a quieter life. After leaving Atlanta in July, 1935, he relocated in Louisville, Kentucky, where he practiced criminal law. He died in November, 1946, at the age of forty-one.[7]

Whitney North Seymour, Herndon's second attorney, returned to the prestigious Manhattan law firm of Simpson, Thacher, and Bartlett, where eventually he became a senior partner. He accumulated numerous honors over the years, including terms as president of the Association of the Bar of the City of New York and chairman of the board of the Carnegie Endowment for International Peace. In 1960 he received the distinction of being named president of the American Bar Association, but not before several critical southern attorneys resurrected his participation in the Herndon case in hope of discrediting his candidacy.[8]

Elbert P. Tuttle, who had assisted Seymour in Atlanta, enjoyed a successful legal and civic career. He served as a trustee for Atlanta University and as head of the legal division of the Treasury Department during 1953–1954. Appointed to the Fifth Circuit Court of Appeals in 1954 by President Dwight D. Eisenhower, Tuttle sat as presiding judge from 1961 to 1967. In the early sixties he was asked to rule on a suit involving civil rights activists, reactionary local officials, and the resurrected Georgia insurrection law. In August, 1963, local authorities in Americus, Georgia, had arrested four civil rights workers and charged them with "inciting to insurrection" following several disturbances in

7. Benjamin J. Davis, *Communist Councilman from Harlem* (New York: International Publishers, 1969), 7–16; Henry Abraham, *Freedom and the Court* (New York: Oxford University Press, 1967), 139–42, 163–67; Mary V. Bennett [formerly Mrs. John Geer] to the author, March 14, 1975.

8. "Whitney North Seymour," *Current Biography, 1961* (New York: H. W. Wilson, 1961), 417–19.

the town. The four had been active in voter registration drives and other civil rights activities in Sumter County. After local officials held them without bail for over two months and declined to bring them to trial, attorneys for the four brought suit in federal court and gained a hearing. Following a two-day session, on November 1, 1963, a three-judge panel headed by Tuttle declared the insurrection law unconstitutional and terminated prosecutions under it. This ruling was significant because it marked the first time that a federal court had intervened in a civil rights case, at the request of a private party, to halt a state court proceeding.[9]

Still, this was not the last gasp of the insurrection statute. In September, 1966, Atlanta police made one additional futile effort to revive the law, this time hoping to prosecute civil rights activist Stokely Carmichael. A federal court, quickly reaffirming the 1963 ruling, dismissed the case.[10] Thus, after one hundred years of existence, Georgia's controversial insurrection law was finally dead. Originally fashioned in response to the unsettled conditions of the South's first Reconstruction, the statute had appropriately met its death amid the second and more permanent Reconstruction of the 1960s.

9. The court, however, declined to grant a general injunction against the local authorities, who continued to harass the defendants by pressing other charges against them as part of an admitted effort to drive all civil rights activists out of the area. New York *Times*, October 22, 1963, p. 31, November 1, 1963, p. 19, and November 2, 1963, p. 1; Atlanta *Constitution*, November 2, 1963; *Economist*, November 9, 1963, pp. 565–66; Michael Meitsner, "Southern Appellate Courts: A Dead End," in Leon Friedman (ed.), *Southern Justice* (New York: Pantheon, 1965), 148–54.

10. Paul D. Bolster, "Civil Rights Movements in Twentieth Century Georgia" (Ph.D. dissertation, University of Georgia, 1972), 321.

Selected
Bibliography

PRIMARY SOURCES

BOOKS, MEMOIRS, AND ARTICLES

Allen, James S. *The American Negro*. New York: International Publishers, 1932.

————. "The Black Belt: Area of Negro Majority." *Communist*, XIII (June, 1934), 581–99.

————. *Negro Liberation*. New York: International Publishers, 1938.

Alsop, Joseph, and Turner Catledge. *The 168 Days*. Garden City, N.Y.: Doubleday, Doran, 1938.

American Civil Liberties Union. *Let Freedom Ring!: The Story of Civil Liberty, 1936–1937*. New York: American Civil Liberties Union, 1937.

Ames, Jesse Daniel. *The Changing Character of Lynching*. Atlanta: Commission on Interracial Cooperation, 1942.

Baldwin, Roger N. "Negro Rights and Class Struggle." *Opportunity*, XII (September, 1934), 264–66.

Browder, Earl. *The People's Front*. New York: International Publishers, 1938.

————. "Recent Political Developments and Some Problems of the United Front." *Communist*, XIV (July, 1935), 625–40.

Burke, Donald. "It's Hard to Believe." *Labor Defender*, October 1, 1935, pp. 7–8.

Burns, Robert E. *I Am a Fugitive from a Georgia Chain Gang!*. New York: Grosset and Dunlap, 1932.

Cason, Clarence. *90 Degrees in the Shade*. Chapel Hill: University of North Carolina Press, 1935.

Coleman, Louis, ed. *Equal Justice: Year Book of the Fight for Democratic Rights, 1936–1937*. New York: International Labor Defense, 1937.

Damon, Anna. "The Struggle Against Criminal Syndicalist Laws." *Communist*, XVI (March, 1937), 279–86.

Davis, Benjamin J. *Communist Councilman from Harlem*. New York: International Publishers, 1969.

————. "Why I Am a Communist." *Phylon*, VIII (Spring, 1947), 105–16.

Dorsey, Hugh M. *A Statement from Governor Hugh M. Dorsey as to the Negro in Georgia*. Atlanta: N.p., 1921.

Ford, James W. "The United Front in the Field of Negro Work." *Communist*, XIV (February, 1935), 158–74.

Foster, William Z. *The Negro People in American History*. New York: International Publishers, 1954.

Gannett, Lewis S. "Skipping Bail." *Nation*, October 22, 1930, pp. 437–38.

"Georgia Chain Gang Awaits Peaceful Demonstrator." *Christian Century*, August 21, 1935, pp. 1052–53.

Guzman, Jessie Parkhurst, ed. *Negro Year Book: A Review of Events Affecting Negro Life, 1941–1946*. Tuskegee, Ala.: Tuskegee Institute Department of Records and Research, 1947.

Hays, Arthur Garfield. "Civil Liberties and Angelo Herndon." *Survey Graphic*, December, 1935, pp. 616–17.

————. *Trial by Prejudice*. New York: Convici and Friede, 1933.

Herndon, Angelo. *Let Me Live*. Originally published in 1937. New York: Arno Press, 1969.

————. "You Cannot Kill the Working Class." In August Meier, Elliott Rudwick, and Francis L. Broderick, eds. *Black Protest Thought in the Twentieth Century*. 2nd ed. Indianapolis: Bobbs-Merrill, 1971.

"Herndon Case, The." *New Republic*, April 10, 1935, pp. 230–31.

Hirsch, Alfred. "On Behalf of Angelo Herndon." *New Masses*, August 20, 1935, pp. 13–14.

Isms: A Review of Alien Isms, Revolutionary Communism, and Their Active Sympathizers in the United States. Indianapolis: National Americanism Commission of the American Legion, 1937.

Kempton, Murray. *Part of Our Time: Some Ruins and Monuments of the Thirties*. New York: Simon and Schuster, 1955.

Lawson, John Howard. *A Southern Welcome*. New York: National Committee for the Defense of Political Prisoners, 1934.

McGill, Ralph E. *The South and the Southerner*. Boston: Little, Brown, 1959.

Mack, Mary. "We Have Them on the Run." *Labor Defender*, January 1, 1937, p. 13.

Mason, Lucy Randolph. *To Win These Rights*. New York: Harper and Brothers, 1952.

Milner, Lucille. *The Education of an American Liberal*. New York: Horizon Press, 1954.

"Nation's Honor Roll, The." *Nation*, January 1, 1936, p. 9.

"Negro Editors on Communism: A Symposium of the American Negro Press." *Crisis*, XXXIX (April, 1932), 117–19, and (May, 1932), 154–56.

North, Joseph. "Chain Gang Governor." *New Masses*, November 12, 1935, pp. 9–12.

_____. "Herndon Is Back in Atlanta." *New Masses*, November 5, 1935, pp. 15–16.

_____. *No Men Are Strangers*. New York: International Publishers, 1958.

_____. "United Front Opens Herndon's Jail." *New Masses*, December 17, 1935, pp. 15–16.

Page, Myra. "Men in Chains." *Nation*, November 13, 1935, pp. 561–63.

Patterson, William L. "The I.L.D. Faces the Future." *Communist*, XIII (July, 1934), 727–40.

_____. *The Man Who Cried Genocide*. New York: International Publishers, 1971.

Powell, Adam Clayton, Jr. *Marching Blacks*. New York: Dial Press, 1945.

"Red, Black, and Georgia." *Time*, January 30, 1933, p. 14.

Shay, Frank. *Judge Lynch: His First Hundred Years*. New York: Ives Washburn, 1938.

Small, Sasha. *Hell in Georgia*. New York: International Labor Defense, 1935.

Stevenson, Elizabeth. "A Personal History of Change in Atlanta." *Virginia Quarterly Review*, XLI (Autumn, 1965), 580–95.

Street, James H. *Look Away!: A Dixie Notebook*. New York: Viking Press, 1936.

Thomas, Jesse O. *My Story in Black and White*. New York: Exposition Press, 1967.

"Trigonometry Problem." *Emory Alumnus*, X (November–December, 1934), 7–8.

White, Walter. "The Negro and the Communists." *Harper's*, CLXIV (December, 1931), 62–72.

Wilson, Walter. "Atlanta's Communists." *Nation*, June 25, 1930, pp. 730–31.

_____. "Georgia Suppresses Insurrection." *Nation*, August 1, 1934, pp. 127–28.

Wisdom, Justice, and Moderation. New York: Joint Committee to Aid the Herndon Defense, 1935.

GOVERNMENT DOCUMENTS

Acts and Resolutions of the General Assembly of the State of Georgia, at a Session in November and December, 1871. Atlanta: W. A. Hemphill and Co., 1872.

Acts of the General Assembly of the State of Georgia, Passed in Milledgeville, at an Annual Session in November and December, 1833. Macon: Polhill and Fort, 1834.

Acts of the General Assembly of the State of Georgia, Passed in Milledgeville, at an Annual Session in November and December, 1866. Macon: J. W. Burke and Co., 1867.

Journals of the Ten-Days Special Session and the Regular Session of the House of Representatives of the State of Georgia, 1935. Atlanta: Stein Printing Co., 1935.

Journals of the Ten-Days Special Session and the Regular Session of the Senate of the State of Georgia, 1935. Atlanta: Stein Printing Co., 1935.

Journals of the Ten-Days Special Session and the Regular Session of the Senate of the State of Georgia, 1937. Atlanta: Stein Printing Co., 1937.

United States House of Representatives. *Investigation of Communistic Propaganda: Hearings Before a Special Committee to Investigate Communistic Activities in the United States.* 71st Cong., 2nd Sess., Pt. 6, Vol. I.

LEGAL CASES AND RECORDS

Carr v. *State*, 166 S.E. 827 (1932).

Carr v. *State*, 167 S.E. 103 (1933).

Carr v. *State*, 169 S.E. 201 (1933).

De Jonge v. *Oregon*, 229 U.S. 353 (1936).

Downer v. *Dunaway*, 53 F.2d 586 (1931).

Gibson v. *Georgia*, 38 Ga. 572 (1869).

Herndon v. *Georgia*, No. 9871, Supreme Court of Georgia. Transcript of Record. Georgia Supreme Court, Atlanta, Ga.

Herndon v. *Georgia*, No. 665, Supreme Court of the United States. Printed Briefs and Transcript of Record. Offices of Sutherland, Asbill, and Brennan, Atlanta, Ga.

Herndon v. *Georgia*, 295 U.S. 441 (1935).

Herndon v. *Lowry*, Nos. 474 and 475, Supreme Court of the United States. Printed Briefs. Offices of Sutherland, Asbill, and Brennan, Atlanta, Ga.

Herndon v. *Lowry*, 186 S.E. 429 (1936).

Herndon v. *Lowry*, 301 U.S. 242 (1937).

Herndon v. *State*, 174 S.E. 597 (1934).

Herndon v. *State*, 176 S.E. 620 (1934).

Lee v. *Maryland*, 161 Atl. 284 (1932).

Moore v. *Dempsey*, 261 U.S. 86 (1924).

Schenck v. *United States*, 249 U.S. 47 (1919).

State v. *Angelo Herndon*, No. 37812, Superior Court of Fulton County. Miscellaneous Documents. Fulton County Courthouse, Atlanta, Ga.

MANUSCRIPT COLLECTIONS

American Civil Liberties Union Archives. Princeton University Library, Princeton, N.J.

Commission on Interracial Cooperation Papers. Trevor Arnett Library, Atlanta University, Atlanta.

Frank P. Graham Papers. Southern Historical Collection, University of North Carolina Library, Chapel Hill.

Angelo Herndon File. Schomburg Collection, New York Public Library, New York.

International Labor Defense Papers. Schomburg Collection, New York Public Library, New York.

National Association for the Advancement of Colored People Papers. Library of Congress, Washington, D.C.

Oral History Collection. Nicholas M. Butler Library, Columbia University, New York.

Glenn W. Rainey Papers. In possession of Glenn W. Rainey, Atlanta, Ga.

Socialist Party Papers. Duke University Library, Durham, N.C.

Nathan Yagol File. Emory University Archives, Atlanta, Ga.

NEWSPAPERS AND MAGAZINES

Atlanta *Constitution*
Atlanta *Daily World*
Atlanta *Georgian*
Atlanta *Journal*
Commonwealth (Atlanta)
Crisis
Daily Worker (New York)
Journal of Labor (Atlanta)
Kourier
Labor Defender
Louisiana Weekly (New Orleans)
Macon *Telegraph*
Nation
Negro Quarterly: A Review of Negro Life and Culture
New Republic
New York *Times*
Pittsburgh *Courier*
Savannah *Tribune*
Socialist Call (New York)

INTERVIEWS

Brennan, Joseph. February 6, 1970, Atlanta, Ga.
Day, R. A. September 22, 1970, Atlanta, Ga.
Ellison, Ralph. April 7, 1972, Washington, D.C.
Gellhorn, Walter. September 10, 1970, New York, N.Y.
Johnson, Edgar H., Jr. August 24, 1970, Atlanta, Ga.

Jones, William H. September 22, 1970, Atlanta, Ga.

LeCraw, J. Walter. August 25, 1970, Atlanta, Ga.

Meyer, Howard N. September 4, 1970, New York, N.Y.

Mitchell, H. L. August 11, 1970, New Orleans, La.

Rainey, Glenn W. August 26, 1970, Atlanta, Ga.

Seymour, Whitney North. September 8, 1970, New York, N.Y.

Tuttle, Elbert P. September 22, 1970, Atlanta, Ga.

Washburn, Nannie Leah Young. September 21, 1970, Atlanta, Ga.

West, Don. September 13, 1970, Pipestem, W.Va.

Woodward, C. Vann. November 8, 1973, Atlanta, Ga.

LETTERS

Baldwin, Roger N., to the author, March 5, 1970.

Bennett, Mary V., to the author, March 14, 1975.

Crawford, Floyd W., to the author, November 21, 1973.

Gellhorn, Walter, to the author, May 6, 1970.

LeCraw, J. Walter, to the author, May 7, 1970.

Mackay, Clifford W., to the author, October 28, 1970.

Mitchell, Clarence, to the author, August 5, 1974.

Patterson, William L., to the author, May 25, 1970.

SECONDARY SOURCES

BOOKS AND ARTICLES

Abraham, Henry. *Freedom and the Court*. New York: Oxford University Press, 1967.

Alexander, Raymond Pace. "The Upgrading of the Negro's Status by Supreme Court Decisions." *Journal of Negro History*, XXX (April, 1945), 117–49.

Bornet, Vaughn D. "Historical Scholarship, Communism, and the Negro." *Journal of Negro History*, XXXVII (July, 1952), 304–24.

Burns, James MacGregor. *Roosevelt: The Lion and the Fox*. New York: Harcourt, Brace, and World, 1956.

Carter, Dan T. *Scottsboro: A Tragedy of the American South*. Baton Rouge: Louisiana State University Press, 1969.

Chafee, Zechariah, Jr. *Free Speech in the United States*. Cambridge: Harvard University Press, 1941.

Coulter, E. Merton. *Georgia: A Short History*. Chapel Hill: University of North Carolina Press, 1947.

Crowe, Charles. "Racial Massacre in Atlanta, September 22, 1906." *Journal of Negro History*, LIV (April, 1969), 150–73.

Dinnerstein, Leonard. *The Leo Frank Case*. New York: Columbia University Press, 1968.

Drake, St. Clair, and Horace R. Cayton. *Black Metropolis*. Rev. ed. New York: Harper and Row, 1962.

Draper, Theodore. *American Communism and Soviet Russia*. New York: Viking, 1960.

Dykeman, Wilma, and James Stokely. *Seeds of Southern Change: The Life of Will W. Alexander*. Chicago: University of Chicago Press, 1962.

Edwards, John C., and Joseph H. Kitchens, Jr. "Georgia's Anti-Insurrection Law: Slave Justice for Twentieth-Century Negro Radicals." *Washington State Research Studies*, XXXVIII (June, 1970), 122–33.

English, Thomas H. *Emory University, 1915–1965: A Semicentennial History*. Atlanta: Emory University, 1966.

Friedman, Leon, ed. *Southern Justice*. New York: Pantheon, 1965.

Gosnell, Cullen B. *Government and Politics of Georgia*. New York: Thomas Nelson and Sons, 1936.

Jackson, Kenneth T. *The Ku Klux Klan in the City, 1915–1930*. New York: Oxford University Press, 1967.

Josephson, Hannah. *Jeannette Rankin*. Indianapolis: Bobbs-Merrill, 1974.

Latham, Earl. *The Communist Controversy in Washington: From the New Deal to McCarthy*. Cambridge: Harvard University Press, 1966.

Leab, Daniel J. "'United We Eat': The Creation and Organization of the Unemployed Councils in 1930." *Labor History*, VIII (Fall, 1967), 300–15.

Leuchtenburg, William E. *Franklin D. Roosevelt and the New Deal*. New York: Harper and Row, 1963.

McMahan, C. A. *The People of Atlanta*. Athens: University of Georgia Press, 1950.

Mason, Alpheus, and William M. Beaney. *The Supreme Court in a Free Society*. New York: Norton, 1968.

Mendelson, Wallace. "Clear and Present Danger—From Schenck to Dennis." *Columbia Law Review*, LII (April, 1952), 313–33.

Miller, Loren. *The Petitioners: The Story of the Supreme Court of the United States and the Negro*. New York: Pantheon, 1966.

Moore, John Hammond. "The Angelo Herndon Case, 1932–1937." *Phylon*, XXXII (Spring, 1971), 60–71.

––––––––. "Communists and Fascists in a Southern City: Atlanta, 1930." *South Atlantic Quarterly*, LXVII (Summer, 1968), 437–54.

Murray, Hugh. *Civil Rights History-Writing and Anti-Communism: A Critique*. Occasional Paper 16. New York: American Institute for Marxist Studies, 1975.

————. "The NAACP Versus the Communist Party: The Scottsboro Rape Case, 1931–1932." *Phylon*, XXVIII (Fall, 1967), 276–87.

Nathanson, Nathaniel L. "The Communist Trial and the Clear-and-Present-Danger Test." *Harvard Law Review*, LXIII (May, 1950), 1167–75.

Nolan, William A. *Communism Versus the Negro*. Chicago: Henry Regnery, 1951.

Potter, David M. "C. Vann Woodward." In Marcus Cunliffe and Robin Winks, eds. *Pastmasters: Some Essays on American Historians*. New York: Harper and Row, 1969.

Prude, Jonathan. "Portrait of a Civil Libertarian: The Faith and Fear of Zechariah Chafee, Jr." *Journal of American History*, LX (December, 1973), 633–56.

Record, Wilson. *The Negro and the Communist Party*. Chapel Hill: University of North Carolina Press, 1951.

Rice, Roger L. "Residential Segregation by Law, 1910–1917." *Journal of Southern History*, XXXIV (May, 1968), 179–99.

Rogers, Ernest. *Peachtree Parade*. Atlanta: Tupper and Love, 1956.

Roy, Ralph Lord. *Communism and the Churches*. New York: Harcourt, Brace, 1960.

Seton-Watson, Hugh. *From Lenin to Khruschev: The History of World Communism*. New York: Frederick A. Praeger, 1960.

Simkins, Francis B. *A History of the South*. New York: Alfred A. Knopf, 1965.

Sternsher, Bernard, ed. *The Negro in Depression and War*. Chicago: Quadrangle, 1969.

Terkel, Studs. *Hard Times: An Oral History of the Great Depression*. New York: Pantheon, 1970.

Thomas, H. Glyn. "The Highlander Folk School: The Depression Years." *Tennessee Historical Quarterly*, XXII (December, 1964), 358–71.

Tindall, George B. *The Emergence of the New South, 1913–1945*. Baton Rouge: Louisiana State University Press, 1967. Vol. X of Wendell Holmes Stephenson and E. Merton Coulter, eds. *A History of the South*. 10 vols. Baton Rouge: Louisiana State University Press, 1949–.

Woodward, C. Vann. *Tom Watson: Agrarian Rebel*. New York: Oxford University Press, 1963.

Work Projects Administration Writers' Program. *Atlanta: A City of the Modern South*. New York: Smith and Durrell, 1942.

THESES AND DISSERTATIONS

Bolster, Paul D. "Civil Rights Movements in Twentieth Century Georgia." Ph.D. dissertation, University of Georgia, 1972.

Entin, David. "Angelo Herndon." M.A. thesis, University of North Carolina, 1963.

Lemmon, Sarah M. "The Public Career of Eugene Talmadge, 1926–1936." Ph.D. dissertation, University of North Carolina, 1952.

Mathews, John M. "Studies in Race Relations in Georgia, 1890–1930." Ph.D. dissertation, Duke University, 1970.

Merrill, Michael. "The Angelo Herndon Case: Free Speech in Georgia, 1932–1937." M.A. thesis, Columbia University, 1972.

Minnis, Fred. "The Attitude of Federal Courts on the Exclusion of Negroes from Jury Service." M.A. thesis, Howard University, 1934.

Moseley, Clement Charlton. "Invisible Empire: A History of the Ku Klux Klan in Twentieth-Century Georgia, 1915–1965." Ph.D. dissertation, University of Georgia, 1968.

Porter, Michael Leroy. "Black Atlanta: An Interdisciplinary Study of Blacks on the East Side of Atlanta, 1890–1930." Ph.D. dissertation, Emory University, 1974.

Index

Abrons, Herbert, 105, 106
Aderhold, Fannie, 212*n*
Ades, Bernard, 14–15
Agnes Scott College, 133
Alexander, Will W.: and Atlanta Six, 24, 29; and Herndon case, 71–72, 158–59; and Communists, 74–75, 202–203; friendship of, with C. Vann Woodward, 78; mentioned, 142
Allen, H. A., 11, 34, 170
Allen, O. W., 88, 91–92
Alling, Kay, 125, 127
Alling, Mrs. R. W., 125, 135, 136–37
Almand, Bond, 143
Amado, Jorge, 212
American Civil Liberties Union: and civil liberties, 17, 190; and the Atlanta Six, 23–24, 27–28, 29, 80, 203–204, 211; and Herndon case, 70–71, 79–80, 157, 158–59, 203–204; and Communists, 80; relations of, with ILD, 80, 152, 156, 195–96, 204; and Effie Cox, 93–94; mentioned, 23, 32, 160*n*, 172
American Federation of Labor, 174
American Legion, 138, 166, 180
American Order of Fascisti, 2
American Youth Congress, 174–75
Amici curiae brief, 153, 157, 158
Anderson, Sherwood, 11–12
Anderson, W. T.: on Atlanta Six, 23, 114; and Herndon case, 73–74, 159, 186–87, 202; on Communists, 123
Andrews, Mrs. J. E., 22*n*
Ansley, David, 126–27
Anticommunism, 10, 130, 143–45, 163–64. *See also* Georgia officials

Anti-Semitism, 18, 113
Aptheker, Herbert, 212
Atlanta: relief crisis in, 1, 3–6, 10; history of, 17–18
Atlanta blacks: and Herndon case, 75–76, 115; and ILD, 84, 98–101, 197, 200–201; and communism, 84–85, 96; on local police, 86–87, 88–89, 91–93; and local officials, 130, 180–81
Atlanta *Constitution*: on relief crisis, 2, 3; on Herndon case, 37, 61, 117, 186, 205; on communism, 126, 134, 138, 163–64; 179–80; mentioned, 123, 125
Atlanta *Daily World*: on local police, 32–33, 87–88, 91; on all-white juries, 36–37; on Herndon case, 37, 76, 186; on Ku Klux Klan, 95–96
Atlanta *Georgian*, 18
Atlanta *Independent*, 37
Atlanta *Journal*, 125
Atlanta Six: arrested, 20, 22–27 *passim*; bonds for, 28, 79–80, 211–12; and Will Alexander, 202; charges of, dropped, 212*n*; mentioned, 29, 35, 193, 203–204

Bailey, A. F., 76
Baldwin, Roger N.: and Atlanta Six, 24, 70, 71, 211; and Herndon case, 70–72, 159, 160*n*, 171; and ILD, 80, 196, 204; mentioned, 32, 93, 102
Baxter, J. A., 99
Bedacht, Max, 129
Bell, John, 120
Benson, Syd, 78–79
Bilbo, Theodore G., 1
Binkley, W. G., 83

Birmingham, 9–10, 19, 25
Birmingham *Post*, 150
Blacks: on discrimination, 16, 29, 34; on communsim, 44, 54, 165–66, 169–70, 174, 191–95, 199–202, 205, 212–13; and Herndon case, 63–66, 75–77, 85, 151, 166, 185–88, 199–202, 209; on Red raids, 169–70
Black Shirts, 2
Blake, Olive, 160n
Blalock, Dr. J. C., 56, 104
Blayton, J. B., 77, 92
Bonus Army, 2
Boykin, John A.: prosecutes Herndon, 38, 153, 166–68; on communism, 114, 207; discovers secret Communist group, 128–29; and anti-Red law, 130, 143–45; political rivals of, 162n, 173, 206; mentioned, 4, 10, 162, 178, 211–12. *See also* Georgia officials
Brady, Gilmer. *See* Newton, Herbert
Brandeis, Louis, 120, 149–50, 182
Braxton, Eugene. *See* Herndon, Angelo
Brenau College, 138
Brodsky, Joseph, 15, 116–17
Brotherhood of Sleeping Car Porters, 174
Broun, Heywood, 187
Browder, Earl, 15, 118
Brown, Joseph E., 21
Brown, Sterling A., 212
Brown, William Montgomery, 8, 12, 46, 50, 126, 147
Browning, L. B., 170n
Burke, Donald, 11
Burlack, Ann, 22, 28, 103–104, 201
Butler, Pierce, 183
Butler Street YMCA, 129

Calloway, A. W., 170, 172
Camp, Lindley, 106, 122–23, 159
Cardozo, Benjamin N., 149–50, 182
Carmichael, Stokely, 215
Carolina Times (Durham, N.C.), 185
Carr, Joseph, 9, 19–20, 22, 25–27
Carr v. *State*, 149. *See also* Atlanta Six
Carter, Alex, 36–37
Carter, Dan T., 193
Chain gang, 81, 154, 161n. *See also* Prison conditions
Chalmers, Allan Knight, 157, 203
Chambers, Hewitt W., 93–94
Chappell, Winifred, 105–106
Chester, John, 7
Chicago *Defender*, 65

Christian Century, 185
Cincinnati *Union*, 66
Civil Rights Congress, 13, 198n
Civil rights movement, 214–15
Clear and present danger test: Georgia Supreme Court on, 120, 170–71; explained, 146, 146n, 189; Whitney North Seymour on, 146, 148, 163, 208–209; Justice Roberts on, 183; modified, 214
Clement, Hunt, Jr., 136, 139
Cleveland *Call and Post*, 171
Colman, Louis, 165
Commission on Interracial Cooperation, 98, 158–59, 202–203
Commonwealth, 134–35
Communism and Christianity, 8, 46, 50, 214
Communist International, 97, 152
Communist party: and ILD, 12; in South, 19, 22, 66; on race, 19, 54; and liberals, 29, 84, 152, 156, 174, 201–204; activities of, 46, 49, 90–91, 163–64; and blacks, 63–66, 83–85, 165–66, 192, 192n, 200n, 201–202, 212–13; and labor movement, 123–24; on Judge Dorsey, 165; on U.S. Supreme Court, 188. *See also* Anticommunism; International Labor Defense (ILD); Scottsboro case
Cone, John L., 87, 95, 124
Connally, Mrs. C. H., 77
Corley, T. J., 54–55, 206n
Court-packing plan, 181–82, 189
Cox, Effie, 93–94
Cox, Harvey W., 133, 137, 158
Craddock, R. L., 40, 40n
Crawford, Bruce, 155
Criminal syndicalism laws, 21, 176
Crisis, 63–64, 166

Dabney, Virginius, 74, 74n, 171
Dabney, W. P., 200
Daily Worker: supports Angelo Herndon, 10, 67–68, 104, 151, 165, 184; on anticommunism, 26, 114; on all-white juries, 34; and Herndon bail drive, 35, 115–16, 118; on ILD, 78, 84; on George Schuyler, 119; on *De Jonge* ruling, 177; on U.S. Supreme Court, 181–82, 188; mentioned, 125, 175
Dalton, Mary, 22, 25
Damon, Anna: and Herndon case, 118, 165, 178, 184, 192n; mentioned, 145, 211
Dangerous tendency test: Georgia Supreme Court on, 120; LeCraw on, 146–48; Justice Roberts on, 183; mentioned, 109, 189, 208
D'Antignac, Edward, 95

David L. Roston Agency, 80
Davis, Benjamin J., Jr.: defends Herndon, 7, 11, 34–59 *passim*, 81; legal skills of, 12, 196–97, 201, 208; early life of, 37–38; and Communist party, 56–57, 57n; and ILD, 76, 90, 100, 200; on Glover Davis' murder, 88–92; on Herndon's health, 103; and white radicals, 112, 201; flees Atlanta, 113; on U.S. Supreme Court, 182, 188; later life of, 213–14; mentioned, 83, 95, 178, 204
Davis, Benjamin J., Sr., 11, 37
Davis, Frank Marshall, 33, 64, 101n
Davis, Glover, 88–89, 91–92, 194
Davis, John P., 182
Davis, Ollis, 91
Deaver, Bascom S., 30–31
De Jonge, Dirk, 176–77, 190
Dennis v. *United States*, 214
Divine, Father, 152
Dodge, Witherspoon, 160n, 178–79
Dorsey, Hugh M.: presides over special hearing, 161–66, 162n; prosecutes Leo Frank, 162; defeats John Hudson, 172, 173, 207; and southern justice, 210; mentioned, 4, 162
Dorsey, J. T., 89–90
Downer, John, 30–31, 98–99, 142, 201
Dreiser, Theodore, 117
Dyer, Maggie, 92

Echols, John, 168
Elaine, Arkansas, riot cases, 31
Eleazer, R. B., 88, 159, 162
Ellison, Ralph, 209, 212, 213
Emergency Relief Committee, 3
Emory University, 50–51, 54–55, 132–34, 136
Engels, Friedrich, 51
Etheridge, Paul S., 171, 173
Evans, Mercer G., 50–51, 121, 131–32, 137, 207

Fain, Grover, 22
Fields, E. E., 76
Fish, Hamilton, 19n
Ford, James W., 118
Fort McPherson, 122
Fosdick, Harry Emerson, 157, 203
Foster, William Z., 80n
Foster-Ford clubs, 10, 46, 49
Fountain, W. A., Jr., 115
Fox, Mary, 156
Frank, Leo, 18, 162, 205

Frazier, E. Franklin, 212
Free speech. *See* Clear and present danger test
Frenwick, Fred, 65
Fryer, Charles, 21
Fulton Cotton and Bag Mill, 205n
Fulton County, 1, 2, 4, 10
Fulton County Civic League, 88
Fulton Tower Prison, 55–56, 102–103, 107, 161

Gaines, R. B., 41–42
Gallagher, Buell G., 142
Geer, John: defends Herndon, 7, 11, 34–44 *passim*, 54, 58; legal skills of, 12, 196–97, 208; early career of, 38; requests prosecution of policeman, 88, 91; defends white radicals, 124, 129, 201; later career of, 214; mentioned, 81–82, 84, 95, 116, 143, 204
Gelders, Joseph, 178
Gellhorn, Walter, 140, 141–42, 147
Georgia legislature, 20, 21, 142–45, 178–79
Georgia officials: and communism, 6–7, 19, 22, 26, 45–46, 83, 90–91, 93, 110–11, 131, 139, 168–69, 204–205, 207, 214–15; mentioned, 178–79, 190
Georgia Supreme Court: and Atlanta Six, 28–29, 35; and Herndon conviction, 108–109, 119–20, 170–71; mentioned, 21
Gewinner, Holt, 2
Gibson, John T., 21
Ginsburg, Sarah, 77
Gitlow v. *New York*, 109, 148, 150, 183. *See also* Dangerous tendency test
Glenn, T. K., 3, 4
Godwin, Ruth, 170n
Googe, George L., 123–24
Gowland, Emmet, 155
Grady Hospital, 104–105
Graham, Frank P., 158–59
Grant, John, 129, 136, 212n
Graves, Bibb, 155
Griggs, A. A., 170n

Hall, Otto, 45
Halley, Mrs. S. D., 93
Hamilton, George B., 86
Hammond, Henry C., 98
Hancock, Oliver C., 7, 23, 26–29
Hardwick, Thomas W., 24, 159, 178
Hardy, A. Gordon, 41
Harper, C. L., 86–87
Harris, Julian, 133, 158
Harris, Martha, 170n

Hart, Robert H., 67, 76–77
Hartsfield, William B., 143, 173
Harvard Law Review, 151
Hawks, Ellie, 170*n*
Hawks, Nina, 170*n*
Hays, Arthur Garfield, 71, 204
Henderson, J. Raymond: on police, 33, 88, 90; and Herndon, 77, 83, 85, 95; and ILD, 99, 100, 200; on Atlanta NAACP, 101*n*; on Red menace, 130–31
Hendrix, Walter C., 4, 6, 52
Henry, T. J., 38, 88
Henson, A. L., 155, 159, 160*n*, 163, 205*n*
Herndon, Angelo: leads relief demonstration, 5; arrested in Atlanta, 7; early life of, 8–9; arrested in Birmingham, 9, 25; converted to communism, 9; as a symbol, 17, 209–10; on trial, 36–61 *passim*; becomes *cause célèbre*, 62; reaction of southern whites to, 72–73, 205–207; bail for, 81–82, 115–16; health of, in prison, 101–105; publicity campaigns for, 105, 174–75; visited by northern delegation, 107; leaves prison, 116–17; on Dubois and Schuyler, 118–19; first appeal of, to U.S. Supreme Court, 146–50, 152–53, 156–58; pardon for, 158–59; returns to prison, 160–61; habeas corpus hearing of, 162–66; and Scottsboro case, 166, 193, 205–206; in American Youth Congress, 174–75; and President Roosevelt, 175; second appeal of, to the U.S. Supreme Court, 182–84; on U.S. Supreme Court, 184, 188, 189; later life of, 212–13; mentioned, 10, 34, 35, 68, 79, 81*n*, 118, 154, 173, 193, 193*n*
Herndon, Milton, 118
Herring, Hubert C., 203
Highlander Folk School, 112
Hirsch, Alfred, 155
Holland, R. N., 56, 81, 107
Holmes, Oliver Wendell, 120, 146, 148
Holsey Temple C.M.E. Church, 94–95, 96
Hope, John, Jr., 130
Hopkins, Shirley, 155
Hornsby, Guy, 180–81
Horton, James E., 165, 166, 201
Horwatt, S., 93–94
Houston, Charles H.: and *amici curiae* brief, 153, 157; and ILD, 156, 174; on insurrection law, 160; compares Herndon and Scottsboro cases, 174; speaks in Atlanta, 180–81
Howard, David T., 39–40, 40*n*
Howard, G. H., 27, 124, 171
Hubert, Dennis, 76*n*

Hubert, H. O., 129
Hudson, John H.: discovers insurrection law, 19, 22; prosecutes Atlanta Six, 24–28, 35; prosecutes Herndon, 38–55 *passim*, 167–68, 206*n*; and communism, 90–91, 110–11, 138, 204–205, 207; prosecutes DeKalb suspects, 126–27; and Judge Dorsey, 162*n*, 171–72, 173, 207; mentioned, 36, 106, 136, 206. *See also* Georgia officials
Hughes, Charles Evans, 145, 153, 176, 182, 208
Hughes, Langston, 212, 213
Hunter, Fannie, 125

Industrial Workers of the World (IWW), 156
Insurrection law: constitutionality attacked, 12, 34, 39, 84, 146–48, 163–64, 177–78, 208; history of, 20–21, 211, 214–15; other radicals arrested under, 93–94, 169–70; Georgia Supreme Court on, 108–109, 119–20, 170–71; application of, to Herndon declared unconstitutional, 164, 182–84; mentioned, 155, 203
International Labor Defense (ILD): and Scottsboro case, 10, 13, 14, 145; and black attorneys, 11, 34, 197; history of, 12; assists blacks, 12, 16, 83–85, 191–95, 201–202; legal strategy of, 12–13, 79, 210; defends Euel Lee, 14–15; defends Atlanta Six, 23, 27–28; and united front, 77–79, 155–56; finances of, 79–80, 193, 193*n*; and ACLU, 80, 204; relations of, with liberals, 84, 152, 156, 202–204; protests Glover Davis' murder, 89; and NAACP, 99, 152, 155–56, 174, 201, 203; and Save Angelo Herndon campaign, 102, 103, 154; selects Whitney North Seymour, 140–41, 156; and sectarianism, 194*n*, 195; quality of legal services of, 196–98; mentioned, 76–77, 82, 84–85, 90, 93–94, 95, 97, 141, 205, 211. *See also* Communist party; Scottsboro case
International Workers' Order, 128, 129
Irwin, Frank, 11–12
Isserman, Abraham, 27–28

Jackson, Carrie, 170*n*
Jackson, Lula, 170*n*
Jefferson, Thomas, 51
Johnson, Edgar A., 133, 207
Joint Committee to Aid the Herndon Defense, 156, 160, 174–75
Jones, I. B., 88
Jones, Jerome, 31

Jones, Julia, 212*n*
Jones, M. Ashby, 132, 137
Jones, Orphan. *See* Lee, Euel
Journal of Labor, 4, 73, 134
Juries: blacks and, 12, 14–15, 34–37, 39–43,
  80–81; for Herndon trial, 44–45; mentioned,
  84, 145

Kane, Edward, 164
Kelley, William D., 65
Key, James L., 86, 173
King, Carol Weiss, 119, 140, 160, 178
King, Edgar, 212*n*
King, Martin Luther, Sr., 170
Klarin, Julius, 22*n*, 45
Klarin, Lizette, 22*n*
Ku Klux Klan (KKK): and Herndon case, 45,
  117, 206; and Ben Davis, 44; and Scottsboro
  rally, 94–95; and John Boykin, 114, 130;
  mentioned, 18, 59, 91

Labor movement: and communism, 22, 203;
  and Herndon case, 174, 203; mentioned, 179
Lampkin, Daisy, 34, 69–70
Lawrence, Lucille, 126, 136, 212*n*
Lawson, John Howard, 105, 107
League for Industrial Democracy (LID), 156
League of Struggle for Negro Rights, 156
Leathers, Annie Mae, 45, 124, 129, 201, 205*n*,
  212*n*
Leathers, Roy C., 128
Leathers, Willie, 111
LeCraw, J. Walter: on insurrection law, 22*n*,
  146–48, 153, 163, 167, 178; prosecutes
  Herndon, 39–60 *passim*; and communism,
  60*n*, 204–205, 207; on Seymour, 199
Lee, Euel, 14–15, 198
Lee, Sarah, 125, 127
LeFlore, J. L., 180
Leibowitz, Samuel, 145
Lenin, Nikolai, 51
Let Me Live, 209
Levinson, David, 14–15
Liberals: and ILD, 83–84, 202–204; and Hern-
  don, 131, 158–59, 202–204; on court-
  packing plan, 182; and Communists,
  201–204
Life and Struggles of Negro Toilers, The, 8, 46
Linder, Tom, 86
Longino, George F., 2
Louisiana Weekly (New Orleans), 65, 66, 185
Lowry, James L., 161, 164
Lynching. *See* Downer, John; Frank, Leo

McClellan, W. A., 23, 26–29, 70–71
McDermott, Arthur V., 213
Mackay, Cliff W., 36, 164
Macon Telegraph, 23, 202, 205. *See also*
  Anderson, W. T.
McRae, William G., 173
McReynolds, James C., 183
Maddox, James M., 104
Manufacturer's Record, 19
Martin, J. A.: and Davis and Geer, 43–44; and
  ILD, 77, 83, 100–101, 201; on police, 88,
  90; meets Talmadge, 106–107; hides Don
  West, 112; mentioned, 44, 76, 130
Marx, Karl, 51
Mass protest: explained, 12–13, 195–96,
  197–98; ILD use of, 79, 210; mentioned, 15,
  87, 165
Mays, Mrs. Benjamin E., 77
Men of Justice, 166
Methodist Federation for Social Service, 157
Michael, Jerome, 140
Michelson, Clarina, 74
Miller, Kelly, 187–88
Millican, G. Everett, 178
Millis, Mary Raoul: and Herndon committee,
  77, 83–84; investigates prison conditions,
  102–103, 103*n*; on local conditions, 113–14;
  describes Boykin, 114, 131; mentioned, 24,
  80, 204
Milner, Lucille, 27
Milton, L. D., 201
Minor, Robert, 118
Miscegenation, 54–55, 108, 206*n*
Mitchell, Clarence, 180
Mizell, R. C., 4
Moates, John, 36–37
Moncrief, Adiel Jarrett, 24
Montgomery, Viola, 68, 84–85, 160
Mooney, Tom, 79, 79*n*, 175
Moore, Virlyn E., 7
Moore v. *Dempsey*, 31
Moreland, Joseph, 125, 212*n*
Moreland, William, 125, 136, 212*n*
Morris, Richard, 81*n*
Morrison, Ansel W., 81, 111, 113
Mulkey, Ruth, 90
Murphey, Carl, 64
Murrell, Kenneth, 138, 155, 159, 168, 205*n*

Nance, A. Steve, 41, 43, 179
Nation, 63, 150, 165, 185
National Association for the Advancement of
  Colored People (NAACP): and gradualism,

12, 15; and ILD, 14, 77, 99, 152, 155–56,
174, 201, 203; Atlanta chapter of, 31–32,
33, 86, 101*n*, 169–70, 180–81; on Newnan
murders, 33–34; seeks control of Herndon
case, 69; follows Herndon case, 152–54,
157, 192, 200; and *amici curiae* brief, 153,
157, 203; seeks pardon for Herndon, 158,
160; and communism, 180–81; mentioned,
32, 66, 70, 72, 100, 130, 184, 192
National Bar Association, 157, 173–74
National Committee for the Defense of Political
Prisoners, 105–108, 117, 155–56
National Guard, 122, 124
Negro Chamber of Commerce, 87
Negroes. *See* Blacks
Negro Publication Society of America, 212
Negro Quarterly, 209, 212–13
Nelson, Claud, 144, 156, 158–59, 172
New Masses, 102
Newnan, Georgia, murders, 32–34
New Orleans *Item*, 185
New Republic, 63, 145–46, 150, 185
Newton, Herbert (alias Gilmer Brady), 22, 116
New York *Age*, 65
New York *Amsterdam News*, 65, 109, 185
New York *Daily News*, 185, 187
New York *Herald-Tribune*, 62
New York *Post*, 150, 165, 185
New York *Times*, 177, 188
New York *World-Telegram*, 62, 185
Nicholson, I. C., 76
Non-Partisan Labor Defense, 156
Norfolk *Journal and Guide*, 65, 66, 187
Norris, Clarence, 145
Norris, Ida, 119
North, Joseph, 160–61

Oglethorpe University, 136
Oklahoma City *Black Dispatch*, 188
O'Neal, Reavis, Jr., 134–35
Order of 21, p. 168

Padmore, George, 8, 46
Palmour, Oscar, 40–41, 42
Park, Orville A., 31
Parker, Jack, 170*n*
Parker, W. O., 125–26
Patterson, William L.: seeks lawyers for Hern-
don, 10–11; and ILD, 13, 15, 72; career of,
13, 198*n*; and united front, 79, 155–56; and
NAACP, 87; on Atlanta police, 92; men-
tioned, 68, 80

Paxon, F. J., 41, 43
Periodicals, liberal, 184–85. See also *Nation;
New Republic*
Petry, O. E., 144, 179
Phagan, Mary, 18
Philadelphia *Tribune*, 64–65
Pickens, William, 70
Pierce, Haywood, Sr., 138
Pittsburgh *Courier*, 66, 151, 166, 171, 185,
200
Police: and Newnan blacks, 32–34; and mis-
treatment of blacks, 83, 86–93 *passim*; and
demand for black police, 88, 92; mentioned,
194
Pomeroy, E. E., 26–27
Poteat, Edwin, 24
Powell, Adam Clayton, Jr., 188, 202
Powell, C. B., 129
Powell v. *Alabama*, 14
Powers, M. H., 19, 20, 22, 26–27
Press, black: on communism, 63–66; on Hern-
don case, 64–65, 165–66, 171, 185–86; on
ILD, 166, 166*n*
Prison conditions: in Georgia, 53, 55, 154. *See
also* Chain gang
Provisional Committee for the Defense of
Angelo Herndon: formation of, 77–78;
finances of, 79; activities of, 83–85; and
appeals to blacks, 84; splits within, 84, 98,
99, 101

Racholin, Alexander, 125, 127–28, 135, 136*n*
Rainey, Glenn W., 24, 77
Randolph, A. Philip, 174
Rankin, Jeannette, 138, 160*n*
Reddick, L. D., 212
Red raids, 110–11, 125, 169
Red scare, 121–39 *passim*, 201
Redwine, Charles D., 172
Relief crisis, 1–6, 10, 52–53
Rhodes, E. Washington, 64
Ricarno, R., 77
Richmond *Planet*, 64, 118, 151, 166, 185
Richmond *Times-Dispatch*, 171, 185, 189. *See
also* Dabney, Virginius
Rivers, E. D., 172
Roberson, Paul, 13*n*
Roberts, Owen J., 154, 182–84, 189, 208
Rollins, William, Jr., 105
Ronin, Ben, 77
Roosevelt, Franklin D., 175, 181–82
Ross, Holt, 179

Rosser, L. Z., 91–92
Russak, Martin, 105
Russell, Richard B., 10, 172

Sacco, Nicola, 13
St. Louis *Argus*, 65, 166, 185
St. Louis *Post-Dispatch*, 62–63, 171, 185, 189
Savannah *Tribune*, 65
Save Angelo Herndon campaign, 103
Schenck v. *United States*, 146, 148–49. *See also* Clear and present danger test
Schuyler, George S., 66, 119
Schwab, Irving, 76, 85
Schwarz, Bess, 76
Scottsboro case: ILD tactics in, 13, 14, 97, 198; Klan pickets rally for, 94–95; and all-white juries, 144–45, 145n; and Judge Horton, 165, 166; compared with Herndon case, 166, 174, 192, 193, 205–206; mentioned, 10, 14, 75, 107, 177, 196, 203
Scottsboro Defense Committee, 152
Seaboard Railroad, 116–17
Sedition bill, 143–45, 178–79. *See also* Anticommunism
Segregation, 31–32, 84
Self-determination for the Black Belt: discussed at Herndon's trial, 45–46, 54–55; and Georgia officials, 59, 109n, 168–69, 204–205; and Justice Sutherland, 210
Serber, William, 105
Seymour, Whitney North: agrees to direct Herndon appeal, 140–41; background of, 141; motivation of, 141, 198–99; argues before U.S. Supreme Court, 146–48, 153, 157, 175, 177–78; argues before Judge Dorsey, 162–63; legal abilities of, 197, 197n, 198–99; later career of, 214; mentioned, 150, 158, 159, 169
Shannon, Georgia, 122–23, 124
Sheppard, Neal, 126
Simmons, J. W., 42
Simmons, William J., 18
Sims, George H., 41–42
Sims, Richard, 81n
Singer, Max, 169, 170n
Slaton, John M., 18
Smith Act, 213–14
Socialist party, 73, 150n–51n, 154, 193n
Sons of the Revolution, 72
Southern Tenant Farmers' Union, 154
Spooner, Ralph, 127–28
Stafford, Martha, 110

Stephens, E. A., 7, 48–49
Steward, Walter, 6, 52–53
Stone, Harlan Fiske, 149–50, 182
Story, Henry, 22
Street, James H., 51n–52n, 54, 205
Strickland, Dinah, 32
Strickland, Oneta, 32
Strozier, Harry S., 31, 98
Sturdivant, T. O., 86, 89, 91–93
Supreme Court of Georgia. *See* Georgia Supreme Court
Sutherland, George, 149, 183, 210
Sutherland, W. A., 31, 75, 140–42, 163, 169, 178
Syndicalism. *See* Criminal syndicalism laws

Talmadge, Eugene: and northern visitors, 106–107, 155, 161, 161n; denies Herndon to be lynched, 117; and textile strike, 122; vetoes anticommunism acts, 137, 144; on pardon for Herndon, 158–59; acts with restraint, 206; mentioned, 102, 160n, 172
Tatham, Louis, 124, 129
Taub, Allan, 83–84
Textile strike of 1934, pp. 121–24
Thomas, E. D., 81
Thomas, Jesse O.: on Herndon case, 5, 186, 201; on communism, 85; on public officials, 88, 128, 130–31; mentioned, 76n, 200
Thomas, Norman, 133n, 151n, 152
Time magazine, 63
Turner, W. T., 55
Tuttle, Elbert P., 141–42, 161–62, 164, 211–12, 214–15
27 Club, 76, 76n

Underwood, Marvin, 24–25
Unemployed Council: national activities of, 4–5, 5n; Herndon's work in, 4–5, 10, 45, 52–53; in Birmingham, 9. *See also* Relief crisis
Unemployment. *See* Relief crisis
United front: established, 77, 152, 156; disrupted, 83–84, 99–101, 193; and liberals, 202; evaluated, 204; mentioned, 165, 193–94
United States Circuit Court of Appeals, 31
United States Supreme Court: hears Scottsboro case, 14; hears Herndon case, 146–50, 156–57, 158, 175, 177–78, 182–84; criticism of, 150–51, 181–82, 185–87, 189; and free speech, 189–90, 208–209

University of Pennsylvania Law Review, 151
Urban League, 77, 88, 128

Van Devanter, Willis, 183, 184
Van Dyke, W. L., 180
Vann, Robert L., 64
Vanzetti, W. L., 180
Veterans of Foreign Wars, 134
Villard, Oswald Garrison, 182

Wagner Act, 189
Walden, A. T.: and John Downer, 30–31, 98;
    on police, 33, 88; and Clarence Weaver, 130;
    mentioned, 32, 34, 38, 153
Walker, Martin, 90
Ware, Zelman, 126, 136, 212n
Washburn, Edith, 170n
Washburn, Walter, 77, 94, 112
Washington, Forrester B., 88, 169–70,
    180–81
Washington *Tribune*, 65
Watkins, Edgar, Sr., 102, 135, 171
Watson, Frank B., 7, 45, 47–50
Weatherwax, L. R., 104–105
Weaver, Clarence, 77, 125, 127–29, 135, 212n
Wechsler, Herbert, 140, 141–42
Weiner, William, 129
West, Don, 110–13, 113n
White, Mose, 81n

White, Walter, 33, 68–69, 99, 153, 155–56
Whitney v. *California*, 120, 148
Wilkins, Roy, 33–34
Wilson, Henry, 170n
Wilson, J. R., 201
Wilson, Walter, 23–24, 115, 158, 202
Wilson, William, 53, 55, 56
Wilson, Woodrow, 182
Wise, Stephen S., 157
Woodward, Comer M., 24
Woodward, C. Vann, 24, 57n, 77–78, 78n,
    83–84, 196
Wright, Ada, 116
Wyatt, Lee B.: presides at Herndon trial, 37–60
    passim; and chain gang, 81; sets bail for
    Herndon, 115, 116; mentioned, 82, 109

X rays: of Herndon, 104–105

Yagol, Nathan: arrested, 95, 125, 127–28; re-
    leased, 135, 136; mentioned, 88, 133, 136n
Yates, C. R., 201
Young, Nannie Leah: describes life of textile
    worker, 124; defended by John Geer, 124,
    129, 201; arrested, 124, 205n; second arrest
    of, 169, 170n; charges against, dropped,
    212n; mentioned, 45
Young Communist League, 8, 163–64, 212